THE TIBERIAN PRONUNCIATION TRADITION OF BIBLICAL HEBREW

VOLUME II

The Tiberian Pronunciation Tradition of Biblical Hebrew

Including a Critical Edition and English Translation of the Sections on

Consonants and Vowels in the Masoretic Treatise

Hidāyat al-Qāri' 'Guide for the Reader'

Volume II

Geoffrey Khan

https://www.openbookpublishers.com

© 2020 Geoffrey Khan.

Semitic Languages and Cultures 1, volume 2.
ISSN (print): 2632-6906
ISSN (digital): 2632-6914

ISBN Paperback: 978-1-78374-857-0
ISBN Hardback: 978-1-78374-858-7
ISBN Digital (PDF): 978-1-78374-859-4
DOI: 10.11647/OBP.0194

Cover image: Cambridge University Library T-S Ar. 31.61 (Hidāyat al-Qāriʾ). Courtesy of the Syndics of Cambridge University Library
Cover design: Luca Baffa.

Volume II

Edition and English Translation of the
Sections on Consonants and Vowels in the
Masoretic Treatise
Hidāyat al-Qāriʾ 'Guide for the Reader'

CONTENTS

II. INTRODUCTION

II.INT.0.1. PRELIMINARY REMARKS

This volume presents an edition and English translation of the sections of the Masoretic treatise *Hidāyat al-Qāriʾ* 'Guide for the Reader' that concern the consonants and vowels. This medieval work constitutes an important primary source for the reconstruction of the Tiberian pronunciation tradition, and it has been constantly referred to in volume 1.

Some general remarks concerning *Hidāyat al-Qāriʾ* in the context of other Masoretic treatises have been made in vol. 1, §I.0.13.1., where references are given to previous scholarship on the text, in particular the important work of Ilan Eldar.

The author of *Hidāyat al-Qāriʾ* was the Karaite grammarian ʾAbū al-Faraj Hārūn, who was active in Jerusalem in the first half of the eleventh century (see vol. 1, §I.0.13.4.).[1] He produced the work in Arabic in both a long and a short version, first writing the long version and subsequently abbreviating this to produce a shortened recension. These underwent further recensions in later centuries in both Arabic and Hebrew (see vol. 1, §I.0.13.1.). The original Arabic versions written by ʾAbū al-Faraj Hārūn contained an introduction, followed by sections on the consonants ,vowels and accents. The listi vowels in both versions. Also included in the edition are some selected passages from the section on the accents that relate to the *gaʿya* and to the interaction of vocalization and stress. Eldar (2018) has made an edition of the section on musical accents and also has published selected passages from other sections of both versions of the treatise (e.g. Eldar 1980; 1987a; 1987b; 1994). There are not, however, any full editions of all the extant portions of the introduction and the sections on the consonants and vowels in the two versions. Moreover, Eldar published the selected passages with a Hebrew translation. The edition in this volume, therefore, complements the work of Eldar by making available the entire text of the introduction and sections on consonants and vowels and by providing an English translation. It is based on many newly identified manuscripts in the Firkovitch collections (National Library of Russia, St. Petersburg), which now allow a complete reconstruction of the text of the short version and a nearly complete reconstruction of the text of the long version. The edition is accompanied by a commentary, which clarifies passages where it has been deemed necessary and contextualizes the ideas of ʾAbū al-Faraj within the linguistic and philosophical thought of his day.

II.INT.0.2. THE LONG VERSION

In his introduction to the long version, ʾAbū al-Faraj indicates (§II.L.0.1.10.) that the work consists of three discourses (*maqālāt*), one devoted to consonants, one to vowels and one to accents. The introduction to the third discourse refers to the division of the work into two parts (*'ajzā'*), with the first two discourses in part one and the third discourse in part two:

> The first part contains two discourses. The first discourse contains a discussion concerning the letters. The second discourse contains a discussion concerning the vowels. This part contains one discourse, which contains a discussion concerning the accents of the twenty-one books and the accents of the three books.[2]

The majority of sections of the long version that are covered by the edition here are extant in their entirety in the surviving manuscripts, with only a few, apparently relatively small, gaps.

The grammatical works of 'Abū al-Faraj reflect a considerable influence from contemporary Arabic linguistic thought and direct parallels can be found between his works and Arabic grammatical literature (Khan 1997; Khan, Gallego, and Olszowy-Schlanger 2003, xi–xxxii; Becker 1996; Basal 1998; 1999). 'Abū al-Faraj's works exhibit convergences with contemporary Arabic texts also in general features of literary form, such as the authorial preface (Goldstein 2014).

The Arabic genre of literature that would be expected to correspond most closely to *Hidāyat al-Qāri'* is that of works on correct Qur'ānic recitation, known as *tajwīd*. A comparison with *tajwīd* works from roughly the same period such as those of al-Dānī (d. 1052-3)[3] and al-Qaysī (d. 1045),[4] reveals some parallels in structure. These *tajwīd* manuals open with an introduction on the requirements of *tajwīd* sanctioned by earlier authorities. This is followed by a series of sections on the pronunciation of the consonants, arranged by place of articulation, which is clearly analogous to the contents of the first discourse of *Hidāyat al-Qāriʾ*. In these *tajwīd* manuals, however, there are no clear counterparts to the various sections of *Hidāyat al-Qāriʾ* on philosophical aspects of letters (§II.L.1.1.), on morphological formations involving the interchange, augmentation and elision of letters (§II.L.1.5., §II.L.1.11., §II.L.1.13.) and on verbal conjugations (§II.L.1.10), which are found in the first discourse of the long version of *Hidāyat al-Qāriʾ*.

The remainder of the contents of the *tajwīd* manuals are concerned mainly with contextual variations in the realization of vowels, in particular with regard to their length. This does not correspond very closely to the second discourse of the long version of *Hidāyat al-Qāriʾ*, which is concerned with philosophical aspects of vowels (§II.L.2.1.–§II.L.2.2., §II.L.2.18.), the role of vowels in various morphological formations (§II.L.2.3.–§II.L.2.8., §II.L.2.16.–§II.L.2.17), the *shewa* (§II.L.2.9.–§II.L.2.13.) and the production and places of articulation of vowels (§II.L.2.14.–§II.L.2.15.).

---

[3] ʾAbū ʿAmr ʿUthmān ibn Saʿīd al-Dānī, *Al-Taḥdīd fī al-ʾItqān wa-l-Tajwīd* (ed. al-Ḥamad 2001).

[4] Makkī ibn ʾAbī Ṭālib al-Qaysī, *Al-Riʿāya li-Tajwīd al-Qirāʾa wa-Taḥqīq Lafẓ al-Tilāwa* (ed. Farḥāt 1996).

The *tajwīd* manuals do not contain sections corresponding to the treatment of cantillation accents in the third discourse of *Hidāyat al-Qāriʾ*, since pitch variation in the recitation of the Qurʾān is not prescribed but is improvised (Nelson 2001).

The various aforementioned components in the three discourses of *Hidāyat al-Qāriʾ* that do not have counterparts in the *tajwīd* manuals have been incorporated from the Masoretic tradition, from material on morphology in other grammatical works of ʾAbū al-Faraj Hārūn, from the Arabic grammatical tradition, e.g. the theory of the production of vowels (§II.L.2.15.),[5] and from philosophical treatments of language in Muslim speculative theological works (*kalām*). The custom of incorporating morphological material into treatments of pronunciation is seen already in earlier Masoretic treatises such as *Kitāb al-Muṣawwitāt* (ed. Allony 1963) and *Seder ha-Simanim* (ed. Allony 1965). It is clear that *Hidāyat al-Qāriʾ* is hybrid with regard to the nature and origin of its contents. It does not replicate exactly the format of Qurʾānic *tajwīd* manuals. It does not, moreover, constitute a simple compendium of material from the Masoretic tradition, despite the statement to that effect in §II.L.0.9. of the introduction.

II.INT.0.3. THE SHORT VERSION

The short version of *Hidāyat al-Qāriʾ* has survived in many more manuscripts than the long version. This

al-Lugha al-ʿIbrāniyya 'The Sufficient Book concerning the Hebrew Language', which is a shortened version of his original grammar book *al-Kitāb al-Mushtamil ʿalā al-ʾUṣūl wa-l-Fuṣūl fī al-Lugha al-ʿIbrāniyya* 'The Comprehensive Book of General Principles and Particular Rules of the Hebrew Language' and is extant in many more manuscripts than *al-Kitāb al-Mushtamil* (Khan, Gallego and Olszowy-Schlanger 2003, xlvii).

In the introduction to the short version of *Hidāyat al-Qāriʾ*, ʾAbū al-Faraj indicates that he may take the opportunity to include 'where necessary what was not mentioned in the (original) *Hidāyat al-Qāriʾ*'. This is analogous to his approach in *al-Kitāb al-Kāfī*, in which he in several places states that he is expanding on material that is dealt with in *al-Kitāb al-Mushtamil* or presenting the material in a different arrangement. In one case he admits that the view he expresses in *al-Kitāb al-Kāfī* should supersede the remarks he made on the subject in *al-Kitāb al-Kāfī* (Khan, Gallego and Olszowy-Schlanger 2003, xxxiii).

The first two discourses of the original long version of *Hidāyat al-Qāriʾ* have been made more concise in the short version by removing sections that relate to philosophical discussions of letters and vowels, and sections that are concerned with morphological patterns and processes. The main sections that are retained in the short version of the first two discourses concern the pronunciation of the consonants, vowels and *shewa*. The division into two discourses has also been eliminated.

The first part of the introduction to the short version (§II.S.0.1.–§II.S.0.2.) includes a variety of titles of the work. It is indicated that the long version was called *Kitāb al-Shurūṭ* 'The

Book of Conditions/Rules', but was generally known (*mulaqqab*) by the name *Hidāyat al-Qāriʾ*. The term *sharṭ* 'rule' is a term that is frequently used in the work. The short version of *Hidāyat al-Qāriʾ* (*mukhtaṣar Hidāyat al-Qāriʾ*) is said in the introduction to have been known as *Kitāb al-Muhja* 'The Book of the Essential Requirements (literally: the lifeblood).' This corresponds closely the title *Muhjat al-Qāriʾ* (מהג'ה אלקאר) 'The Essential Requirements of the Reader' that appears in a booklist datable to the 13th century (Allony 1975, 56). A Genizah fragment of the short version has a scribal note that refers to the work as *Kitāb al-Hidāya fī ʿIlm Shurūṭ al-Miqrā* 'The Book of Guidance regarding the Knowledge of the Rules of Scriptural Reading' (JRL A 694). A Genizah fragment of an anonymous Masoretic treatise (CUL T-S NS 311.113) refers, moreover, to what appears to be *Hidāyat al-Qāriʾ* by the title *Kitāb al-ʾAlḥān* 'The Book of the Accents'.

Some other works of ʾAbū al-Faraj are referred to with different forms of title. This applies, for example, to his glossary of biblical words, which is referred to in the sources with various titles, including *Tafsīr ʾAlfāẓ al-Miqrā* 'Explanation of Biblical Words', *Sharḥ ʾAlfāẓ allatī fīhā Ṣuʿūba fī al-Miqrā wa-Dhikr Ishtiqāqihā* 'The Explanation of Words in the Bible that have Difficulty and the Mention of their Derivation', *ʾAlfāẓ al-Ṣaʿba allatī li-l-Torah* 'The Difficult Words of the Pentateuch' (Goldstein 2014, 357).

II.INT.0.4. THE MANUSCRIPT CORPUS

The edition of the long version of *Hidāyat al-Qāriʾ* is based on all manuscripts of the work that are known to me. These are extant predominantly in the Second Firkovitch collection of the National Library of Russia in St. Petersburg. The corpus includes the following manuscripts. Full class-marks are given together with the abbreviations that are used in the edition:[6]

St. Petersburg, National Library of Russia:

> II Firkovitch, Evr.-Arab. I 2390 = L1
> II Firkovitch, Evr.-Arab. I 2505 = L2
> II Firkovitch, Evr.-Arab. I 4477 = L3
> II Firkovitch, Evr.-Arab. II 307 = L4
> II Firkovitch, Evr.-Arab. II 418 = L5
> II Firkovitch, Evr.-Arab. II 604 = L6

Cambridge University Library:

> T-S NS 301.23 = L7

New York, The Jewish Theological Seminary:

> JTS 8110, EMC 829, 832 = L8

The number of extant manuscripts of the short version is much larger and only a selection of those that are extant were

---

[6] These include some manuscripts that were identified by Ilan Eldar. I identified the remainder in my investigations in the Firkovitch collection.

used for the edition. These again are predominantly from the Second Firkovitch collection, which preserves the longest manuscripts. My corpus includes the following:[7]

St. Petersburg, National Library of Russia:

II Firkovitch, Evr.-Arab. I 2347 = S1
II Firkovitch, Evr.-Arab. I 2477 = S2
II Firkovitch, Evr.-Arab. I 2478 = S3
II Firkovitch, Evr.-Arab. I 2480 = S4
II Firkovitch, Evr.-Arab. I 2481 = S5
II Firkovitch, Evr.-Arab. I 2528 = S6
II Firkovitch, Evr.-Arab. I 2542 = S7
II Firkovitch, Evr.-Arab. I 2544 = S8
II Firkovitch, Evr.-Arab. I 2551 = S9
II Firkovitch, Evr.-Arab. I 2557 = S10
II Firkovitch, Evr.-Arab. I 2772 = S11
II Firkovitch, Evr.-Arab. I 2794 = S12
II Firkovitch, Evr.-Arab. I 2795 = S13
II Firkovitch, Evr.-Arab. I 2813 = S14
II Firkovitch, Evr.-Arab. I 2814 = S15
II Firkovitch, Evr.-Arab. I 2897 = S16
II Firkovitch, Evr.-Arab. I 2928 = S17
II Firkovitch, Evr.-Arab. I 2941 = S18
II Firkovitch, Evr.-Arab. I 2945 = S19
II Firkovitch, I

II Firkovitch, Evr.-Arab. I 3384 = S21

II Firkovitch, Evr.-Arab. I 3944 = S22

II Firkovitch, Evr.-Arab. II 297 = S23

II Firkovitch, Evr.-Arab. II 323 = S24

II Firkovitch, Evr.-Arab. II 325 = S25

II Firkovitch, Evr.-Arab. II 326 = S26

II Firkovitch, Evr.-Arab. II 420 = S27

II Firkovitch, Evr.-Arab. II 488 = S28

Cambridge University Library:

Mosseri I, 57.2 = S29

In addition to these manuscripts, there are also several ex-tant Genizah fragments containing the short version, which were used by Eldar (1987a; 1987b) in his edition of selected passages from the short version. For my own edition I decided to give pref-erence to the longer manuscripts that are now available in the Firkovitch collection.

The manuscripts of the corpus that are used for the edition of the long and short versions are all written in Judaeo-Arabic (Arabic in Hebrew script). They do not include any colophons. Their scribal hands and codicology, however, are similar to the manuscripts from the Firkovtich collection that formed the basis of the edition of 'Abū al-Faraj's grammatical work *al-Kitāb al-Kāfī* (Khan, Gallego, and Olszowy-Schlanger 2003, xlvii–lxix). Based on this comparison, therefore, they can be dated to a period rang-ing from the eleventh to the thirteenth centuries. Their ultimate origin would in all likelihood have been the Karaite synagogue in Cairo, which appears to have been the source of most of the Second Firkovitch collection (Harviainen 1996).

II.Int.0.5. The Edition and Translation of the Texts

The edition of the two texts follows the same basic method as was applied in the edition of ʾAbū al-Faraj's *al-Kitāb al-Kāfī* (ed. Khan, Gallego, and Olszowy-Schlanger 2003). The objective of this method is to produce a text that is as clear and readable as possible but still remains close to the philological reality of the manuscripts.

For each section of the works a single manuscript was chosen to act as the basis of the edition. Preference was given to a manuscript that contains the section in undamaged folios. As is the case with most manuscripts of the Second Firkovitch collection, individual folios are often out of order in the manuscripts of the corpus. This has often necessitated re-ordering the folios. Where the complete section is not contained in one base manuscript, various base manuscripts are used for the section.

As far as possible, the text is presented in the edition exactly as it appears in this base manuscript for a particular section, following its orthography and reproducing the diacritical marks and vocalization. Where scribes make corrections or additions to the text, these are incorporated into the edition. No indication is made, however, of deleted text. Similarly, when text is inserted as an afterthought in the margin, it has been included in the main text of the edition .

If the reading in another manuscript is clearly superior to that of the base manuscript, the superior reading is adopted in the edited text and distinguished by enclosing it in angled brackets < .... >. Editorial judgements as to superiority in reading do not include cases where another manuscript has a linguistic construction that conforms more closely to the conventions of Classical Arabic than the one found in the base manuscript, so long as the construction in the base manuscript could be interpreted as exhibiting a difference only in linguistic register and is not the result of a scribal error. In some cases where the reading of the base manuscript makes little sense and no superior reading is available in other manuscripts, an emended reading is proposed, enclosed in angled brackets, which is as close as possible in form to the reading in the manuscript .

If small lacunae occur in the base manuscript and the text has been supplied from another manuscript or the missing text is easily reconstructable, the supplied text is enclosed in square brackets [...].

As remarked, the diacritical marks of the base manuscript are reproduced in the edition. These include marks on letters and vocalization. In most cases diacritical dots on letters are inconsistently marked in the manuscripts and this inconsistent marking is reproduced in the edition. It was decided, however, to mark a dot consistently over the letters *ṣade* and *ṭet* when they represent Arabic *ḍād* and *ẓāʾ*, respectively, even if they do not have a diacritical dot in the manuscript. The purpose of this was to make the text more readable. Missing or inconsistently marked diacritics of other letters were judged not to reduce the readability of the text. Indeed, it cannot be excluded that the omission of diacritical marks on the letters *dalet* and *tav* representing Arabic *dhāl* and *thāʾ* may, in some cases, be a reflection of the pronunciation of these consonants by the scribe as stops rather than fricatives due to the interference of his vernacular dialect .

Hebrew words and Biblical quotations are vocalized in some manuscripts. If vocalization appears in the base manuscript, this is reproduced in the edition exactly as it is written by the scribe. The vocalization always consists of Tiberian signs, but in many cases it deviates from the standard Tiberian Masoretic vocalization. These reflect idiosyncracies of vocalization and pronunciation of individual scribes who transmitted the text. The standard Tiberian vocalization of the Hebrew words is given in the translation on the page facing the edited text. The most common deviations from standard Tiberian vocalization include the following:

Interchange of *segol* and *pataḥ* (cf. vol. 1, §I.4.3.3.), e.g.

בֶּרֶע (long version, §II.L.1.10. | Standard Tiberian: בֶּרַע Gen. 14.2 'Bera')

בֶּעֶר (long version, §II.L.1.10. | Standard Tiberian: בַּעַר Psa. 92.7 'stupidity')

גֶּם (long version, §II.L.2.12.7 | Standard Tib...

יִרְבַּה (long version, §II.L.1.13. | Standard Tiberian: יִרְבֶּה 'it multiplies')

Simple vowel sign in place of a *ḥatef* sign on gutturals, e.g.

וַעֲלֵי (long version, §II.L.1.11.4. | Standard Tiberian: וַעֲלֵי Psa. 92.4 'and on')

עֲדֵי (long version, §II.L.1.11.4. | Standard Tiberian: עֲדֵי 'until')

וַיְמַהֲרֹוּ (long version, §II.L.2.12.4.2. | Standard Tiberian: וַיְמַהֲרֹוּ Josh. 8.14 'they made haste')

Non-standard distribution of *shewa* and *ḥatef* signs, e.g.

יִמְחֲאוּ כָף (long version, §II.L.2.12.1.6. | Standard Tiberian: יִמְחֲאוּ־בֶף Psa. 98.8 'let them clap their hands')

אֱלָהֲהֹום (long version, §II.L.2.12.1.6. | Standard Tiberian: אֱלָהֲהֹם Ezra 7.16 'their God')

בְּיֹום הַהוּא (long version, §II.L.2.12.2.2. | Standard Tiberian: בַּיֹּום הַהוּא Isa. 27.2 'on that day')

The edited texts have been divided into numbered sections and subsections, which correspond to sense units. In some cases these paragraph divisions are also marked in the base manuscript by various means, such as section titles or blank spaces. In numerous cases, however, they are not marked in the manuscript. It was decided that the imposition of a system of paragraph division produced a text that is far more readable and also would facilitate reference to specific passages. The numbers of the paragraphs consist of three elements: A roman numeral II, denoting volume 2 of the book, a capital L or S, denoting the long or short version respectively, and a series of Arabic numerals indicating sections and subsections, e.g. II.L.1.7.11 (= vol. 2, long version, section 1.7.11.). Where the original text does not have a title at a major section division, a title indicating the contents of the section is supplied in the translation in brackets. Where the original text has only a generic title at such divisions, such as פצל *faṣl* 'section', the specific content of the section is likewise supplied in the translation in brackets.

Section numbers of this introduction have the prefix II.Int.

The folio divisions of the base manuscript are shown in the edited text by a superscribed abbreviation of the manuscript with the folio number after a colon, indicating where the following text begins, e.g. (L5:17v) denotes that the following text begins on fol. 17 verso of the manuscript L5.

The English translation is intended to be read either in conjunction with the original text or independently of it. An attempt has been made to convey to the reader as clearly as possible the sense of the author. The translation is not, therefore, a slavishly literal rendering of the text, since this would often remain obscure for the English reader on account of the predilection of ʾAbū al-Faraj for complex syntax. Biblical quotations are reproduced in the original Hebrew, with standard Masoretic vocalization and an English translation. Occasional footnotes clarify some details of the translation. Longer explan-

II.Int.0.6. Terminology

The technical terminology used by ʾAbū al-Faraj in *Hidāyat al-Qāriʾ* corresponds closely to what is found in his grammatical works (Khan, Gallego, and Olszowy-Schlanger 2003, xxxix–xlvi). Much of the grammatical terminology is that which was used in the mainstream Baṣran school of Arabic grammar of the period. There are also a number of survivals of Hebrew and Aramaic terms from the Masoretic and early Karaite grammatical tradition. Some of these have been Arabicized. The main technical terms that are used in *Hidāyat al-Qāriʾ* are as follows.

II.Int.0.6.1. Arabic Terms

אמר *ʾamr* 'imperative'

אנחא *ʾanḥāʾ* 'vowels'

אסאס *ʾasās* 'basic noun'

אסם *ism* 'noun'

אסתפהאם *istifhām* 'interrogative'

אצל *ʾaṣl* 'basic form'

בי *bē* 'bet'

דאל *dāl* 'dalet'

ואו *wāw* 'vav'

זג *zujj* 'arrow-head' (term for the vowel sign *qibbuṣ*)

חרף *ḥarf* 'letter'

חרף אללין *ḥarf al-līn* 'soft letter' (see commentary on §II.L.1.1.7.)

חרף מסתעמל *ḥarf mustaʿmal* 'auxiliary letter' (see commentary on §II.L.1.12.3.)

טעאם *ṭaʿām* 'taste (of a vowel)', 'perceived quality (of a vowel)' (see commentary on §II.L.1.1.)

כאדם *khādim* 'subordinate particle'

כאף *kāf* 'kaf'

כבר *khabar* 'assertion'

כסדאני *kasdānī* 'Aramaic'

כסרה *kasra* (*i* vowel)

כֿפֿץ *khafḍ* 'lowering' (vowel quality) (see commentary on §II.L.2.3.)

לגה *lugha* 'lexical class' (see commentary on §II.L.0.1.1.)

מאצֿי *māḍī* 'past tense'

מדגוש *madgūsh* 'with *dagesh*'

מדכר *madhakkar* 'masculine'

מונת *muʾannath* 'feminine'

מלך (pl. מלוך) 'vowel' (literally: 'king')

מסתקבל *mustaqbal* 'future tense'

מפעול *mafʿūl* 'passive participle'

מצדר מסתעאר *maṣdar mustaʿār* 'transposed infinitive' (see commentary on §II.L.2.7.2.)

מקטע *maqṭaʿ* 'prosodic stopping point', 'place of prosodic division' (§II.L.2.10.3., §I.2.5.2.)

מרפי *marfī* 'with *rafe*'

נגמה *naghama* 'vowel'

נצב *naṣb* 'holding level' (vowel quality) (see commentary on §II.L.2.3.)

נקטה ואחדה *nuqṭa wāḥida* 'single dot', i.e. *ḥireq*

נקטה מן אספל *nuqṭa min ʾasfal* 'dot below', i.e. *ḥireq*

נקטין *nuqṭatayn* 'two dots', i.e. *ṣere*

סאכן *sākin* 'silent, without a following vowel'

עבראני *ʿibrānī* 'Hebrew (language)'

עטף *ʿaṭf* 'conjunction'

ערׁץ *ʿaraḍ* 'abstraction, abstract property, verbal property'

פאעל *fāʿil* 'agentive participle'

פאעל באלגיר *fāʿil bi-l-ghayr* 'transitive agent'

פאעל בנפסה *fāʿil bi-nafsihi* 'reflexive agent'

פאתחה *'pataḥ'*

פעל *fiʿl* 'verb'

פעל אלדי לם יסם פאעלה *fiʿil alladhī lam yusamma fāʿiluhu* 'action whose agent has not been mentioned', i.e. passive.

פעל פי אלנפס *fiʿl fī al-nafs* 'intransitive verb'

פרע *far‘* 'secondary, derivative form'

פתחה *fatḥa* (*a* vowel)

צַמה *ḍamma* (*u* vowel)

קאמצה (pl. קואמץ) '*qameṣ*'

קטע *qaṭ‘* 'disjoined state'

ראכב *rākib* 'affix'

רפע *raf‘* 'raising' (vowel quality) (see commentary on §II.L.2.3.)

שוא '*shewa*'

שוא מתחרך *shewa mutaḥarrik* 'mobile *shewa*'

שוא סאכן *shewa sākin* 'silent *shewa*'

תלת נקט *thalāth nuqaṭ* 'three dots', i.e. *segol*

תצריף *taṣrīf* 'verbal conjugation'

תקדיר *taqdīr* 'virtual form' (see commentary on §II.L.1.4.8.)

II.Int.0.6.2. Hebrew and Aramaic Terms

אוֹגֶרָה 'collection' of exceptional words with regard to the occurrence of *dagesh* on initial בגדכפת consonants (§II.L.1.7., §II.S.2.0.)

אינת the person prefixes of the ~~f~~

גמאל 'gimel'

גַּגִּי symbol representing verbal conjugations with imperatives containing *pataḥ* in the first syllable and past forms
containing *ḥireq* in the first syllable (§II.L.2.7.2.,
§II.L.2.8.2.)

גְּעְיָה 'gaʿya'

דָּגֵשׁ 'dagesh'

דְּדְחִיק 'what is compressed', *dehiq*, compression of a vowel
that brings about the occurrence of *dagesh* at the beginning
of a following word (§II.L.1.7., §II.S.2.0.)

דִּפְסִיק 'what is paused', a pause due to *paseq* (§II.L.1.7.,
§II.S.2.0.)

הֵי, הא 'he'

וָו 'vav'

חית 'ḥet'

חֹלֶם 'holem'

חֶרֶק 'hireq'

טית 'tet'

טַעַם (i) 'accent'; (ii) 'taste (of a vowel)', 'perceived quality
(of a vowel)' (see commentary on §II.L.1.1.)

יוד 'yod'

כּוֹנֵן symbol representing verbal conjugations with imperatives containing *holem* in the first syllable and past forms
containing *pataḥ* in the first syllable (§II.L.2.5.)

למאד 'lamed'

לָשׁוֹן 'lexical class', 'linguistic form' (see commentary on §II.L.0.1.1.)

מְיֻדָּע 'definite'

מאם, מים 'mem'

מַכֶּה symbol representing verbal conjugations with impera-tives containing *patah* in the first syllable and past forms containing *segol* in the first syllable (§II.L.2.7.2.)

מֻכְרָת 'disjoined' (see commentary to §II.L.1.5.21.)

מְנֻכָּר 'indefinite'

מֵסַב symbol representing verbal conjugations with impera-tives containing *ṣere* in the last syllable and past forms con-taining *patah* in the last syllable (§II.L.2.8.2.)

מַפֵּק, מַפִּיק *mappiq*

נון 'nun'

סגולה 'segol'

סמאך 'samekh'

סָמוּךְ 'conjoined' (see commentary to §II.L.1.5.21., §II.L.2.17.)

עָבַר 'past tense'

פתח 'patah'

צדי 'sade'

צֵרִי 'sere'

קוֹף 'qof'

קָמֶץ 'qames'

רֵיש 'resh'

רָפֶה 'rafe'

שׁוּעָל symbol representing verbal conjugations with imperatives containing *shureq* in the first syllable and past forms
containing *qames* in the first syllable (§II.L.2.6.)

שִׁין 'shin'

שִׁירָה symbol representing verbal conjugations with imperatives containing *hireq* in the first syllable and past forms
containing *qames* in the first syllable (§II.L.2.8.2.)

שִׁירוֹ symbol representing verbal conjugations with imperatives containing *hireq* in the first syllable and past forms
containing *holem* in the first syllable (§II.L.2.5.)

שרק 'shureq'

תָּיו, תָּו 'tav'

תֵּמַה 'interrrogative'

HIDĀYAT AL-QĀRIʾ

HIDĀYAT AL-QĀRIʾ (LONG VERSION)

II.L.0.0. (INTRODUCTION)

GAP

II.L.0.1.

[...] לְיוֹם קוּמִי לְעֵד 'for the day when I arise as a witness' (Zeph. 3.8), יְהוָה| אוֹרִי וְיִשְׁעִי 'The Lord is my light and my salvation' (Psa. 27.1), which are two masculine nouns, since the accent is at the end and not the beginning of the word. Another example is הַשָּׁבָה עִם־נָעֳמִי (Ruth 2.6), which means 'who returned' and is a past verb, since the accent is on the first letter. Similar to this in letters and form is וְשָׁבָה אֶל־בֵּית אָבִיהָ (Lev. 22.13), which means 'and she became one returning (to her father's house)', 'she became one doing', since the accent is not on the first letter. A similar case is כָּל־הַנֶּפֶשׁ הַבָּאָה לְיַעֲקֹב (Gen. 46.26), which means 'every soul (belonging to Jacob) that is entering'. Since the accent occurs on the ʾalef, (it means) the soul became one doing, as opposed to כָּל־הַנֶּפֶשׁ לְבֵית־יַעֲקֹב הַבָּאָה מִצְרַיְמָה (Gen. 46.27), which means '(all the persons belonging to Jacob who) arrived' or 'who entered'. The he in the first word (i.e. הַבָּאָה Gen. 46.26) is the he of the definite article, whereas in the second word (i.e. הַבָּאָה Gen. 46.27), it is in place of אֲשֶׁר. The accent has changed two things: the meaning (of the word) and the meaning of the affixed he. Likewise, שָׁבוּ עַל־עֲוֺנֹת אֲבוֹתָם 'They have turned back to the iniquities of their forefathers' (Jer. 11.10), since the accent is on the shin, this is from the lexical class of 'returning', as opposed to שָׁבוּ וַיָּבֹזּוּ 'They captured and made their prey' (Gen. 34.29), which should be interpreted as being from the lexical

https://doi.org/10.11647/OBP.0194.02

הדאיה אלקאר

GAP

(L5:17r) [ ] לֹא לְיוֹם קוּמִי לְעַד יְיָ אוּרִי וְיִשְׁעִי פְצַארא <אסמִין>

למדכר למא תאכר אללחן ען אול אלכלמה וכדלך הַשָּׁבָה עִם

נָעֳמִי ותפסירה אלתי רגעת פעלא מאצֹיא למא כאן אלטעם מע

אלחרף אלאול מתל דלך פי אלחרוף ואללפט כקוֹ ושָׁבָֿה אל בית

5 אביה אלדי תפסירה ותציר ראגעה צארת פאעלה למא תאכר

אלטעם ען אול חרף וכדלך כל הנפש הבאה ליעקב אלדי יפסר

כל אלנפס אלדאכלה למגי אללחן עלי אלאלף (L5:17v) צארת

אלנפס פאעלה מכאלפא לקוֹ [כל] הַנֶפֶשׁ לבית יעקב הַבָּאָה

מִצְרַיְמָה אלדי תפסירה אלדי חצלת או אלדי דכלת ויכון אלהֵא

10 עלי אלכלמה אלאולי הא אלתעריף ועלי אלכלמה אלתאניה

מקאם אֲשֶׁר גייר אללחן שיין אלמעני ומעני אלהא אלראכב

class of 'capturing', since the accent is on the *bet*. Likewise עוּרִי עוּרִי דְּבוֹרָה עוּרִי עוּרִי דַּבְּרִי־שֵׁיר (Jud. 5.12), in which the first (two cases of עוּרִי) mean 'my rousing, my rousing', since the accent occurs on the *resh*, whereas the second (two cases of עוּרִי) mean 'rouse yourself, rouse yourself', feminine singular imperative, on account of the occurrence of the accent on the *ʿayin*. Similarly, וְדִבַּרְתִּי עַל־הַנְּבִיאִים 'and I spoke to the prophets' (Hosea 12.11) should be interpreted as a past verb, since the accent falls on the *bet*, as opposed to וְדִבַּרְתִּי עַל לִבָּהּ 'I will speak tenderly to her' (Hosea 2.16), which should be interpreted as a future verb. (To these could be added) other similar examples. On account of this, the accents have an important status and there is a need to learn them.

II.L.0.2

If one were to say 'What do you say concerning the formation of these accents?', the response would be that they originated by convention among the people of the language, by the help of which they fully expressed their purposes, as in the aforementioned examples and others. They established them by convention, just as they established the vowels by convention, as will be explained. It is not impossible that the established form was based on a particular type of arrangement of the Levites in [Ezra], peace be upon him, because [   ] the accents were established [   ] his time [   ], for if he investigates what [   ] the forms, he would realize that it was fixed by the Levites [   ] on the basis of the principles of singing and according to the established arrangement [   ] [ ] serves *pashṭa* [   ] close to [   ] two conjunctive accents, namely inverted *shofar*[1] and *merkha*, as will be explained.

---

[1] I.e. *mahpakh*.

עוּרִי דברי (L1:4r) אללחן עלי אלבא וכדלך עוּרֵי עוּרִי דבוֹרָה עוּרִי

15 שיר אלדי תפסיר אלאול תוראני תוראני למגי אלטעם עלי

אלריש ואלבّ יפסר תורי תורי אמר למונת למגי אלטעם עלי

אלעין וכדלך וְדִבַּרְתִּי עַל־הַנְּבִיאִים יפסר מאצّיא [למגי] אללחן

עלי אלבא מכאלפא לקולה ודברתי על לבה אלדי יפסר

מסתקבלא אלי גיר דלך ממא יגרי הדא אלמגרי פאדא כאן דלך

20 כדלך כאן ללאלחאן מוקף כביר ואלחאגה תדעו אלי עלמהא

II.L.0.2.

פאן קיל פמא [ת]קול פי הדה אלאלחאן מן רתבהא קיל לה

אנהא מואצّעה פי אלאצל בין אהל אללגה כמלו בע[ונהא]

אגראצّהם כאלאמתלה אלמדכורה וסואהא פתואצّעו עליהא

כמא תואצّעו עלי אלמלוך עלי מא יגי ביאנה ומא ימתנע

25 אלת[ואצّע] עלי וגה מכצוץ מן תרתיב אללוים פי [   ] עזרא[

עֹ אّל לאן [   ] [אלאלחאן מוצّוע] [   ] זמאנה] [   ] לאן אדא

תאמל מא [   ] [   ] אלאחכאם עלם אנה מן תקריר אל[לוים

[   ] [   ] (L1:4v) [   ] טלי אצול אלשיר ועלי מואצّעה תרתי[ב

Likewise, *tevir* is served by two conjunctive accents, namely *merkha* and *darga*. Each has its own special melody, and a particular number of tones in various different pitches according to the accent when it is followed by a vowel in the word, as will be explained. If it be said 'What is the origin of the melodies of the accents before the aforementioned arrangement was fixed?', the response would be as follows. It is possible that the people of the language paused on one letter and made it slightly longer than another one to the extent that they could make thereby their intentions known. My claim that the accents have been fixed since the time of the prophets, peace be upon them, is supported by three things.

II.L.0.3

One of these is that the nation has not been cut off from the holy land. The period in which they were cut off from it was between the two temples, concerning which it is stated אָ֣ז תִּרְצֶ֣ה הָאָ֗רֶץ אֶת־שַׁבְּתֹתֶ֔יהָ בׇּהְשַׁמָּ֖ה מֵהֶ֑ם 'Then the land shall enjoy its sabbaths while it lies desolate without them' (Lev. 26.34, 43).[2] When the land completed its rest in the periods of its lying fallow, הֵעִ֣יר יְהֹוָ֗ה אֶת־ר֙וּחַ֙ כֹּ֣רֶשׁ מֶֽלֶךְ־פָּרַ֔ס 'the Lord stirred up the spirit of Cyrus king of Persia' (Ezra 1.1 etc.) and he sent up the two groups (of returnees) to the holy land, the group of Ezra and the group of Nehemiah, according to what [   ] Ezra. After they arrived in the Holy Land they were not cut off from it until this day. Now the reading that Ezra, peace be upon him, and his congregation used to read is the reading of the Land of Israel today. It has remained the way (of reading) that has been transmitted among them from generation to generation, from

---

[2] The wording is a conflation of the two verses Lev. 25.34 and Lev. 26.43 in the Masoretic Text.

יכדמה כאדמין אלמארכה ואלסלסלה ולכל כא[ן] תנגים מכצוץ

וחרכאת מעדודה עלי וגוה מכתלפה חסב <אללחן> אדא בקי

בעדה מלך פי אלכלמה עלי מא יאתי ביאנה פאן קיל פכיף כאן

אצל אלאלחאן פי תנאגימהא קבל אן תקרר אלתקריר אלמדכור

35 קיל לה ימכן אן כאן אהל אללגה יוקפון אלחרף ויתקלונה ען

גירה יסירא במקדאר מא יעלם בה גרצׄהם יאיד מא דכרתה מן

אן אלאלחאן מקררה מן זמאן אלאנביא על אלס̇ אמור ג̇

אחדהא אן לם תנקטע אלאמה ען ארץ הקדושה ואלמדה אלתי

אנקטעו מנהא בין אלביתין והו אלדי קאל פיהא אז תרצה הארץ

40 את שבתותיה בהשמה מהם פלמא אסתופאת אלארץׄ עטלהא

אלדי כאן פי אלשמטות העיר יְיָ [את רוח] כרש מלך פרס

וצע[ד] אלגמעין אלי [ארץ הקדושה והמא ג]מע עזרא וגמע

נחמיה עלי מא [   ] [   ] עזרא ומן בעד חצולהם פי ארץ [הקדוש]ה

מא אנקטעו מנהא ועד היום הזה (L1:5r) פאלקראה אלדי כאן

_____ כי הראה ארץ ישראל אליום

one offspring to another, until now. If it be said: the wicked Edom deported the people, filled ships with them, left them without a sailor or a helmsman, and caused the hot baths to overwhelm them with smoke until they died, in accordance with what is said to have happened during the conquests of Jerusalem by Edom; the response should be: Although it did to them what you have mentioned, Edom only cut them off from Jerusalem. This is demonstrated by the fact that there was pilgrimage to Tiberias from the direction of the Levant and the East and to Gaza from the direction of the West during the period the people of Edom were in control of the Land of Israel, which was about five hundred years, in accordance with what is mentioned in their chronicles. Those who dwelt in the land all taught their children the Torah and the Scriptures, I mean the remainder of the twenty-four books. If all this is indeed so, then it must be the case that the people used to teach their children what they knew and were familiar with concerning the correct division of the accents and their musical rendition.

II.L.0.4.

The second point is that those who were exiled and did not come back with Ezra and Nehemiah, peace be upon them, remained scattered and they lost (knowledge of) the accents, and began to read with different cantillations. Therefore, you see that the (Jews of) Byzantium read in a way that is different from that of the people of Iraq. The (Jews of) Persia have a way of reading that is different from that of the (Jews of) Byzantium and the Iraqis. The people of the West have (a reading) different from all of the aforementioned. Indeed, perhaps some community that you do not know has a way (of reading) that differs from all of these, such as those whom Edom drove away to remote countries, as we have mentioned. It is the general

אלאן פאן קיל אן אדום הרשעה אגלת אלאמה ומלת מנהם

אלמראכב וכלתהא בלא נותי ולא מדבר ודכנת עליהם

אלחמאמאת חתי מאתו עלי מא קיל אנה גרי פי פתוח ירושלים

עלי יד אדום קיל לה ואן כאן קד פעלת בהם מא דכרת פלם   50

תקטעהם אדום אלא מן ירושלים פקט יאייד דלך אן אלחג כאן

אלי טבריה מן גהה אלשאם ואלשרק ומן גהה אלגרב אלי גזה

מדה מא קאמת גמאעה אדום מאלכה ארץ ישראל והו נחו כמס

מאה סנה עלי מא הו מדכור פי אכבארהם ומא כאנו מקימין פי   55

אלבלד אלא ויעלמו אולאדהם אלתורה ואלקראן אעני בקיה

ארבעה וכׄ ספר פאדא תבתת הדה אלגמלה יצח אן אלקום

כאנו יעלמו אולאדהם מא עלמוה וערפוה מן תעדיל אלאלחאן

ותנאגימהא

II.L.0.4.

תאניהא אן אלדי אנגלא ולם יגי מע עזרא ונחמיה עׄ אׄ בקיו

משתתין ותשתת ענהם אלאלחאן פצארו יקרו בגיר לחן ולדלך   60

תרי אלרום יקרו בטריקה ליס הי לאהל אלעראק וללעגם

[faded illegible line]

consensus of those just mentioned[3] that the way of reading of the Land of Israel is the original one and this is what is called the Tiberian reading. This is demonstrated by the fact that the people in the communities of the exile would press any teacher who travelled (from Tiberias) to these distant lands to teach their children the reading of the Land of Israel and eagerly imbibed that from him, making him sit down so that they could assiduously learn it from him. Whoever came from the exile to the Land of Israel had a desire for the teaching of the reading of the Land of Israel that was equally ardent as that of those absent and (a desire) for abstaining from his own (tradition of reading). This is evidence for what I have stated.

II.L.0.5.

The third point is that if somebody were to read בְּרֵאשִׁית (Gen. 1.1) with the accent *tevir* or an accent other than the *ṭifḥa*, he would provoke the congregation to point out his error and angrily censure him. This demonstrates what I have stated. Likewise, if somebody were to read the three books with the cantillation of the twenty-one books or read the twenty-one books with the cantillation of the three books, the congregation would declare him to be in error and reject it. Likewise, if somebody were to read *merkha* in place of *darga*, or *darga* in place of *merkha*, or *reviaʿ* in place of *pazer*, or the like, he would be declared to be in error. Now, if all this is the case, it strengthens my claim that the accents have been established since the time of the prophets. If this were not the case, then anybody who wished to change (the reading) could change it without being called to account for this, just as there would be

---

[3] I.e. the various Jewish communities outside of the Land of Israel.

65 חכמה מא דכרנאה ובאגמאע מן דכר אן טריקה ארץ ישראל הי

אלאצל והי אלדי יסמונהא אלקראן אלטבראני יאייד מא

דכרתה אן מן סאפר מן אלמעלמין אלי הדה אלבלאד אלנאאיה

עלקת בה אלגואלי ליעלם אולאדהם קראה ארץ ישראל ותנשף

דלך מנה ואגלסוה ליתעלמו דלך מנה באגתהאד ומן גא מן

70 אלגולה אלי ארץ ישראל חכמה חכם אלגאיבין פי שהותה

לתעלים קראה ארץ ישראל וזהדה במא פי ידה אמארה עלי מא

דכרתה מן דלך

II.L.0.5.

ואלג אן לו קרא אלאנסאן בראשית בלחן תביר או מא כאן מן

אלאלחאן גיר אלטפחה <לכאן> פי תגליט אלגמאעה לה

75 ואלרד עליה באלזגר דלאלה עלי מא דכרתה וכדלך לו קרי

קאריא אלג אספאר בלחן אלואחד ועשרין ספר או קרי

<אלואחד> ועשרין ספר בלחן אלתלתה אספאר לגלטה

אלגמע ורד עליה דלך וכדי מן קרי מוצע סלסלה מארכה או

מוצע מארכה סלסלה או מוצע פזר רביע ומא גרי הדה אלמגרי

80 לגלט פאדא אסתקרת הדה אלגמלה תקוא מא דכרתה מן אן

לכאן ללמגייר

no calling to account of somebody who wanted to recite in prayer the Psalms or some passage from the twenty-four books without the intention of reading (the text) in order.

II.L.0.6.

Some people have considered the following passage to demonstrate that the accents are the work of the Levites: וְשׂ֣וֹם שֶׂ֔כֶל וַיָּבִ֖ינוּ בַּמִּקְרָ֑א 'and they gave the sense, so that they understood the reading' (Neh. 8.8). The argument is that there was no one preceding the time of Ezra, as has been mentioned before, and what is referred to (in this passage) is an innovation in relation to earlier practice. This is not improbable, since neither reason nor textual tradition confutes this claim.

II.L.0.7.

It is an established fact that the reading has various characteristic features, which the reader must learn in order to ensure a correct cantillation of what he reads. When he does not know this, the cantillation is produced in a corrupt fashion. If it be said 'So what benefit is there in the accents apart from what you have stated?', the response would be that their benefit is that they enable the congregation, however numerous, small or large, all to read one word together, and that they continue, whatever they read, in a coordinated way. Such a thing cannot be achieved without the established accents. Surely you see that Muslims, whether they be two or more, cannot read with the same degree of coordination as the Jews read, since each one has his own way (of reading). One makes long a place that another makes short. One reads melodically a place that another reads flat. For this reason they are unable to achieve what Jews do, because a group and individuals intone according to specific

אראד אן יצלי אלתהלות <ומא כאן> מן ד וכ ספר אדא לם

יכון גרצّה תרתיב אלקראה

II.L.0.6.

85 וקד אסתדל בעצהם באן אלאלחאן עמל אללוים בקו ושום שכל

ויבינו במקרא הדא אן לם יכון מתקדמא ען זמאן עזרא כמא

דכר מן קבל ויכון מא דכר תגדיד למא תקדם ומא הו בעיד לאן

לא יחיל מא דכר לא עקל ולא שרע

II.L.0.7.

פקד תבת אן אלקראה להא טרק יחתאג אן יעלמהא אלקאר

90 ליעדל תנגים מא יקראה פמתי לם יעלמה כרג אלתנגים מפסוד

פאן קיל ומא פי אלאלחאן מן אלמנפעה גיר מא דכרתה קיל לה

אן מנפעתהא אנה יתם ללגמע אלכתיר אלצגיר ואלכביר אן

יקראו גמיעא פי כלמה ואחדה ויסתמר דלך מהמא הם יקרון

עלי תרתיב ולא יתם מא הדא סבילה בגיר הדה אלאלחאן

95 אלמקררה אלי תרי אן ישמעאל לא יקדר אתנין מנהם ומא זאד

‎—————— לכל ואחד מנהם

rules, and they do not change that from letter to letter. If somebody were to change something, (his reading) would be rejected and declared to be incorrect.

II.L.0.8.

For this purpose and others, they fixed the rules of the accents and the masters of this discipline composed books and treatises that discuss the principles that have brought about their particular effects. They recorded what has deviated from a particular principle. This includes cases where the reason for the deviation is stated and cases where a reason is not stated. Know that the rules of the discipline of the accents involve the consideration of a particular accent that exhibits some inconsistency and stating what the reason is for this inconsistency. This involves, for example, consideration of the fact that the accent *tevir* is served sometimes by the conjunctive accent *merkha* and sometimes by *darga*, this being a case where the same accent has two alternating conjunctive accents. When somebody considers the reason for this, it is clear to him what the cause is that conditions the *darga*. The other rules are formulated in a similar manner. It is a discipline that is known by all who have investigated it carefully. If somebody has not investigated carefully, he only knows it from somebody who has investigated carefully. It is possible that the person who established these accents founded a discipline derived from them, which was transmitted with its practitioners. Some of this was lost and some remained, just as some of the knowledge of a language may be lost while some remains. This applies to the rules (of the accents). Whoever investigates carefully achieves his goal, or at least part of it. Since earlier scholars—may God have mercy

ואלפראד ינגמו עלי אלחק בעינה ולא יגיירו דלך מן חרף אלי

חרף פאן גייר מגייר רד עליה וגלט   100

II.L.0.8.

פלהדא אלוגה וגירה צבט[ת] (L1:6v) [ש]רוט אלאלחאן וצעו

ארבאב הדה אלעלם לה כתבא ותצאניפא יתכלמו עלי אלעלל

אלתי ותרת פי מעלולאתהא וצבטו מא כרג ען תיך אלעלה

פמנהא מא דכר אלסבב פי כרוגה ומנהא מא לם ידכר לה

סבבא ואעלם אן אלשרוט פי עלמהא תחתאג אן ינטר לחן ואחד   105

יכון פיה כלאף מא פיקול אלנאטר מא אלסבב פי הדא אלכלאף

כמן נטר פי לחן תביר אנה יכדמה תארה מארכה ותארה

סלסלה והו לחן ואחד ואלכאדמין מתגאיראן פאדא נטר מא

אלסבב פי דלך באן לה מא >אלעלה< אלמוגבה ללסלסלה

וכדי יגרי אמר סאיר אלשרוט פהו עלם יעלמה כל מן נטר פיה   110

באלסבר ואן לם יסבר לם יעלם אלא ממן סבר ומא ימתנע אן

יכון אלואצע להדה אלאלחאן געל להא עלמא מסתמדא וכאן

מע אצחאבה ואנדרס מנה אלבעץ ובקי אלבעץ כמא אנדרס מא

upon them—investigated this discipline very carefully, they achieved an expert knowledge of it.

II.L.0.9.

When, however, somebody wishes to learn about this, he is not able to find a complete book of theirs on this subject, only fragmentary writings. I have, therefore, been requested to strive to complete this short treatise that I have begun, and I have acceded to this request, acknowledging my deficiencies with regard to it and transmitting what I have learnt from their writings and from their pupils, and seeking help (in this task) from the God of Israel.

II.L.0.10.

This book consists of three sections. The first section concerns the letters and their pivots, I mean their places (of articulation) in the mouth, including those that are heavy and those that are light. The second section concerns the vowels, those that are long and those that are short, their places of articulation, their basic form and their accidental properties. The third section concerns the accents, those of low pitch and those of high pitch, and their subordinate accents.

רח אללה קד סבר הדא אלעלם סברא ג׳יידא אתבתו מא עלמוה

II.L.0.9.

ולמא ראם אלראים עלם דלך לם יציב להם פי דלך כתאבא

כאמלא בל כתב מקטעה פסאל אלסאיל אן אג׳ד פי מא אבתדית

בה מן תכמיל הדא אלמכתצר פאג׳בת אלי דלך מקר בקצורי

פיה חאכי מא תעלמתה מן כתבהם ומן (L1:7r) תלאמידהם   120

ובאלהי ישראל אסתעין

II.L.0.10.

הדא אלכתאב ישתמל עלי תלת מקאלאת אלמקאלה אלא פי

אלחרוף ומראכזהא אעני מחאלהא פי אלפם ואלתקיל מנהא

ואלכפיף אלמקאלה אלב פי אלמלוך ותקילהא וכפיפהא

ומחאלהא ואסהא ‹וערצֿהא› אלמקאלה אלג׳ פי אלאלחאן   125

ווצֿעהא ורפעהא וכדאמהא

_____

125 וערצֿהא] וערצֿעהא L1

II.L.1.0.
THE FIRST DISCOURSE: ON THE LETTERS

II.L.1.1. (Preliminary Discussion concerning the Nature of Letters)

II.L.1.1.1.

It should be noted that a letter by itself in isolation does not convey meaning. What we say is demonstrated by the fact that if you say אלף (ʾalef), although you may think it is a single letter, it is not one but three letters, viz. א ל פ. Likewise, the בא (bāʾ, i.e. bet) is two letters. Similarly, when you say גמאל (gimel), this is four letters. Similarly, the דאל (dāl, i.e. dalet) is three letters, and so forth for the remainder of the inventory of letters. This is because one cannot communicate only with the (phonetic) property of the letter itself, but when two letters follow each other, it is possible to do this with them, whether they are identical or different, as when you say גַּג ('roof'), דַּד ('breast'), גַּגּוֹת ('roofs'), דַּדֶּיהָ ('her breasts' Prov. 5:19). One cannot communicate concerning the (phonetic) property of gimel or the (phonetic) property of dāl (i.e. dalet) (by uttering the sounds) in isolation. This shows that the original conventional agreement was on the properties of the letters, and since the property could not be talked about (by uttering it) by itself, it needed something else to allow it to stand as an independent expression [ ]. So, to ʾalef was added a lamed and pe, to bāʾ (i.e. bet) was added an ʾalef, and to gimel mem, ʾalef and lamed so that it is possible to communicate about their property in isolation.

II.L.1.1.2.

If somebody were to say 'Why was the conventional agreement not on the ʾalef without its property, and on the bāʾ (i.e. bet) and gimel without their property', the response would be that ʾalef

II.L.1.0.
אלמקאלה אלאולי אלכלאם פי אלחרוף

II.L.1.1.

II.L.1.1.1.

אעלם אן אלחרף וחדה לא יפיד במגרדה יביין מא קולנא אן
קולך אלף ואן כאן ענדך אנה חרף ואחד פליס הו ואחד בל ג̇

130 חרוף אלﬞף וכדלך אלבא איצֹא חרפאן וכדלך קולך גמאל ד'
חרוף וכדלך אלדﬞאל ג̇ חרוף ועלי הדא אלמגרי יגרי אמר בקיה
אלקבאלה ודלך אן מחﭏ אלחרף וטעמה לא יצח אלתכאתב
במפרדה בל אדא תראדפא צח דלך פיהמא מתלין כאנא או
גירהן כקולך ג̇ג̇ דﭏ דתּ ג̇גיִﬞ דדיה פכאציה̇ אלגמאל לא יצח

135 אלתכאתב בהא ולא כאציה̇ אלדﬞאל עלי אלתפריד פדל דלך עלי
אן אצל אלמואצֹעה עלי כואﬕ אלחרוף ולמא לם תכן אלכאציה
תנהﭏ בנפסהא פי אלתכאתב אחתאגת אלי אמר אכר יקלהא
וינהצֹהא [   ] [   ] דלך פאזיד עלי אלאלף למﬞאד ופא ואזיד עלי
[אלבא] אלף עלי אלגמאל מאיִ ואלף ולמﬞאד חתי יצח

140 אל[תכאטב] (L1:7v) באלכאציה עלי אלתפריד

II.L.1.1.2

פאן קאל קﬞאﬕל פלﬞם לﬞא כﬞאן אלתﬞואצֹיִע עﬞלﬞי אלﬞאלﬞף דﬞון כﬞאﬞצﬞיﬞתﬞה
ואﬞלﬞבﬞא ואﬞלﬞגﬞמﬞאﬞל דﬞון כﬞאﬞצﬞיﬞתﬞהﬞמﬞא קﬞיﬞל לﬞה אﬞן אﬞלﬞאﬞלﬞף פﬞיﬞיִה ג̇ חרוף

has three letters and each letter has a different property, so how could they aim to know the property of one letter, then two further letters when no property is known to them. Rather it is necessary for them to know the distinctive property of the three letters and then pronounce a single word. My claim that the conventional agreement was initially on the property of the letter is supported by the fact that people differ with regard to the number of the letters that are added to the quality of the letter and its phonetic property, whereas no difference is permitted with regard to the quality of the letter and its phonetic property. This is because the Tiberians add only *yod* to the essence of *bāʾ*, whereas other towns add to it *yod* and *tav* and they say 'bet'. Likewise, they (the Tiberians) add *ʾalef* and *lamed* to the property of *dāl*, whereas others add *lamed* and *tav* and say 'dalet'. They add *ʾalef* and *yod* to the quality of *zāy* and say 'zāy', whereas others add *nun* to this and say 'zayin'. To *lamād* they add *mem*, then *ʾalef*, then *dāl*, where others reverse this and add *ʾalef*, then *mem*, then *dāl* and say 'lamed', and so forth. This is also the practice with the remaining letters. The variation has not taken place in the property (of the letter) but rather in the occurrence of the added letters in order for the property to be articulated in a single utterance. If this (i.e. the addition of letters) is what existed in the establishment (of the language), there would be no variation.

II.L.1.1.3.
Since the property of the letter requires other (elements), the additions have been added to the property and the letter has become a free-standing entity consisting of a combination of its property with additional elements. After this, however, the

ולכל חרף כאציה מתגאאירה פכיף יקצדו כאציה חרף ואחד ותם

חרפאן מא ערף להם כאציה ואנמא ינבגי אן יערפו כצוציה

145   אלתלת חרוף תם ינטקו בהא כלמה ואחדה יאייד מא דכרתה

מן אן אלמואצעה וקעת עלי כאציה אלחרף פי אלאבתדא הו אן

אלחרוף אלמצֿאפה אלי טעם אלחרף וכאציתה קד יכתלף

אלנאס פי כתרתהא וקלתהא וטעם אלחרף וכאציתה לא יצח

בתה אלכרוג ענה ודלך אן אלטבראניין יזידון עלי כאציה אלבא

150   יוד פקט ומדן אכר יזידון עליה יוד ותֿו פיקולון בית וכדלך יזידון

עלי כאציה אלדאל אלף ולמאד וגירהם יזיד למאד ותֿו פיקולון

דלת וכדלך יזידון עלי טעם אלזאי אלף ויוד פיקולון זאי וגירהם

יזיד עלי דלך נון פיקולון זאין וכדלך אללמאד יזידון עליה מאם

תם אלף תם דאל וגירהם יעכס דלך פיזיד אלף תם מאם תם

155   דאל פיקול לאמד אלי גיר דלך ומא גרי הדה אלמגרי פי בקיה

אלחרוף פאלתגייר לם יקע [פי אל]כאציה בל <פי וקוע>

אלחרוף אלמזידה <לנהוֿ> [אלכא]ציה באללפטֿ פי אלתפריד

פלו כאן ממא הו [וקע] פי אלמואצֿעה לם יתגייר

II.L.1.1.3.
פלמא אפתקרת (L1:8r) אלכאציה אלי גירה זידת אלזואיד עלי

160   אלכאציה ואסתקל אלחרף בטעמה מע אלזואיד ולם יכן מן בעד

156 פי וקוע] וקוע פי L1   157 לנהוֿ] בל ללנהוֿ L1

letter still cannot communicate meaning by itself, because if somebody said 'ᵓalef', he would not thereby communicate to the hearer more than what he already knows, namely that ᵓalef is distinct from (other letters such as) *ṭet*. The letter, therefore, requires other letters to be combined with it in order for meanings to be understood. So it is required, for example, to have the combination ᵓalef, *resh* and *ṣade* to (form the word) ארץ, and the combination *shin, mem* and *resh* to form שמר.

II.L.1.1.4.

Just as the property of a letter requires added elements, the combinations of letters required something else, without which no meaning can be understood by the joining of letters, namely the vowels (literally: 'kings'), which are called also vocalization (literally: inflectional vowels). This is because if (vowels such as) *qameṣ* and *pataḥ* were missing from שמר, you would not know to what form to assign the word, whether to שָׁמוֹר, or to שְׁמֹר or to שׁוֹמֵר. This would have been after the vowels were fixed among those who established (the language) by convention. If the vowels are removed, the meaning is not understood at all.

II.L.1.1.5.

The letters and vowels also require something else, namely the accents. This is the case as remarked above with (a pair of) words that have identical combinations of letters and identical vowels with no difference (between them), and that require (the placement of) the accent in order for the meaning to be understood, as in קוּמִי אוֹרִי 'Arise! Shine!' (Isa. 60.1), קוּמִי לְעֵד 'my arising as a witness' (Zeph. 3.8), יְהוָה| אוֹרִי וְיִשְׁעִי 'The Lord is my light and salvation' (Psa. 27.1).

דלך אלחרף יפיד מעני במפרדה לאן לו קאל קאיל אלף למא

אפאד אלסאמע מנה גיר מא עלמה אנה אלף מכאלף לטית

פאחתאג אלחרף איצא אלי גירה מן אלחרוף ינטם אליה ליפהם

בדלך אלמעאני פאחתיג אלי אלאלף ואלריש ואלצדי פי ארץ

165   ואלי אלשין ואלמים ואלריש פי שמר

II.L.1.1.4.

וכמא אפתקרת כאציה אלחרף אלי אלזואיד אפתקרת אלחרוף

אלמנצֹומה אלי אמר אכר לולאה מא פהם באנצֹמאם אלחרוף

מעני והם אלמלוך אלדי תסמא אנחא >לאן< לו עדם מן שמר

אלקאמצה ואלפאתחה למא עלמת אלי אין תרדהא אלי שָׁמוֹר

170   אם אלי שָׁמֵר אם אלי שׁוֹמֵר הדא בעד אסתקראר אלמלוך בין

אלמתואצֹעין ואמא בארתפאע אלמלוך מא יפהם מעני אלבתה

II.L.1.1.5.

ואפתקר איצא אלחרוף ואלמלוך אלי אמר אכר והו אלאלחאן

כמא מצֹא פימא אנצֹמת חרופה עלי סוא ואסתות מלוכה מן גיר

כלף ואחתאג אלי אללחן ליפהם אלמעני מתל קוֹמִי אָו[רי] קוּמֵי

175   לעד ייי אוֹרִי וישעי

II.L.1.1.6.

So, there are four cases of need (of complements): the need of the property (of a letter) for added elements in order for it to be an autonomous utterance, the need of a letter for another letter, the need of (a combination of) letters for vowels—these three are necessarily interdependent—and the need of (combinations of) letters and vowels for accents, not in all circumstances but in certain cases. For this reason I have presented the section on letters first, then I have presented second the section on vowels and I have presented third the section on accents, according to this order of obligatory complementarity.

II.L.1.1.7.

Now, meaning is not expressed by a letter alone and so the Hebrew grammarians have called a 'letter particle' a 'functional particle', since a functional particle does not express meaning in relation to itself but expresses meaning in relation to something else. This terminology (i.e. 'functional particle' rather than 'letter') is appropriate because אֶל consists of two letters, and likewise כִּי, מִן, אַךְ, עִם and similar cases. When some letters are combined with each other, unwritten letters are concealed between written letters. The main case of this are the vowels in words such as שָׁם, בָּם, עָם, יָד, שָׂם. In each of these words a letter ʾalef is hidden, which is one of the soft letters. When some letters are combined and a vowel occurs with them, a letter is not hidden between them, as in כִּי, בּוֹ, מִי, בִּי, in which another letter is not hidden between the two (written) letters, as a yod is hidden between the *kaf* and *nun* in נֶגֶב כִּנְּרוֹת 'south of Chinneroth' (Josh. 11.2). There are many cases of this, but I have cited here one example.

II.L.1.1.6.

פצאר ארבעה אפתקאראת אפתקאר אלכאציה אלי אלזואיד

לתסתקל פי אללפט ואפתקאר חרף אלי חרף ואפתקאר

אלחרוף אלי אלמלוך הדה תלתה לא בד מן חאגה בעצהא אלי

בעץ ואפתקאר אלחרו[ן] (L1:8v) ואלמלוך אלי אלאלחאן לא עלי

כל וגה בל פי בעץ אלמואצע ולהדא געלת מקאלת אלחרוף

מתקדמה פי אלאול ותנית במקאלה אלמלוך ותלת מקאלה

אלאלחאן עלי תרתיב אלאפתקאר ואלחאגה

II.L.1.1.7.

פאדן אלחרף וחדה לא יפאד מנה מעני ועלי הדא אלוגה סמא

אלדקדוקיין <אלחרף כאדמא> מן חית אן אלכאדם וחדה לא

יפיד מעני פי נפסה בל יפיד מעני פי גירה והדה אלתסמיה תגוז

לאן אֶל חרפאן וכדלך כִּי ומֶן ואַךְ ועֹם ומא שאכל דלך ואלחרוף

פיהא מא אדא אנצֹם בעצֹהא אלי בעץ אנכתמת חרוף גיר

מכתובה בין אלחרוף אלמכתובה ואלאצל פי דלך אלמלוך

כקולך שֵם בם עם יד שֵם פקד אנכתם פי כל לפטֹה חרף אלף

והו מן חרוף אללין ופי אלחרוף מא אדא אנצֹמת וחצל מעהמא

מלך לא ינכתם בינהמא חרף כך כִּי בוֹ מֶי בִּי אלדי מא כפי בין

אלחרפין חרף סואהמא כמא כפי ואנכתם פי נֶגֶב כְּנֻרֹות אליוד

בין אלכאף ואלנון ואמתאל דלך כתיר ואנמא אורדת באנמודגא

──────────

II.L.1.2. Section (concerning the Inventory of Letters)

The traditional inventory of letters consists of twenty-two basic letters. To the basic letters are added five letters, which are called 'straight', namely דסזʼץ. To the basic letters are added six letters, namely בגדכפת. The Tiberians add to these six letters the letter *resh*, making it (i.e. the group of non-basic letters) בגדכפרת, so that the total comes to thirty-four with the *resh* of the Tiberians. It is said that there are some who attribute a particular feature to *zayin* and call it *zāy makrūkh*. I have not, however, been able to identify their purpose in using the term *makrūkh*, in order for me to be able to describe it, as I shall describe the purpose of the Tiberians (in the use of this term *makrūkh*) with regard to the *resh*.

II.L.1.3. Chapter concerning the Place (of Articulation) of the Letters

II.L.1.3.1.

Know that according to the traditional inventory (of letters) there are five groups in five places (of articulation). These are בומף, זסצש, דטלנת, גיכרק, אהחע.

II.L.1.3.2.

The letters אהחע have a single place of articulation. This is the throat and the root of the tongue. The Tiberians call it the 'root of the tongue' and the 'place of swallowing'. This is the first place of articulation in the mouth. For this reason they are the lightest letters, as a group or individually. The meaning of their 'lightness' is that they never take *dagesh*. It has been said that *dagesh* is placed in *ʾalef* in some specific places in Scripture, namely in the following four cases: וַיָּבִיאוּ לוֹ אֶת־הַמִּנְחָה 'and they brought him the present' (Gen. 43.26), וַיָּבִיאוּ לָנוּ כְּיַד־אֱלֹהֵינוּ 'and they brought to us by the hand of our God' (Ezra 8.18), מִמּוֹשְׁבֹתֵיכֶם תָּבִיאּוּ׀ 'from your dwellings you shall bring'

II.L.1.2. פצל

אלקבלה כֹּב חרף אצולא וינצّاف אלי אלאצול כמסה חרוף והי
אלתי יסמונהא פשוטות והם דֹסֹזֹףֹץֹ ינצّاف אלי אלאצול איצֹא
סתה חרוף והי בֹגֹדֹכֹפֹתֹ אלטבראניין יזידו עלי הדה אלסתה
אחרף חרף ריש ויגעלונהא בֹגֹדֹכֹפֹרֹתֹ פיציר אלכל ארבעה (L1:9r)
ותלאתין בריש אלטבראניין וקד קיל אן תם מן יגעל ללזאי חכם
ויסמיה זאי מכרוך ומא וקפת להם עלי גרץֹ פי קולהם מכרוך
פכנת אדכרה כמא אדכר גרץֹ אלטבראניין פי אלריש

II.L.1.3. באב פי מחל אלחרוף

II.L.1.3.1.
אעלם אלקבלה תגי כמסה אקסאם פי כמסה מחאל והי אֹהֹחֹעֹ
גֹיֹכֹרֹקֹ דֹטֹלֹנֹתֹ זֹסֹצֹשֹ בֹוֹמֹףֹ

II.L.1.3.2.
אֹהֹחֹעֹ מחלהא מחל ואחד והו אלחלקום ואצל אללסאן ויסמונה
אלטבראניין עקר הלשון ובית הבליעה והו אול מחל פי אלפם
ולדלך צארת אכף אלחרוף מגמועה או מפתרקה ומעני אלכפה
פיהא הו אן לא ידכלהא דגש בתה וקד קיל אן אלדגש ידכל פי
אלאלף פי מואצֹע מכצוצה מן אלמקרא והו ארבעה ויביאו לו
את המנחה ויביאו לנו כיד אלהינו ממשבותיכם תביאו ושפו

(Lev. 23.17), וְשֻׁפּוּ עַצְמוֹתָיו לֹא רֻאּוּ 'and his bones, which were not seen, are laid bare' (Job 33.21). I shall clarify this in response to those who have adduced this as a counterargument. *Ḥet* and *ʿayin* do not take *dagesh* in any circumstances. As for *he*, it takes what could be thought to be *dagesh*, but it is not what it is thought to be. This is because *dagesh* makes a letter heavy and *rafe* makes it soft, as in גָּג 'roof'.

II.L.1.3.3.

The quality of the letter is uttered with *dagesh* and with *rafe* in the realization of its phonetic property. *Dagesh* is placed on a letter at the beginning of a word, the middle and the end. This is not the case with *he*, since it is in a place (of articulation) in which heaviness is not possible. This is because heaviness is for the purpose of a pressure[4] that is applied to the place of articulation, so that the letter is made heavy. The tongue root and the place of swallowing are not a place that permits closure or contraction, or what resembles this, like the lips, which can be closed and receive pressure,[5] so that from them can be heard בְּי and בֵּי, as will be described below. It is only at the end of a word that a point occurs in it (i.e. *he*) in order to cause its property to appear and distinguish it from places where it does not appear, such as חֶרְפָּה וּגְדוּפָה 'a reproach and a taunt' (Ezek. 5.15), in which the quality of the *he* is not pronounced, rather it is pronounced with the pronunciation of *ʾalef*. This differs from the other letters in which *dagesh* is permitted, such as *kaf* and *pe*, which have two types of pronunciation that both necessarily entail the articulation of the property of the letter.

---

[4] Literally: leaning. | [5] Literally: leaned upon.

עצמותיו לא ראו וסאביין אלכלאם פיה פי גואב מן עארﭏ בה

ואלחית ואלעין פלא ידכלהא דגש לא בוגה ולא בסבב ואלהא

קד ידכלה בטן אלטאן אנה דגש וליס דלﭏ כמא טן לאן אלדגש

יתקל אלחרﭏ ואלרפי ירכיה כﭏ גﱢ

215   קד כרג טעם אלחרﭏ פי אלדגש ואלרפי למעני כאציתה ואלדגש

ידכל פי אלחרﭏ פי אול אלכלאם ואלוצט ואלאכר ואלהא מא

הדא חאלה לאנה פי מחל לא יצח פיה אלתקל לאן אלתקל

ללאעתמאד יפעל פי אלמחל פיתקל דלﭏ אלחרﭏ ועקר הלשון

(L1:9v) ובית הבליעה מא המא מחל יגוז פיה אלטבק או אלצﭏם או

220   מא מאתל דלﭏ כאלשפתין אלתי יצח אן תטבקא ויעתמד עליהא

ויסמע מנהא בﱢ ובﱢ עלי מא ידכר מן בעד ואנמא יגי פי אואכר

אלכלאם פקט פיה נקטה פתﭏהר כאציתה ותבינה פי מא לא

יטהר חַרְפָﺓ וﭏדוּפָﺓ אלדין מא כרג ללהא טעאם בל כרג בכרוג

אלאלף אלדי הו מכאלף לבקיה אלחרוף אלדי יצח פיהמא

225   אלדגש כאלכאﭏ ואלפא אלדי עלי חאלתין פי אלנטק לא בד מן

אללפﭞ פי כאציה אלחרﭏ

II.L.1.3.4.

As for *he*, this is not pronounced at the end of a word unless it
has a dot in it. This is is not called *dagesh* but rather
'appearance'. Do you not see that if a dot appears in it, (it is) at
the end of a word, as in אֲהָהּ 'Oh!' (Josh. 7.7), מַחֲצִיתָהּ 'half of it'
(Lev. 6.13). It may occur in the middle of a word and be
pronounced in the way that it is pronounced when it has a dot
in it, as in תַּהְכְּרוּ־לִי 'you wrong me' (Job 19.3), מַהְבְּלִים 'filling
with vain hopes' (Jer. 23.16), וְהַהַרְאֵל 'and the altar hearth'
(Ezek. 43.15). So it is clear to you that this (dot) denotes
appearance and is not *dagesh*, for *dagesh* is a strengthening that
occurs in the letter after the articulation of its property: מֶלֶךְ
'king', מַלּוּךְ 'Malluch' (1 Chron. 6.29), הֶרְאֲךָ 'He made you see'
(Deut. 4.36), הַרְאִיתֶם 'Have you seen?' (1 Sam. 10.24). It is clear,
therefore, from this that the dot in *he* is to indicate the
appearance of the property (of the letter) and not for making it
heavy.

II.L.1.3.5.

It follows from all of this that these four letters are never made
heavy since they are in the first place of articulation from which
speech is sounded. If it were said: Surely the *dagesh* may be
inserted in some of the four letters of this place, namely in the
ʾalef in the four passages that you have just mentioned, and this
disproves your statement that *dagesh* is not put on the letters of
this place of articulation, the response would be: If one
examines carefully the so-called *dagesh* in the ʾalef in these four
passages, one sees that it is not *dagesh*, since the speaker strives

II.L.1.3.4.

ואלהא לא ילפט בה פי אכר אללפט אלא אן יכון פיה נקטה

פלא יסמא הדא דגש בל טהור אלי תרי אנה אדא חצל פיה

אלנקטה פי אכר אלכלמה כך אֱהָהּ מַחֲצִיתָהּ וקד יכון פי וצט

אלכלאם מן גיר הדא אלנקטה וילפט בה עלי מא ילפט בה ופיה   230

אלנקטה כך תַּהְכְּרוּ לִי מַהְבָּלִים וְהַהַרְאֵל פקד באן לך אן הדא

טהור לא דגש לאן אלדגש הו תשדיד יחצל פי אלחרף בעד

‹אלנטק› בכאציתה כך מֶלֶךּ מלוך הָרָאְךּ הַרְאִיתֶם פבאן בדלך

אן אלנקטה פי אלהא אנמא הי לטהור אלכאציה לא ללתתקיל

II.L.1.3.5.

פחצל מן הדה אלגמלה אן הדה אלדّ חרוף לא תתקל בתה למא   235

כאנת אול מחל יתצות מנה אלכלאם פאן קיל אוליס ‹קד

ידכל› אלדגש פי בעץ אלחרוף אלדّ חרוף הדא אלמחל והו

אלאלף פי אלארבע מואצّע אלתי דכרתהא אנפא פקד   (L1:10r)

כסר מא דכרתה מן אן הדא אלמחל לא ידכל חרופה דגש קיל

אן הדה אלארבע מואצّע אדא תאמל אלדגש אלמדכור פי   240

אלאלף ירי אנה לא בדגש מן חית אן אלמתכלם מתכלף

---

233 אלנטק] אלנקט L1   236 קד...ידכל] קד L1   237 קד L1

to introduce heaviness into it but it is not made heavy. Surely you see how heaviness occurs in *bet*, *kaf* and other letters without effort and strengthening takes place. This is not the case with *ʾalef*. If one examines carefully whether *ʾalef* is made heavy in this way, one will see that it is not made heavy. Rather it is as if the speaker is taking it out of a pit, unlike the other letters in which *dagesh* is permitted. It is said that the reason for the impossibility of heaviness in the letters of this place of articulation is that it is the first of the places of articulation, and the more the articulation progresses upwards from place to place, the more heaviness can be applied.

II.L.1.3.6.

From the second of the places of articulation are heard גֿ and כֿ *rafe*. This is the third of the tongue that is adjacent to the pharynx, opposite the (soft) palate. In fact this is not a primary place of articulation, but it functions like one. This is because when *gimel* and *kaf* have *dagesh*, their place of articulation is the middle of the tongue, in its wide part. The primary places of articulation are five in number. The third of the tongue that is the place of articulation of the two (aforementioned) letters with *rafe*, I mean גֿ and כֿ, is secondary. So, the total number of places of articulation are six, five primary and one secondary. The middle of the tongue is the place of articulation of five letters, namely גיכרק.

II.L.1.3.7.

From the third place of articulation are heard five letters, namely דטלנת. This is the extremity of the tongue in combination with the flesh of the teeth. If you press gently, you hear from it לֿ and נֿ *rafe*. If you press with force, you hear from it דּ

לאדכאל אלתתכיל פיה והו לא יתקל אלי תרי כיף יגי אלתתכיל
פי אלבי ואלכאף וגירהמא בגיר תכלף ויקע אלתשדיד מוקעה
וליס כדלך אלאלף ואן תאמל דלך פי תתכיל אלאלף עלם אנה
245 לא יתקל ואנמא אלמתכלם כאנה יכרגה מן גב מכאלפא למא
יצח פיה אלדגש מן סאיר אלחרוף וקיל אן אלעלה פי סקוט
אלתתכיל ען חרוף הדא אלמחל לאנה אול אלמחאל וכל מא
צעד מן מחל מחל אלי מחל יתקל

II.L.1.3.6.

ואלמחל אלתאני מן מחאל אלחרוף יסמע מנה גׄ דׄ אלמרפיין והו
250 תלת אללסאן ממא ילי אלחלקום קדאם אלחנך והדא אלמחל
ליס הו אלאצל פי אלחקיקה בל יגרי מגראה לאן מתי צאר
אלגמאל ואלכאף מדגושה כאן מחלהמא וסט אללסאן בערצׄה
פאצול אלמחאל כמסה ותלת אללסאן אלדי הו מחל אלחרפין
אלמרפיין אעני גׄ דׄ הוא פר[ע] פגמלה אלמחאל סתה כמסה
255 אצול ואאח[ד] (L1:10v) פרע פוסט אללסאן מחל לכמסה חרוף והי
גׄכׄרקׄ

II.L.1.3.7.

ואלמחל אלתאלת ‹יסמע מנה› כמסה חרוף והי דׄטׄלׄנׄת והו
טרף אללסאן מע לחם אלאסנאן ואן אלצקת ברפק סמעת
מנהא דׄ תׄ אלמרפיין ואן אלצקת בקוה סמעת מנה ד ת

---

257 יסמע מנה] יסמע L1

and ת with *dagesh*. This differs from the second place of articulation, which is divided into two places (when the letters are pronounced) with *dagesh* and *rafe* respectively, namely the (back) third of the tongue and its middle. *Dalet* and *tav* are not like that, rather their place of articulation does not change, whether they have *dagesh* or *rafe*. *Dagesh* denotes pressing with force and *rafe* (pressing) lightly.

II.L.1.3.8.

The fourth place of articulation is the teeth, from which are heard four letters, namely זסצש. In this place of articulation the letters are not divided into light and heavy as in the preceding places of articulation. Know that when you pronounce (the word) שִׁין, you pronounce three letters from three different places of articulation, the *shin* from the teeth, the *yod* from the middle of the tongue, in its wide part, and the *nun* from the extremity of the tongue and the flesh of the teeth. If you taste a letter (by pronouncing it) in its place of articulation, you will taste its property.

II.L.1.3.9.

The fifth place of articulation is the lips, which is that of the four letters בומף. If you close the lips with force, ב and פ with *dagesh* are heard. If you close them gently and lightly, you hear from them ב and ף with *rafe*. This place of articulation is like the place of articulation of דטלנת, where two letters with *dagesh* and two letters with *rafe* are heard.

אלמדגושין והדֹא מכֹאלף ללמחל אלבֹ אלדי אנקסם אלי מחלין

ענד אלדגש ואלרפה המא תלת אללסאן וסטה ואלדאל ואלתו

ליס המא כדלך בל מחלהמא לא יתגייר לא פי אלדגש ולא פי

אלרפי ואנמא אלדגש לאלאלצאק באלקוה ואלרפי באלכפה

II.L.1.3.8.

ואלמחל אלראבע הו <אלאסנאן> יסמע מנה דֹ חרוף והי זֹסֹצֹשֹ

והדֹא אלמחל לא ינקסם פיה אלחרף אלי כפה ותקל מתל

אלמחאל אלדי תקדמתה ואעלם אנֹך אדא לפטֹת בשין פקד

לפטֹת בגֹ חרוף מן תלת מחאל מתגאירה פאלשין מן אלאסנאן

ואליוד מן [וסט] אללסאן בערצֹה ואלנון מן טרף אללסאן ולחם

אלאסנאן פאדֹא דקת אלחרף פי מחלה אנמא דקת מנה

כֹאציתה

II.L.1.3.9.

ואלמחל אלֹה הו אלשפתין מחל ארבע חרוף בֹוֹמֹף פֹאן

אטבק[ת] אלשפתין בקוה סמע מנהמא ^(L1:11r) ב פֹ אלמדגושין

ואן אטבקתהמא ברפק וכפה סמעת מנהמא ב ו ף אלמרפיין

פקד צאר הדֹא אלמחל מתל מחל דֹטֹלֹנֹת אלדי יסמע מנה

חרפין מדגושין וחרפין מרפיין

II.L.1.4. Section (concerning some General Issues relating to Letters)

II.L.1.4.1.

If somebody were to say 'What is the value of knowing the places of articulation of the letters?', the response to him would be as follows. If somebody asked and said 'What is language?', I would say: It consists of expressions that its original speakers[6] established by convention among themselves to make their intentions understood to one another. It needs to be known that before this they established by convention specific letters in various places of articulation, from which the expressions could be constructed. They were, therefore, the foundations of the expressions. Through knowledge of the places of articulation the thinking of the establishers (of the language) can become clear, in that they taught that the meaning that one intends can be fully expressed with twenty-two letters, but cannot be fully expressed with less than this. They took them from five basic places of articulation, and one secondary place of articulation, as has been explained. Either it was the case that only the aforementioned letters could have been produced from each place of articulation or they knew that letters other than those mentioned could have been produced from the places of articulation but they had no need of more than the ones they proclaimed. It seems that it will be impossible for us to know the truth with regard to this issue.

II.L.1.4.2.

[   ] not true. Since it is of this nature, knowledge [   ] than ignorance. Since the knowledge of the technique of reading is explicated through (its analysis into) letters, vowels, accents and

---

[6] Literally: the masters.

פצל .II.L.1.4

II.L.1.4.1.

אן קאל מא אלפאידה פי מערפה מחאל אלחרוף קיל לה לו

סאל סאיל פקאל מא אללגה לקלת הי עבאראת תואצֹע עליהא

ארבאבהא ליפהמו אגראצֹהם לבעצֹהם בעץֹ ויחתאג אן יעלם

קבל הדא אנהם תואצֹעו עלי חרוף מכצוצה פי מחאל מכתלפה   280

אלתי מנהא יצח אן תנבני אלעבאראת פהי ללעבאראת אצֹולא

פאתצֹח בעלם אלמחאל חכמה אלמתואצֹעין באן עלמו אן

אלגרץֹ יכמל באתני ועשרין חרפא ובדון דלך לא יכמל

ואתכדוהא מן כמסה מחאל אצול ומחל ואחד פרע עלי מא

מצֹא ביאנה פאמא אן יכון לא יצח מן כל מחל גיר מא דכר מן   285

אלחרוף או עלמו אן יצח מן אלמחאל גיר אלחרוף אלמדכ[ורה]

גיר אן לם תדעהם אלחאגה אלי אכתר ממא דכרוה וקריב אנא

תתעדד מערפה צחה דלך

II.L.1.4.2.

מן ל[   ] אלעלם סבילה הדא כאן פמא יצח לא [   ] (L1:11v) [   ]

אלגהל ולמא כאן עלם צנאעה אלקראה יעלל בחרוף ומלוך   290

the *shewa*, it is appropriate for the necessary description to be made of each of these, in order for me to demonstrate the superiority of this language over other languages, since it is 'a pure language' (Zeph. 3.9). Given that among the letters of Hebrew there are several letters, as explained above, that are 'straight', there are בֹּגֹדֹכֹפֹתֹ letters, and *dagesh* and *rafe* in all remaining letters except אֶהֶחֶעֶ, if one were to say 'What is the function of *dagesh* and *rafe*?', the response would be as follows. There is clearly a function. This includes the change of meaning by means of *dagesh* and *rafe*, for example שְׂמַח בָּחוּר 'Rejoice, oh young man!' (Ecc. 11.9), which is an intransitive verb, since the *mem* in it is light. If it has *dagesh*, the verb becomes transitive, as in שַׂמֵּחַ נֶפֶשׁ עַבְדֶּךָ 'Gladden the soul of your servant' (Psa. 86.4). Likewise הַכֹּהֵן הַמְטַהֵר 'the priest who cleanses' (Lev. 14.11) is a transitive agent, whereas אֶת הָאִישׁ הַמִּטַּהֵר 'the man who is cleansed' (Lev. 14.11) is a reflexive agent, and similar cases.

II.L.1.4.3.

The people of the language used words from one place of articulation, such as אֲהָהּ 'Oh!', which is from the place of articulation of אֶהֶחֶעֶ, דְּלֶת from the place of articulation of דֹטֹלֹנֹת, מִפּוֹ וּמִפּוֹ 'on this side and that' (Ezek. 40.34) from the place of articulation of בֹוֹמֹף, and similar cases.

GAP

II.L.1.4.4.

[...] The third category is what interchanges in one place of articulation, for example בִּזַּר 'He scattered' (Psa. 68.31), which is said to be like פִּזַּר | נָתַן לָאֶבְיוֹנִים 'He has distributed, he has given to the poor' (Psa. 112.9). The place of articulation of *bet* and *pe* is the lips. (Another case) is וְשׁוֹבַךְ 'and Shobach' (2 Sam. 10.16) and וְשׁוֹפַךְ 'and Shopach' (1 Chron. 19.16), which are said to be

ואלחאן [ו]שוא חסן אן ידכר פי כל ואחד מא יסנח ויתגה פיה

לאביין שרף הדה אללגה עלי סאיר אללגאת לאנהא שפה

ברורה ואדא פי חרוף אלעבראני כאנת חרוף עדה עלי מא דכר

פי מא תקדם מן אלפשוטות ובْגْדْכْפֿת ואלדגש ואלרפי אלדי פי

בקיה אלחרוף סוא אֹהֹחֹע פאן קיל פמא אלפאידה פי אלדגש   295

ואלרפי קיל לה לא בד מן פאידה מן דלך תגייר אל[מע]נא

באלדגש ואלרפי מתל שָׂמַח בָחוּר אלדי הו פעל פי אלנפס לכון

אלמים גאת פיה כפיפה ואדא גאת מדגושה תעדי אלפעל כْק

שָׂמֵחַ נפש עבדך וכדלך הכהן הַמְטַהֵר פאעל באלגיר את האיש

הַמְטַהֵר פאעל בנפסה ואמתאל דלך   300

II.L.1.4.3.

ואסתעמל אהל אללגה אלכלאם מן אלמחל אלואחד מתל אַהָה

מן מחל אֹהֹחֹע ומן מחל דْטْלْנْת דלת ומן מחל בْוֹמֹף מפו ומפו

ומא מאתל

GAP

II.L.1.4.4.

אלארוזי ואלקסם אלתאלת מא ינבדל פי מחל ואחד מתל   (L3:14r)

בזר אלדי יקאל אנה מתל פזר נתן לאביונים אלבא ואלפא   305

מחלהמא אלשפתאן ושובך ושופך אלדי יקאל אנהמא אסם

the same name; and likewise הִטְעוּ אֶת־עַמִּי 'They have misled my people' (Ezek. 13.10)—הִתְעוּ '(God) caused (me) to wander' (Gen. 20.13), עוּשׁוּ 'Hasten!' (Joel 4.11)—חוּשׁוּ.

II.L.1.4.5.

The fourth category is what interchanges from different places of articulation, which includes scribal error and ciphers, for *dalet* and *resh* (which are sometimes confused by scribal error) are from two different places of articulation and the cipher (consisting of the interchange of) *bet* and *shin* is from two different places of articulation. Interchanges that are from a single place of articulation do not fall into this category, as will be explained in a separate chapter (see §II.L.1.5.).

II.L.1.4.6.

Take note that it is said that some letters are contracted. Their contraction is indicated by two things: meaning and grammar. Some letters are augments at the beginning, middle or end of a word.

II.L.1.4.7.

An example of an augmented letter at the beginning of a word is הַשְּׁלִשִׁי לְאַבְשָׁלוֹם 'The third is Absalom' (1 Chron. 3.2). It is said that the presence of this *lamed* has no meaning and the meaning would remain the same if it were elided. An example of an augmented letter in the middle of a word is said to be יְלָדִים אֲשֶׁר אֵין־בָּהֶם כָּל־מְאוּם 'youths without blemish' (Dan. 1.4). It is said that the *ʾalef* in מְאוּם is augmented, without any function, because the lexical class of 'blemish' does not contain a root letter *ʾalef*. Examples of an augmented letter at the end of a word are אֹסְרִי לַגֶּפֶן עִירֹה 'binding his foal to the vine' (Gen. 49.11)

ואחד וכדלך הטעו את עמי התעו עושו חושו

II.L.1.4.5.

ואלקסם אלראבע מא ינבדל מן מחאל מתגאירה והו יעם
אלתצחיף ואלגמטריא לאן אלדאל ואלריש מן מחלין גירין
ואלגמטריא אלבא ואלשין מן מחלין <מתגאירין> פמא כאן מן
מחל ואחד אנבדאלה לא ידכל פי הדא אלקסם עלי מא סיגי
ביאנה פי באב מפרד

II.L.1.4.6.

ואעלם אן קד קיל אן פי אלחרוף איצֹא מא יכתצר וידל עלי
אכתצארה שיין אלמעני ואללגה ופיהא מא יגי זאיד פי אול
אללפטֹ ואלוסט ואלאכר

II.L.1.4.7.

פאלזאיד פי אול אללפטֹ השלישי לאבשלום קיל אן הדא
אללמאד לא מעני לתבותה בל ינ[תטֹ]ם אלמעני בחדפה
ואלזאיד פי וסט אלכלאם קיל מתל ילדים אשר אין בהם כל
מאום פקיל אן אלאלף פי מאום זאיד לא פאידה פיה לאן לגה
אלעיב מא פיה אלף אצלי ואלזאיד פי אכר אללפטֹ כקולה ^(L3:14v)

תֹ[תֹ]ם L1:3r

and בְּנוֹ בְעֹר 'the son of Beor' (Num. 24.3), where the *vav* of בְּנוֹ has no meaning, and likewise the *yod* in אֹסְרִי, since it is not a pronoun, and similar cases.

II.L.1.4.8.

As for cases of the contraction of a letter that is reflected by the meaning, it is said to include examples such as אֲשֶׁר נִתָּנְךָֽ יְהוָה׀ הַיּוֹם בְּיָד 'for the Lord gave you into my hand today' (1 Sam. 26.23), where it is said that a *yod* has been contracted in יָד, and its virtual form is בְּיָדִי, since it does not say בְּיַד, in which it would be conjoined to an underlying noun, but rather it is pronounced in its disjoined form, which is with *qameṣ*. Likewise in אַתָּה זֶה בְּנִי עֵשָׂו 'Are you my son Esau?' (Gen. 27.24), it is said that a *he* has been contracted in אַתָּה, since it does not have the function of a declarative but rather of an interrogative, and its virtual form is הַאַתָּה. Likewise in תַּרְקִיעַ עִמּוֹ לִשְׁחָקִים 'Can you like him spread out the skies?' (Job 37.18) an interrogative *he* is contracted in it and its virtual form is הֲתַרְקִיעַ עִמּוֹ, so that it would be like הֲתָשִׂים אַגְמוֹן 'Can you put a rope?' (Job 40.26), הֲתְשַׁלַּח בְּרָקִים 'Can you send forth lightnings' (Job 38.35).

II.L.1.4.9.

As for cases of the contraction of a letter that is reflected by the grammar, these include examples like בְּכַשִּׁיל וְכֵילַפּֽׂת 'with hatchets and hammers' (Psa. 74.6), since it should according to rule have been וּבְכֵילַפּוֹת, so that it would be like אַכֶּה בְדָוִד וּבַקִּיר 'I will pin David to the wall' (1 Sam. 18.11), בַּחֲמוֹרִים וּבַגְּמַלִּים וּבַפְּרָדִים׀ וּבַבָּקָר 'on asses and on camels and on mules and on oxen' (1 Chron. 12.41), for this is the rule for the co-ordination of two nouns after one another with the particle *bet*.

אסרי לגפן עירה בנו בעור אלדי אלואו פי בנו לא מעני לה

וכדלך אליוד פי אסרי לאנה ליס צֻמיר ומא מאתל דלך

II.L.1.4.8.

ואמא מא יכתצר ויתבתה אלמעני פקיל אנה מתל אשר נתנך יֵי

היום ביד אלדי יקאל אנה מכתצר יוד פי יד ותקדירה בידי לאנה

325 מא קאל בִיַד פיכון מצֹאף אלי אסם מצֹמר בל אכרגה בכרוג

אלקטע והו אלקֻמֵצ וכדלך אתה זה בני עשו קיל אן אלהא מן

אתה מכתצר לאן ליסה מוצֹע כבר בל אסתפהאם ותקדירה

האתה זה ומתלה תרקיע עמו לשחקים הא אלתמה מכתצר מנה

ותקדירה התרקיע עמו ליגרי מגרי התשים אגֹ התשלח ברקים

II.L.1.4.9.

330 ואמא מא יכתצר פתתבתה אללגה הו כקו בכשיל וכלפות אד

כאן חקה אן יגי ובכלפות ליגרי מגרי אכה בדוד ובקיר בחמורים

ובגמלים ובפרדים ובבקר אד דלך מן חק אלעטף פי אלאסמין

אלמעטוף אחדהמא עלי אלאכר בחרף בא

II.L.1.4.10.

When two identical letters succeed one another at the end of
one word and the beginning of another and the two words are
linked by an accent, if the reader is not careful to pronounce
them both, one of them would become coalesced and they
would be pronounced as one letter. The reader must pronounce
them clearly in order to distinguish, for example, the two *ṣades*
in וַיָּצֵץ צִיץ 'it produced blossoms' (Num. 17.23), to ensure that
the two *nuns* are pronounced in בֵּאדַיִן נְבוּכַדְנֶצַּר 'then Nebuchad-
nezzar' (Dan. 3.13, etc.) and to ensure that the two *mems* are
pronounced in כַּאֲשֶׁר הָיִיתִי עִם־מֹשֶׁה 'as I was with Moses' (Josh.
1.5, etc.), and similar cases of two letters succeeding each other
in this manner.

II.L.1.5. Chapter on the Interchange of Letters

II.L.1.5.1.

It is said that among the letters are those that interchange from
the same place of articulation, so that, for example, *ʾalef*
interchanges with *he* in a case such as וְאַחֲרֵיכֵן אֶתְחַבַּר 'after this
he joined' (2 Chron. 20.35). This is in place of הִתְחַבֵּר, because
the *ʾalef* in אֶתְחַבַּר is not the *ʾalef* of the first person future, but is
the expression of the narrator. Likewise יֶתֶר הָאָמֹן 'the rest of the
multitude' (Jer. 52.15), which is in place of הֶהָמוֹן, כִּי־שֶׁקֶר אַתָּה
דֹּבֵר אֶל־יִשְׁמָעֵאל 'for you are speaking falsely of Ishmael' (Jer.
40.16), which is in place of עַל־יִשְׁמָעֵאל, and similar cases.

II.L.1.5.2.

From the place of articulation of בֹּומֹף, *bet* interchanges with *pe*,
as in יְבַזֵּר—יְפַזֵּר 'he scatters', פִּזַּר—בִּזַּר 'he scattered'. As for what
interchanges from two different places of articulation, this is like
the interchange of *bet* with *he* in וְהִכִּיתָ בַצּוּר 'you shall strike the
rock' (Exod. 17.6), which is said to be in place of הַצּוּר.

II.L.1.4.10.

ואלחרוף אדא תראדף מנהא חרפאן פי אכר אלכלמה ואחד ופי

335 אול אלאכרי אכר מתלה וכאנתא אלכלמתאן מכתלטתין

באללחן אן לם ^(L3:15r) יגעל אלקאר באלה אליהמא ליטהרהמא

ואלא אנדגם אלואחד וכרגא מכרג חרף ואחד פיגב אן

יטהרהמא אלקאר ליבין אלצאדין פי וְיֵצֶץ צִיץ ויכון אלנונין פי

באדין נבוכדנצאר ויכרג אלמאמין פי כאשר הייתי עם משה ומא

340 מאתל דלך מן אלחרפין אלמתראדפה עלי הדא אלוגה

II.L.1.5. באב פי אבדאל אלחרוף

II.L.1.5.1.

קיל אן פי אלחרוף מא ינבדל מן מחל ואחד פינבדל אלאלף

באלהא כקו ואחריכן אתחבר פהו מקאם התחבר לאן ליס

אלאלף פי אתחבר אלף אלאסתקבאל אלדי ללמתכלם בל הו

345 קול אלמכבר וכדלך יתר האמון מקאם ההמון כי שקר אתה

דובר אל ישמעאל הו מקאם על ישמעאל ומא מאתל דלך

II.L.1.5.2.

ומן מחל בֹומִף ינבדל אלבא באלפא כקו יבזור יפזור בְּזַר פְּזַר

ואמא מא ינבדל מן מחאל מתגאירה מתל מא ינבדל אלבא

באלהא בק והכית בצור קיל אנה מקאם הצור

II.L.1.5.3.

Gimel interchanges with *kaf* in סוּגָה בַּשּׁוֹשַׁנִּים 'encircled with lilies' (Cant. 7.3), which is said to be סוּכָה, from יָשָׁר מִמְּסוּכָה 'the upright from a thorn hedge' (Micah 7.4), since it does not make sense for it to be derived from נָסֹגּוּ אָחוֹר 'they shall be turned back' (Isa. 42.17, etc.). These two letters are from the same place of articulation. *Mem* interchanges with *gimel*, as in נְגַשְׁשָׁה כַעִוְרִים 'We grope like the blind' (Isa. 59.10), which is in place of נְמַשְׁשָׁה, as in יְמַשְׁשׁוּ־חֹשֶׁךְ 'They grope in the dark' (Job 12.25).

II.L.1.5.4.

Dalet interchanges with *zayin*, as in דְּהַב—זָהָב. (The interchange of) *resh* with *dalet* is due to scribal error, as in רְעוּאֵל 'Reuel'—דְּעוּאֵל 'Deuel', רִיפַת 'Riphath' (Gen. 10.3)—דִּיפַת 'Diphath' (1 Chron. 1.6), רוֹדָנִים 'Rodanim' (1 Chron. 1.7)—דֹּדָנִים 'Dodanim' (Gen. 10.4).

II.L.1.5.5.

He interchanges with *ʾalef*, as in אֲשֶׁר־יִקְרֶה לְעַמְּךָ 'what is to befall your people' (Dan. 10.14), in which (the *ʾalef* of the qere) is in place of *he*. A similar case is כַּד הַקֶּמַח לֹא תִכְלֶה 'The jar of meal shall not be spent' (1 Kings 17.14). This is from the same place of articulation. A case of interchange from two places of articulation is עֹצֶה עֵינָיו 'he who closes his eyes' (Prov. 16.30), in place of עוֹצֵם from וַיְעַצֵּם 'and he closed' (Isa. 29.10).

II.L.1.5.6.

Vav interchanges with *bet*, as in שָׁכְרוּ וְלֹא־יַיִן נָעוּ וְלֹא שֵׁכָר 'They were drunk, but not with wine; they staggered, but not with strong drink' (Isa. 29.9), in place of בְּלֹא יַיִן, בְּלֹא שֵׁכָר. This is from the same place of articulation. From two places of articulation it interchanges with *ʾalef*, as in מִפְּנֵי גֵוָה 'because of pride' (Jer. 13.17), which is said to be in place of גֵּאָה.

II.L.1.5.3.

אלגמאל ינבדל בכאף סוגה בשושנים קיל אנה סוכה מן ישר

ממסוכה אד כאן לא מעני להא מן נסוגו אחור והדין אלחרפין

מן מחל ואחד ואלמאם ^(L3:15v) ינבדל בגמאל כך נגששה כעורים

מקאם נמששה כקו ימששו חשך

350

II.L.1.5.4.

אלדאל ינבדל בזאי כקו זהב דהב ואלריש באלדאל מן אלתצחיף

רעואל דעואל ריפת דיפת רודנים דודָנים

355

II.L.1.5.5.

אלהא ינבדל באלף כקו אשר יקרא לעמך מקאם הא וכדלך כד

הקמח לא תכלה והדא מן מחל ואחד ומן מחלין עוצה עיניו

מקאם עוצם מן ויעצם

II.L.1.5.6.

אלואו ינבדל בבא כך שכרו ולא יין נעו ולא שכר מקאם בלא יין

בלא שכר והדא מן מחל ואחד ומן מחלין ינבדל באלף כך מפני

גֵוה קיל אנה מקאם גֵאה

360

II.L.1.5.7.

Zayin interchanges in the same place of articulation with *ṣade*, as in יַעֲלֹז 'he rejoices'—יַעֲלֹץ 'he rejoices', מִזְעָר 'a little' (Isa. 10.25, etc.)—מִצְעָר 'a little one' (Gen. 19.20, etc.). An example from two places of articulation is קִפֹּד 'hedgehog' (Isa. 14.23, etc.)—קִפּוֹז 'hedgehog' (Isa. 23.15).

II.L.1.5.8.

Ḥet interchanges with *resh*, as in מֶלֶךְ עַל־כָּל־בְּנֵי־שָׁחַץ 'He is king over all creeping creatures' (Job 41.26), which is in place of שֶׁרֶץ. These are from two places of articulation.

II.L.1.5.9.

Ṭet interchanges in the same place of articulation with *tav*, as in פְּסַנְתֵּרִין 'harp' (Dan. 3.5, etc.)—פְּסַנְטֵרִין 'harp' (Dan. 3.7).

II.L.1.5.10.

It is said that *yod* interchanges with *ʾalef*, as in וּמִמַּעֲמָדְךָ יֶהֶרְסֶךָ 'and I shall cast you down from your station' (Isa. 22.19), in place of אֶהֶרְסֶךָ, which corresponds to the meaning of וַהֲדַפְתִּיךָ 'and I shall cast you down' (Isa. 22.19).

II.L.1.5.11.

It is said that *kaf* interchangs with *bet*, as in כְּאָכְלָם מֵהַנָּזִיד (2 Kings 4.40), which is in place of בְּאָכְלָם, so that its meaning is 'while they were eating (pottage)', since a comparison here is not relevant. A similar case כַּעֲלוֹת הַמִּנְחָה 'when bringing up the offering' (2 Kings 3.20), so that it is like בַּעֲלוֹת הַלַּהַב 'when the flame went up' (Jud. 13.20). This is from two places of articulation. A case from the same place of articulation is וַיְרַגֵּל בְּעַבְדְּךָ 'He has slandered your servant' (2 Sam. 19.28), which is said to be in place of וַיְרַכֵּל, from לֹא־תֵלֵךְ רָכִיל 'You shall not go as a slanderer' (Lev. 19.16).

II.L.1.5.7.

אלזאי ינבדל מן מחל ואחד בצדי יעלץ יעלז מזער מצער ומן

מחלין קפוד קפוז

II.L.1.5.8.

אלחית ינבדל בריש כֹק מלך על כל בני שחץ אנה מקאם שרץ

365   והמא מן מחלין

II.L.1.5.9.

אלטית ינבדל מן מחל ואחד בתֶו פסנתרין פסנטרין

II.L.1.5.10.

אליוד קיל אנה ינבדל באלף כֹק וממעמדך יהרסך מקאם אהרסך

ויואפק מעני והדפתיך

II.L.1.5.11.

אלכאף קיל אנה ינבדל בבא בֹק כאכלם מהנזיד הו מקאם

370   באכלם ליכון מענאה ענד אכלהם (L3:16r) לאן אלתמתיל מא לה

הונא מדכל ומתלה כעלות המנחה ליגרי מגרי בעלות הלהב

והדא מן מחלין ומן מחל ואחד וירגל בעבדך קיל אנה מקאם

וירכֶל מן לא תלך רכיל

II.L.1.5.12.

Lamed interchanges with *bet,* as in לְמִכְמָשׁ יַפְקִיד כֵּלָיו 'At Michmash he stores his baggage' (Isa. 10.28), in place of בְּמִכְמָשׁ. It is said that וְהָיָה כִּי־יֶאְשַׁם לְאַחַת מֵאֵלֶּה 'when a man is guilty in any of these' (Lev. 5.5) is in place of בְּאַחַת. These two are from two places of articulation. An example from one place of articulation is וְיַרְכָתוֹ עַל־צִידֹן 'and his border shall be up to Sidon' (Gen. 49.13), which is said to be in place of עַד־צִידֹן.

II.L.1.5.13.

It is said that *mem* interchanges with *bet,* in the same place of articulation, in אָכֵן בָּגְדָה אִשָּׁה מֵרֵעָהּ 'Surely, (as) a wife is faithless against her husband' (Jer. 3.20), in place of בְּרֵעָהּ.

II.L.1.5.14.

Nun interchanges with *mem* from two places of articulation, for example לַמְּלָכִים 'to the kings' (2 Chron. 1.12, etc.)—מְלָכִין 'kings' (Prov. 31.3), לְקֵץ הַיָּמִין 'at the end of days' (Dan. 12.13), the virtual form of which is הַיָּמִים.

II.L.1.5.15.

Samekh interchanges with *ṣade* in the same place of articulation, as in נָתְסוּ 'they have broken' (Job 30.13)—נָתְצוּ 'they broke' (2 Kings 25.10, etc.). It is also said that יְקוֹסֵס 'he will cut' (Ezek. 17.9) is in place of יְקוֹצֵץ.

II.L.1.5.16.

It is said that *ᶜayin* interchanges with *ḥet,* as in עוּשׁוּ 'hasten' (Joel 4.11)—חוּשׁוּ.

II.L.1.5.12.

אללמאד ינבדל בבא מתל למכמש יפקיד כליו מק במכמש

וקאלו אן והיה כי יאשם לאחת מאלה אנה מקאם באחת והדין

מן מחלין ומן מחל ואחד וירכתו על צידון קאלו אנה מקאם עד

צידון

II.L.1.5.13.

ואלמים קיל אנה ינבדל בבֵא והו מן מחל ואחד אכן בגדה אשה

מרעה מקאם ברעה

II.L.1.5.14.

אלנון ינבדל מן מחלין בֵמֶים מתל למלכים מלבין קץ הימין

תקדירה הימים

II.L.1.5.15.

אלסמאך ינבדל בצדי מן מחל ואחד נתסו נתצו וקיל אן יקוסס

מקאם יקוצץ

II.L.1.5.16.

אלעין קיל אנה ינבדל בחית מתל עושו חושו

375

380

II.L.1.5.17.

Pe interchanges with *bet* from the same place of articulation in
מְטַר סֹחֵף 'sweeping rain' (Prov. 28.3), which is said to be in place
of סוֹחֵב. Likewise it is said that נִסְחַף אַבִּירֶיךָ 'Your warriors have
been dragged away' (Jer. 46.15) is in place of נִסְחַב. An example
from two places of articulation is said to be יְרוֹפְפוּ 'they shake'
(Job 26.11) in place of יְרוֹחֲפוּ from רָחֲפוּ 'they shake' (Jer. 23.9).

II.L.1.5.18.

It is said that *ṣade* interchanges with *samekh* in the same place
of articulation, as in חֲמוּץ בְּגָדִים 'blood red of garments' (Isa.
63.1).

II.L.1.5.19.

It is said that *qof* interchanges with *kaf* in the same place of
articulation, as in קוֹבַע 'helmet' (1 Sam. 13.38, etc.)—כּוֹבַע
'helmet' (1 Sam. 17.5, etc.).

II.L.1.5.20.

It is said that *resh* interchanges with *kaf*, as in חַשְׁרַת־מַיִם
'darkness of water' (2 Sam. 22.12)—חֶשְׁכַת־מָיִם 'darkness of water'
(Psa. 18.12).

II.L.1.5.21.

Shin interchanges with *samekh* in the same place of articulation
in שְׁתֻם הָעָיִן 'shut of eye' (Num. 24.3, etc.), which is in place of
סָתוּם from סְתֹם הַדְּבָרִים 'shut up the words' (Dan. 12.4). Its
interpretation as 'placed' is not plausible. This is because שְׁתֻם is
a conjoined passive participle. The disjoined form would be
שָׁתֻם, like שָׁמוּר, זָכוּר, and its imperative would have to be שְׁתוֹם or
שְׁתֹם. This would lead to the conclusion that there is a root letter
mem in the lexical class of 'placing', but this is not the case,
because (we see from examples such as) שָׁת שָׁתוּ הַשְּׂעֹרָה 'They

II.L.1.5.17.

385 אלפא ינבדל מן מחל ואחד בבא מטר סוחף קיל אנה מקאם

סוחב וכדלך נסחף אבירّיך קיל אנה מקאם נסחב ומן מחלין קיל

ירופפו מקאם ירוחפו מן רחפו

II.L.1.5.18.

אלצّדי קיל אנה ינבדל בסמאך מן מחל ואחד מתל חמוץ בגדים

II.L.1.5.19.

אלקוף קיל אנה ינבדל (L3:16v) מן מחל ואחד בכף מתל קובע

390 כובע

II.L.1.5.20.

אלריש קיל אנה ינבדל בכַף מתל חשרת מים חשכת

II.L.1.5.21.

אלשׁין ינבדל מן מחל ואחד בסמאך והו שתום העין מק סתום

מן סתום הדברים ואלדי פסרה מגעול מא הו תפסיר קריב ודלך

אן שתום מפעול מצّאף ואלמכרת יכון שָׁתום מתל זָכור שָׁמור

395 ויגב אן יכון אמרה שָׁתום או שָׁתַם והדא יודי אלי אן יכון פי לגה

אלאגעאל מים אצלי וליס אלאמר כדלך לאן קו שת שָׁתו

placed (themselves) at the gate' (Isa. 22.7), שָׂתוּ בַשָּׁמַיִם פִּיהֶם 'They set their mouths against the heavens' (Psa. 73.9), כֹּל שַׁתָּה תַּחַת־רַגְלָיו 'You have put everything under his feet' (Psa. 8.7), (that) all forms from the lexical class of 'placing' lack *mem*.

II.L.1.5.22.

It is said that *tav* interchanges with *ʾalef*, as in וַיִּקַּח תִּרְזָה וְאַלּוֹן 'He took a cedar tree and an oak' (Isa. 44.14), which is in place of אֶרֶז 'cedar' (Zeph. 2.14). This is a short sample of the interchange of letters.

II.L.1.6. Chapter concerning the Influence of the Four Letters *ʾalef, vav, yod* and *he*, I mean אוֹיה, on the Six Letters בֿגֿדֿכֿפֿתֿ

When one of these four is at the end of a word and the word is conjoined with what follows it by the accent, and the second word begins with one of the letters בֿגֿדֿכֿפֿתֿ, this letter is pronounced light with *rafe*, as in וְאֶקְחָה פַת־לֶחֶם 'and I shall fetch a morsel of bread' (Gen. 18.5), כִּי בְאַפָּם 'for in their anger' (Gen. 49.6), אוֹ בְדֶרֶךְ רְחֹקָה 'or on a far journey' (Num. 9.10), אֵלֶּה בְנֵי־אֶפְרַיִם 'These are the sons of Ephraim' (Num. 26.35), וּסְקַלְתּוֹ בָאֲבָנִים 'and you shall stone him to death with stones' (Deut. 13.11), וַיְהִי דְבַר־יְהוָה 'and the word of the Lord was' (1 Kings 17.2, etc.), and very many similar examples of what is not disjoined from the (preceding) accent. In every case where there is no disjunction from the (preceding) accent in this way, the בֿגֿדֿכֿפֿתֿ letters are light, with *rafe*.

II.L.1.7. Section (on Deviations from the General Rule)
II.L.1.7.1.

The cases that deviate from what I have stated are nine exceptions to the rule concerning which there is, to my knowledge, no disagreement. I shall exclude from the discussion

השערה שתו בשמים פ֗ כל שתה תחת רג֗ כל לגה אלאגעאל מא

פיהא מֵים

II.L.1.5.22.

אלתָו קיל אנה ינבדל באלף בק ויקח תרזה ואלון מקאם ארזה

פהדא טרף מן אבתדאל אלחרוף באכתצאר 400

II.L.1.6. (L1:14r) **באב פי מא תותרה אלארבעה חרוף והי אלאלף**
ואלואו ואליוד ואלהא אעני אֹוֹהֹ פי סתה חרוף בֹגֹדֹכֹפֹת

הדה אלד֗ אדא כאן אחדהא פי אכר כלמה וכאנת אלכלמה

מצֿאפה אלי מא בעדהא באללחן וכאנת אלכלמה אלתאניה

אולהא אחד חרוף בֹגֹדֹכֹפֹת֗ כרג֗ דלך אלחרף מרפיא כפיפא כק 405

וְאֶקְחָ֥ה פַת־לֶ֛חֶם כִּ֥י בְאַפָּ֖ם או֚ בְדֶ֣רֶךְ רְחוֹקָ֑ה אֵ֚לֶּה בְּנֵי־אֶפְרַ֔יִם

וּסְקָלְתּ֥וֹ בָאֲבָנִ֖ים (L1:14v) וַיְהִ֥י דְבַר־יְיָ֖ ואמתאל דלך כתיר גדא

ממא לא ינפצל מן אללחן פכל מא לא ינפצל מן אללחן עלי

הדא אלמנהאג תכון חרוף בֹגֹדֹכֹפֹת֗ מרפיה כפיפה

II.L.1.7. **פצל** 410

II.L.1.7.1.

אלדי כרג֗ ען מא דכרת תסעה כואסר ממ[א ל]ם יכתלף פיהא

עלי עלמי ואנא אפרד מא אכתלף פיה פי אלדכר דאך אן מא

cases concerning which there is disagreement. This is because when there is no disagreement about a case, the reader cannot change anything, but when disagreement has occurred concerning a case, the reader makes a choice. He reads whatever variant he wishes. Nobody who may wish to reject it is able to reject it, since he would be rejecting something concerning which there is disagreement, involving one (reading) and an alternative. He (the reader) may read the one reading or the two alternatives (i.e. with *dagesh* or *rafe*) interchangeably. So long as this is the situation, a rule cannot be fixed. A rule can only be fixed for something concerning which there are no disagreements. Cases concerning which there is no disagreement include, as far as I can see, the following nine exceptions to the rule: *ʾoghera, di-fsiq, di-dhḥiq, ʾathe me-raḥiq, mappiq he, mappiq vav, mappiq yod*, two identical letters, *bet* and *pe*.

II.L.1.7.2.

As for *ʾoghera*, this is the 'collection' of only seven words. People, however, often add to them what does not belong to them, and introduce variant readings with regard to them. What is contained in this exception to the rule are four words in the song וַיּוֹשַׁע (Exod. 14.30, 'the Song of the Sea'). These are: גָּאֹה גָּאָה 'He has triumphed gloriously' (Exod. 15.1, 21), which Moses said, and the twin phrase that Miriam said, יִדְּמוּ כָּאָבֶן 'They are as still as a stone' (Exod. 15.16), מִי כָּמֹכָה 'Who is like you?' (Exod. 15.11). In this song there is one word that one may think is analogous to these four, but it is not the case, rather there is disagreement concerning it. This is עַם־זוּ גָּאָלְתָּ 'the people whom you have redeemed' (Exod. 15.13). There are only these four in the song that belong to the exceptional group *ʾoghera*. In the

לם יכתלף פיה לא יקדר אלקאר יגייר מנה שיא ואלדי חצל פיה

אלכלף אלקאר מכייר אי אלאכתלאף אראד קרי ולא יתסע למן

415　ירד עליה אן ירד לאן ירד אלכלף אלואחד וכלאפה לה אן

יקראה או יקרא אלכלאפין עלי סביל אלבדל פמא כאן הדא

חאלה לא ינצבט בה אצלא ואנמא ינצבט מן אלאצול מא לם

יקע פיה כלף פאלדי מא וקע פיה כלאף פיה עלי טֹני הי הדה

אלתסעה כואסר אוֹגֵֿיֵרָֿה · דְּפָֿסִֿיק · דְּדחִֿיק · אתא מרחק · מפֿקֹ

420　הא · מפֿקֹ ואו · מפֿקֹ יוד · חרפין מתראדפין · בֿאֹ ופא

II.L.1.7.2.

פאמא אלאוגירה פהי אלגֿאמעה לסבעה כלם פקט ואלנאס

כתיר ‹מא› יצֿיפו עליהא מא ליס מנהא וידכלו פיהא אלכלף

ואלדי פי הדה אלכאסרה ארבע לפטֹאת פי שירת ויושע והי

גָּאָֿה גָּאָֿה אלדי קאלה משה וחבירו אלדי קאלתה מרים (L1:15r)

425　יִדְמוּ כָּאָֿבֶֿן מֵי כָֿמָֿבָֿה ופי אלשירה לפטֹה ואחדה ממא יטן אנהא

תגרי מגרי אלדֿ וליס אלאמר כדלך בל הי כלף והי עם זֹו גָּאָֿלָֿתָֿ

וליס פי אלשירה מן כאסרה אוֹגֵֿירֶה סוא הדה אלדֿ ואלארבע

---

first four books there is nothing, except that there is what may be imagined belongs to the exceptional group, but it is not the case, rather there is disagreement concerning it, viz. וַיַּעַשׂ יָרׇבְעָם| חָג בַּחֹדֶשׁ הַשְּׁמִינִי בַּחֲמִשָּׁה־עָשָׂר 'and Jeroboam appointed a feast in the eighth month on the fifteenth (day)' (1 Kings 12.32). There is disagreement concerning the *bet* in בַּחֲמִשָּׁה. In Isaiah there is one word from the ʾ*oghera* group, viz. וְשַׂמְתִּי כַּדְכֹד 'and I shall make (your pinnacles) of agate' (Isa. 54.12), in Jeremiah, viz. וְנִלְאֵיתִי כַּלְכֵל 'and I am weary of holding it in' (Jer. 20.9) and in Daniel וְחׇכְמָה כְּחׇכְמַת־אֱלָהִין 'and wisdom like wisdom of the gods' (Dan. 5.11). These seven aforementioned cases are called ʾ*oghera*. As for אֲדַרְגָּזְרַיָּא גְדָבְרַיָּא דְּתָבְרַיָּא 'the counselors, the treasurers, the justices' (Dan. 3.2, 3), סַבְּכָא פְּסַנְתֵּרִין 'trigon, harp' (Dan. 3.5), they are cases of disagreement. I do not know for what reason this group of (seven) exceptional cases breaks the rule of the letters אֹוִיה. I have only documented them by listening to the transmitters of the reading.

II.L.1.7.3.
The second type of case that breaks the rule is *di-fsiq* (i.e. 'what is paused'). Whenever *paseq* comes between one of the letters אֹוִיה and the letters בְּגַדְכְּפַת, the letters אֹוִיה have no influence, because they only have influence when there is nothing cutting (them off from what follows). The *paseq* cuts (them off) in a way and so this is the reason why the rule of אֹוִיה is not observed, as in עָשׂוּ| כָלָה 'they have done completely' (Gen. 18.21), יֹסֵף יְהוָה עַל־עַמּוֹ| כָּהֵם 'May the Lord add to his people (a hundred times as many) as them' (1 Chron. 21.3). There is no exception at all to this type of case that breaks the rule. Whenever a *paseq* occurs, the rule of אֹוִיה is broken.

אספאר אלאולה מא פיהא מנהא שי גיר אן פיהא מא יתוהם

אנה מנהא וליס אלאמר כדלך בל הו כלף ויעש ירבעם| חג

בחדש השמיני בֵחמשה עשר פאן אלבא פי בחמשה כלף ופי

ישעיה מן אוגירה לפטה ואחדה והי וַשַׂמְתִּי כַּדְכֹּוד ופי ירמיה

וְנָלְאֵיתִי כַּלְכֵל ופי דניאל וחכמָה כחכמת אלהין פהדה אלסבעה

אלדי תקדם דכרהא והי אלמסמאה אוֹגֵירָה ואמא מא כאן

אדרגזריא גדבריא דתבריא ‹פסנתרין› פהו כלף ומא עלמת

לאי עלה כסרת הדה אלכאסרה עלי שרט אלאֹוֵֹיֹה ואנמא

נאכדהא מן אהל אלקראה סמעא

II.L.1.7.3.

אלכאסרה אלבֹ דפסיק כל מא חצל אלפָסֵק בין חרף אלאֹוֵֹיֹה

ובין אחד חרוף בֹגֹדֹכֹפֹת לם יכון ללאויה תאתיר לאן אנמא

תותר אדא לם יכון מא יקטע ואלפסק קטע עלי וגה פצארת

הדה אלעלה לא יתבת מעהא שרט אלאֹוֵֹיֹה כֹך עָשֹוֹ| (L1:15v)

כָּלָה יוסף ייי על עמו| כֹהֵם וליס עלי הדה אלכאסרה אסתתני

בתה פכל מא חצל אלפסק כסר שרט אלאויה

---

434 פסנתרין] פסנתרין פסנטרין L1

II.L.1.7.4.

The third type of case that breaks the rule is *di-dhḥiq* (i.e. 'what is compressed'). Know that this breaking of the rule consists of what is compressed with regard to the rule regarding them (i.e. the letters אוי״ה), and that is why they say *di-dhḥiq*. The meaning of *di-dhḥiq* is that between the accent that is in the word containing one of the אוי״ה letters and a בֹּגֹדֹכֹפֹת letter there is a vowel and this vowel is not dwelt upon or prolonged in pronunciation. On account of this compression (of the vowel) the rule of the אוי״ה is broken, as in וְאָעִידָה בָּ֫ם 'that I may call to witness against them' (Deut. 31.28), וְהָגִיתָ בּוֹ 'you shall meditate on it' (Josh. 1.8) and similar cases. The compression may occur in a word that does not have an accent but is a small word, as in מַה־תֹּאמַר 'whatever (your soul) says' (1 Sam. 20.4), זֶה־בְּנִי 'This is my son' (1 Kings 3.23), מַה־בְּרִי 'What, my son?' (Prov. 31.2), וּמַה־תַּעֲשֶׂה 'and what will you do?' (Josh. 7.9), and other cases. If it is said that this condition may hold for אוי״ה and בֹּגֹדֹכֹפֹת but its effect does not come about, namely *dagesh*, as in אֲשֶׁר הוֹרַדְתֵּנוּ בּוֹ 'through which you let us down' (Josh. 2.18), וְלֹא־הָיָה בָם עוֹד רוּחַ 'and there was no longer any spirit in them' (Josh. 5.1), רְאֵה נָתַתִּי בְיָדְךָ 'See, I have given into your hand' (Josh. 6.2), and the vowel that you mentioned in וְאָעִידָה בָּם and וְהָגִיתָ בּוֹ is present in הוֹרַדְתֵּנוּ בּוֹ and *dagesh* does not occur in the *bet*, the response should be that the difference between what you mentioned (and the cases with compression) is that the vowel that is after the accent in וְאָעִידָה בָּ֫ם does not have an exhalation of breath but is very compressed, but the vowel in הוֹרַדְתֵּנוּ בּוֹ is not compressed in the joining (of the words) but is expansive with an exhalation breath, and is like other (long) vowels, or nearly so. Whoever examines this closely will perceive the difference.

II.L.1.7.4.

אלכאסרה אלֹג דדחיק אעלם אן הדה אלכאסרה אלצֹיק

אלשרט פיהא והו קולהם דדחיק ומעני דדחיק הו אן יכון בין

אלטעם אלדי פי אלכלמה אלדי פיהא חרף אלאֹוֹיֹהֹ ובין חרף   445

בֹגֹדֹ כֹפֹתֹ מלך ואחד ולא יתאנא ולא יטול פי אלנטק בדלך

אלמלך פלאגל הדא אלצֹיק כסר שרט אלאויה כקולה וְאָעִֽידָֽהֹ

בֹֿם והֹגֵּֽיתָ בֹוֹ ומא מאתל דלך וקד יכון אלצֹיק חאצל פי כלמה

לא יכון פיהא טעם גיר אנה תכון כלמה צגירה כך מֶה־תֹּאמֵר

זֶה־בְּנִי מֶה־בְּרִי ומֶה תעשה אלי גיר דלך פאן קאל אן הדה   450

אלעלה קד תחצל פי אֹוֹיֹהֹ ובֹגֹדֹכֹפֹתֹ ולא יחצל מעלולהא והו

אלדגש כך אשר הורדֹתֶּנו בו ולאֹ־הָֹיָה בָּם עוֹדֹ רוח ראה נָתַֽתִּי

בְֽיָדֹֽךֿ פאלמלך אלדי דכרתה פי ואעידה בם והגֵּיתָ בו תאבת פי

הורדתֶנו בו ולם יחצל אלדגש פי אלבא קיל לה אלפרק בין מא

דכרתה הו אן אלמלך אלדי בעד אלטעם ⁽ᴸ¹:¹⁶ʳ⁾ פי ואעידה בם   455

ליס פיה תנפס בל הו מצֹיק גדא וליס כדלך אלמלך אלדי פי

הורדתנו בו מצֹיק פי אלנסק בל הו מוסע בתנפס יגרי מגרי מלך

אכר או קריב מנה ומן תאמל דלך וגד אלפרק

II.L.1.7.5.

The fourth type of case that breaks the rule is *ʾathe me-raḥiq*. This is the opposite of the previous type of case that breaks the rule, because the latter (i.e. *ʾathe me-raḥiq*) is on account of what is far and the former (i.e. *di-dhḥiq*) is on account of what is near, and so there is a fundamental difference between them. This (i.e. *ʾathe me-raḥiq*) arises from the fact that due to the distance of the accent (from the preceding conjunctive accent), one comes upon it (the accent) like a ballista and so the בֹּגֹדכֹפֹת letter is pronounced with *dagesh*, as in הוּא יִבְנֶה־בַּיִת לִשְׁמִי 'He will build a house for my name' (2 Sam. 7.13), הֲלַמֵּתִים תַּעֲשֶׂה־פֶּלֶא 'Do you work wonders for the dead?' (Psa. 88.11), סוּרָה שְׁבָה־פֹּה 'Turn aside, sit here' (Ruth 4.1). Also (included in this category) are cases in which there is no (conjunctive) accent, so (such cases must be considered) to have a virtual (conjunctive) accent before them in order to conform to (cases such as) הוּא יִבְנֶה־בַּיִת לִשְׁמִי, as in וְאֵלְכָה אֵלֶיהָ וְאֶדְרְשָׁה־בָּהּ 'that I may go to her and inquire of her' (1 Sam. 28.7), and similar cases.

II.L.1.7.6.

The fifth type of case that breaks the rule is *mappiq he*. The meaning of their term *mappiq he* is the (consonantal) pronunciation of the *he*. It is derived from וְדָתָא נֶפְקַת 'and the decree went forth' (Dan. 2.13). This is because when the *he* is pronounced at the end of a word, the rule of the אֹוֹיֹה letters is broken, as in מַחֲצִיתָהּ אֹתָהּ בַּבֹּקֶר 'half of it in the morning' (Lev. 6.13), וְכָל־אֲשֶׁר אִתָּהּ בַּבַּיִת 'and all those who are with her in the house' (Josh. 6.17), וְלָהּ גַּפִּין אַרְבַּע 'and it has four wings' (Dan. 7.6), and similar cases. There are no exceptions to this breaking of the rule at all.

II.L.1.7.7.

The sixth type of case that breaks the rule is *mappiq vav*. This is because every *vav* at the end of a word is pronounced according

II.L.1.7.5.

אלכאסרה אלד אתא מרחיק הדה באלעכّס מן אלכאסרה

אלמתקדמה להא לאן הדה למא בעד ותיך למא קרב פשתאן

בינהמא והו אן כמא יבעד אללחן ינצב עליה כّאלמנגניק פידגש

חרף בֶֹגֶד כֹּפֹת כך הֹוא יִבְנֶה־בַּיִת לְשִׁמְי הַלַמֵתָים תַּעֲשֶׂה־פֶּלֶא

סֻוֻרָה שֶׁבָֹה־פֹּה ומא לם יכון פיה אללחן פהו בתקדיר לחן קבלה

ליגרי מגרי הֹוא יבנה־בַּיִת ואלכה אליה וְאַדְרְשָֹה־בָּה ומתל דלך

II.L.1.7.6.

אלכאסרה אלכאמסה מפק הא מעני קולהם מפק הא הו כרוג

אלהא ישתק מן ודתא נפّקת והו אן אלהא אדא טהר וכרג פי

אכר אלכלמה כסר שרט אלאّוّיֹה כקול מַחֲצִיתָהֶ בַּבֹּקֶר וכל אשֶׁר

אתֶה בַּבֶּית וְלַה גֻּפֶּין ארבע ומא מאתל דלך ומא עלי הדה

אלכאסרה שיא מסתתנא בתה

II.L.1.7.7.

אלכאסרה אלסאדסה מפק ואו ודאך אן כל ואו פי אכר כלמה

to the Palestinians as a *bet rafe*, which breaks the rule of the
אֹוֽיֹה, as in חֲצֵרֹתָיו בִּתְהִלָּה '(enter) his courts with praise' (Psa.
100.4), אֵלָיו פִּי־קָרָאתִי 'I cried aloud to him' (Psa. 66.17), and
similar cases. There are two words that are exceptions to this
breaking of the rule, namely וְנָטָה עָלֶיהָ קַו־תֹהוּ 'He will stretch the
line of confusion over it' (Isa. 34.11), וְקֹול הָמֹון שָׁלֵו בָהּ 'The sound
of a carefree multitude was with her' (Ezek. 23.42). Although
according to the principle of breaking the rule what follows the
two *vavs* should have had *dagesh*, this has not occurred.

II.L.1.7.8.

The seventh type of case that breaks the rule is *mappiq yod*. Take
note that whenever *yod* occurs at the end of a word and the next
word begins with one of the בֹּגֹדֹכֹפֹת letters, and *ḥireq* or *ṣere*
occurs under the letter before the *yod*, then the rule of אֹוֽיֹה is
observed, as in לְבְנִי בְנֹו 'Libni his son' (1 Chron. 6.14), כִּי בְקָקֻום
'for they have stripped them' (Nahum 2.3), שָׂרֵי פְלִשְׁתִּים 'the
princes of the Philistines' (1 Sam. 18.30), and similar cases. If
vowels that are different from the aforementioned occur under
the aforementioned letter, the *yod* is strengthened and the rule
of אֹוֽיֹה is not observed, as in אוּלַי תַּעֲרֹוצִי 'perhaps you may inspire
terror' (Isa. 47.12), יְאָתְרַי בְנֹו 'Jeatherai his son' (1 Chron. 6.6), כִּי
מִי־גֹוי גָּדֹול 'for what great nation' (Deut. 4.7), לְגֹוי־גָּדֹול וְעָצֻום 'into a
great and mighty nation' (Num. 14.12), סִינַי בַּקֹּדֶשׁ 'Sinai into the
holy place' (Psa. 68.18). One word is an exception to this
breaking of the rule, namely אֲדֹנָי בָּם 'the Lord in them' (Psa.
68.18). What should have occurred according to the principle of
the breaking of the rule is אֲדֹנָי בָּם with *dagesh*, because there is
no *ḥireq* or *ṣere* on the letter before the *yod*. I do not know for
what reason it contravenes the breaking of the rule.

יכרג עלי ראי אלשאמיין בבא מרפי הו יכסר שרט אלאۏّۀ כֹּ

חַצֵרוֹתָיו בִּתְהִלָּה אֵלָיו פֵּי (L1:16v) קראתי ואמתאלהמא ואלדי

יסתתנא עלי הדה אלכאסרה לפטתין והמא ונטה עליה קו תהו

וקול הָמוֹן שָׁלֵו בָהּ פאן כאן עלי אצל אלכאסרה אן יגי מא

בעד אלואוין מדגושא ולם יגי כדלך   475

אלכאסרה אלסאבעה מפק יוד אעלם אן כל יוד פי אכר כלמה

ואול אלאכרי מן חרוף בֹּגֹּדֹכֹּפֹּתֹ ותחת אלחרף אלדי קבל אליוד

חֵרֶק וא צֵרי פאן שרט אלאۏّۀ יתבת פיה כֹּ לבָנֵי בָּנו כֵּי בָּקקֹום

שָׂרֵי פְּלִשְׁתִּים ומֹֹ דֹ פאן צאר תחת אלחרף אלמדכור סוי

אלמלכין אלמדכורין אשתד אליוד ולם יתבת שרט אלאۏّۀ כֹּ   480

אוּלַי תַּעַרֹוֹצִי יאתרֵי בְּנֵו וּמִי גֹּוֹי גָּדֹול לגוי גָּדֹול ועצום סיני בַּקֶֹדֶש

יסתתני עלי הדה אלכאסרה בלפטה ואחדה והו אדֹנָי בֹּם וקד

יגב אן תגי עלי מקתצֹא אלכאסרה אדֹנָי בם דגש לאן ליס תחת

אלחרף אלדי קבל אליוד נקטה ולא נקטתין ומא עלמת לאי עלה

גא מכאלֹף ללכאסרה   485

II.L.1.7.9.

The eighth type of case that breaks the rule is the succession of two letters. If two *bets* or *kafs*, but not the remaining בֹּגדכֹפֹּת letters, succeed one another and under the first of them there is a *shewa*, then the rule of אֹוֹיֹהֹ is broken, as in וַיְהִי בְּבוֹאָהּ 'and when she came' (Josh. 15.18), וַתִּתְפְּשֵׂהוּ בְּבִגְדֹו 'and she caught him by his garment' (Gen. 39.12), הֲלֹא כְּכַרְכְּמִישׁ 'Is it not like Carchemish?' (Isa. 10.9), and other cases. If a vowel occurs under the first of the two instead of *shewa*, the rule of אֹוֹיֹהֹ is observed, as in וְהֹוא אִשֶּׁה בִבְתוּלֶיהָ 'And he (shall take) a wife in her virginity' (Lev. 21.13), אֲזַלוּ בִבְהִילוּ 'They went in haste' (Ezra 4.23), and similar cases.

II.L.1.7.10.

The ninth type of case that breaks the rule is *bet* and *pe*. The statement concerning them is similar to the statement regarding the preceding type of case that breaks the rule, without there being any disagreement. This is that when *bet* is followed by *pe* and *shewa* is below the *bet*, the rule of אֹוֹיֹהֹ is broken, as in וְאִכְּבְדָה בְּפַרְעֹה 'and I will get glory over Pharaoh' (Exod. 14.4), וּדְבָרַי אֲשֶׁר־שַׂמְתִּי בְּפִיךָ 'and my words which I have put in your mouth' (Isa. 59.21), and similar cases. If a vowel occurs instead of *shewa*, then the rule of אֹוֹיֹהֹ is observed, as in אַל־יֵרֶא בִפְלַגּוֹת 'He will not look upon the rivers' (Job 20.17). I do not know any exception to this breaking of the rule.

II.L.1.7.11.

Take note that Ben Naftali, and perhaps some of those who preceded him, had a particular opinion about the *dagesh* of seven cases of *kaf* after וַיְהִי, namely וַיְהִי כִשְׁמֹעַ אֲדֹנָיו 'when his master heard' (Gen. 39.19), וַיְהִי כְשָׁמְעֹו 'and when he heard' (Gen.

II.L.1.7.9.

אלכאסרה אלתאמנה חרפין מתראדפין כל באאין ובׄאפׅין
תראדפא אלואחד בעד אלאכר מן דון <בקיה חרוף> בׅגׅדׅכׄפׄת
וכאן תחת אלאול מנהא שוא כסר שרט אלאׄוׄיׄה מתל ויהי
בבואה ותתפשהו בבגדו הלא ככרכמיש אלי גיר דלך פאן כאן
תחת אלאול מנהמא מא עוׄץ (L1:17r) מן אלשוא מלך תבת שרט
אלאׄוׄיׄה כך והוא אשה בבתוליה אזל׳ בבהילו ומא שאכל דלך

II.L.1.7.10.

אלכאסרה אלתאסעה בא ופא אלכלאם פיהא כאלכלאם פי
אלכאסרה אלתי קבלהא מן גיר כלף והו אן כל בא ובעדהא פא
אדא כאן תחת אלבא שוא כסר שרט אלאׄוׄיׄה כקול ואכבדה
בפרעה וּדְבָרַי אֲשֶׁר־שַׂמְתִּי בְּפִיךָ ואמתאלהא פאן צאר עוׄץ
אלשוא מלך תבת שרט אלאויה כך אל ירא בפלגות ומא ערפת
עלי הדה אלכאסרה מסתתני

II.L.1.7.11.

ואעלם אן בן נפתלי ולעל מן תקדמה קד ראי ראיה פי דגש זׄ

כאפאת בעד ויהי והי כשמׄע אדׄ כשמעו כראות כראותו

39.15), וַיְהִ֤י כִרְא֣וֹת 'and when (the king) saw' (Esther 5.2), וַיְהִ֤י
כִרְאוֹת֗וֹ 'and when he saw' (Jud. 11.35), וַיְהִ֤י כְהוֹצִיאָ֤ם 'and when
they brought (them) out' (Gen. 18.17), וַיְהִ֤י כִמְלֹכ֗וֹ 'when he
became king' (1 Kings 15.29), וַיְהִ֗י כַּאֲשֶׁר־תַּ֔מּוּ 'and when they had
perished' (Deut. 2.16).[7] According to him, each of the seven
cases of *kaf* that occurs after וַיְהִי in Scripture has *dagesh*. This is
known from his codices. Others, however, pronounce these *rafe*.
I do not know for what reason Ben Naftali pronounced them
with *dagesh*, for those who pronounce them *rafe* follow the
principle of the influence of the soft אהוֹי letters on the בֹּגֹדֹּכֹפֹּת
letters. The reader, therefore, has two options. Either to read
with the reading of Ben Naftali, in which case he must read all
forms that he (Ben Naftali) reads, whether they be good
readings or difficult readings, or to read with the reading of Ben
Asher, which also is authoritative. If somebody reads what he
deems to be the best reading of this one and of that one, he
would (read) without any rule, because he deviates from the
rationale of each of them.

II.L.1.8. Section (on Further General Issues Relating to אהוֹי)

II.L.1.8.1.

Take note that the criterion of the (rule of) the אהוֹי letters and
the בֹּגֹדֹּכֹפֹּת letters should be based on the pronunciation and not
on the writing. This is demonstrated in וַיַּ֥רְא בָּלָ֖ק 'and Balak saw'
(Num. 22.2). The word וַיַּרְא ends in ʾalef, one of the אהוֹי letters,
and (the next word) begins with *bet*, one of the בֹּגֹדֹּכֹפֹּת letters,
but this letter is not pronounced *rafe*, despite the ʾalef being
adjacent to the *bet* and their being linked by the accent. The *bet*
of בָּלָק occurs with *dagesh*, since the end of וַיַּרְא (in pronunci-

---

[7] The fuller citation כַּאֲשֶׁר־תַּ֔מּוּ וַיְהִ֗י as opposed to simply כַּאֲשֶׁר וַיְהִי in the text
of *Hidāyat al-Qāriʾ* is given in *Kitāb al-Khilaf* (ed. Lipschütz, 1965, 19).

500   כהוציאם כמלכו כאשר ענדה אן כל ויהי פי אלמקרא יגי בעדה

אחד הדה אלז̇ כאפאת אנהא תגי כלהא מדגושה ודלך מערוף

מן מצאחפה וגירה ירפיהא ומא ערפת לאי עלה דגשהא בן

נפתלי לאן מן רפאהא משא עלי אלאצל אלמוצ̇וע פי תאתיר

אוֹזֹה אלרפי לחרוף בֹגֹדֹכֹפֹת פאלקאר אדן עלי אחד אמרין אמא

505   אן יקרא קראה בן נפתלי פילזמה אן יקרא גמיע מא יקראה מן

מסתחסנאת (L1:17v) ומסתתקלאת ואמא אן יקרא קראה בן אשר

ודלך איצֹא חכמה ואמא מן קרא מסתחסנאת הדא והדא פאנה

יבקא בלא שרט לאנה יכרג ען עלה הדא והדא

II.L.1.8. פצל

II.L.1.8.1.

510   אעלם אן אלמעול פי אוֹזֹה ובֹגֹדֹכֹפֹת עלי אללפֹט לא עלי אלכט

יביין דלך אן וירא בלק אכר וירא אלף מן אויה ואולה בא מן

בֹגֹדֹכֹפֹת ולם יגי אלחרף רפי מע אסתנאד אלאלף אלי אלבא

ואכתלאטהמא באללחן ואנמא גא אלבא מן בלק מדגוש לאן

מחט וירא אלריש לא אלאלף פצאר אלמעול עלי אללפֹט לא

ation) is the *resh* not the *ʾalef*, and the criterion is the pronunciation not the writing. An opposite case is וְעָשִׂיתָ בַדֵּי 'and you will
make poles of' (Exod. 25.13). The last letter of the word וְעָשִׂיתָ is
tav, but the *bet* is *rafe*. The reason for this is that when *tav* has
qameṣ, it is pronounced with two letters, and if you were to
write וְעָשִׂיתָה in full orthography, it would have *he*. So the
criterion is the pronunciation. The other cases of the breaking of
the rule are also based on this principle, since this is the
principle that forms the basis for the rule of אֹוִיה and בֹּגְדְכֹּפַת.
Surely you see that in וַעֲבָדֶיךָ בָאוּ 'and your servants have come'
(Gen. 42.10) the *bet* occurs with *dagesh* on account of the
breaking of the rule known as *di-dhḥiq*.

II.L.1.8.2.

Perhaps somebody may ask why the letters אֹוִיה have caused
what is after them to be *rafe* in accordance with the preceding
discussion. The response could be that this is because these four
letters are the letters of softness and prolongation, as has been
stated by Yaḥyā ibn Dāʾūd the Maghribī, the author of the *Book
of Prolongation and Softness*, and letters that come after them
that are not one of the letters of softness become soft due to
their proximity. It may also be said that this is a custom adopted
by the people of the language for a good reason known to them,
and the knowledge of this has been transmitted by us and we
read what we have received from the people of the language,
and we should not abandon it until the people of the language
come and we know the function of what they adopted as their
convention. So whoever does not read according to the rule of
אֹוִיה and בֹּגְדְכֹּפַת is reading incorrectly. Blessed is He who knows
secrets (cf. Psa. 44.22).

עלי אלכט ובאלעכּס מן דלך וְעָשִׂיתָ בַּדֵּי אכר לפטה ועשית תו ‏515

וגא אלבא מרפّי ואלעלה פי דלך אן אלתו אדא כאן מקמוצא

כרג בחרפّין ולו כתבת ועשיתה מלא כאן בהא פאלמעّול אדן

עלי אללّפט וסאיר אלכואסר תתם פי הדא אלאצל לאנה הו

אלאצל אלדי בני ללّאْוֹיֹה ובّגّדّכּפّת אלי תרי אלי ק וְעַבְדֶּיךָ בָּאוּ

אן אלבא [יגّי] מדגוש מן כّאסרה דדחיק ‏520

II.L.1.8.2.

ולעל סאיל [יّס]אל עّל חّרّוף אْוֹיֹה לם כّאנת תרّפّי מא בّעّדّהّא

עלי אלّשّרّוح אלמדכורה פّימّכּן אן יّגّאב אן לّמّا כّאנת הדה

אלّארّבّע חّרّוף הّי חّרّוف אללّין ואלّמّד עّלّי מّא דّכּרّה יחّיّי בّן

דّאוّוד אלّמّגّרّבّי ‏(L1:18r) צّאّחّב כّתّאّב אלّמّד ואّללّין פّילّין מّא

בّעّדّהّא מّמّא לّיّס הّו מّן חّרّוף אללّין ללّמّגّاّورّה וّימّכّן אן יّקّאّל ‏525

איّצّא אّן הّדّא אّן אّצّטّלّاّح אّצّטّלّחّו עّליّה אّהّל אّللّغّה לّגّרّץ צّחّיّח

עّלّמّوّה הّם وّاّنّשّد עّנّا נّחّן עّלّمّה פّنّחّن נّקّرّا מّا תّسّلّמّנّاّه מّن

אّהّל אّללّغّה וّلّا נّכّلّיّه אّلّي אّن יّגّو אّהّל אّללّغّה פّنّעّلّם פّاّيّدّה

מّا אّצّטّلّחّو عّليّה פّمّن קّرّا בّגّיّر שّرّט אْ

وَ2#2 אْوֹיֹה ובّגّدّכّפّت כّاّن

לّاّחّנّا وّبّרّוֹך יّוֹדֵעַ תַּעֲלוֹמוֹת ‏530

II.L.1.9. Chapter concerning Letters that Occur in Three Grades

II.L.1.9.1.

Take note that just as there are among the letters those that when they are adjacent to another letter, the latter makes them light with *rafe*, likewise among the letters are those that occur in three grades with regard to heaviness and lightness. The first grade is lightening. The second is the normal *dagesh*. The third is the major *dagesh*. This includes the *tav*.

II.L.1.9.2.

Take note that the *tav*, unlike the other letters, may occur *rafe*, as in וְתָאֵי הַשַּׁעַר 'and rooms of the gate' (Ezek. 40.10); it may occur with *dagesh*, as in תַּחַת הַנְּחֹשֶׁת 'instead of bronze' (Isa. 60.17), תּוֹרֵי זָהָב 'ornaments of gold' (Cant. 1.11); and it may occur with major *dagesh*. The latter includes three *tav*s: וַיְשִׂימֶהָ תֵּל־עוֹלָם 'He made it an eternal heap of ruins' (Josh. 8.28), וְאֶת־בָּתָּיו וְגַנְזַכָּיו 'and its houses and its treasuries' (1 Chron. 28.11), וְגֻבְרַיָּא אִלֵּךְ תְּלָתֵּהוֹן 'and these three men' (Dan. 3.23). I do not know anybody who differs (in reading) with regard to these three *tav*s. As for the form בָּתִּים, there were differences (of reading) with regard to it.

II.L.1.9.3.

Take note that the Tiberians said that they have a *resh* that is not read (in the same way) by anybody else. It is likely that the climate of their town caused this. It has the same status as the *tav* in the word בָּתִּים according to the view of Ben Naftali, who gives it a grade in between two grades.

II.L.1.9.4.

The *resh* in their tradition is associated with specific letters, just as the בֹּגֹדְכֹּפֹת are associated with the letters אֹוֹיֹה, namely דֹזֹצֹתֹטֹס

II.L.1.9. באב פי מא יגי מן אלחרוף עלי תלאתה מנאזל

II.L.1.9.1.

אעלם אן כמא גא פי אלחרוף מא אדא אסתנד אלי גירה כפפה
ורפאה כדאך פי אלחרוף מא יגי עלי ג̇ מנאזל פי אלתקל
ואלכפה אלמנזלה אלא̇ אלתכפיף אלב̇ אלדגש אלמעהוד אלג̇
אלדגש אלכביר והו אלתו 535

II.L.1.9.2.

אעלם אן אלתו מן דון סאיר אלחרוף קד יגי רפי כך וְתָאֵי השער
וקד יגי דגש כקול תחת הנחשת תורי זהב וקד יגי דגש כביר והו
תלת תאואת וְיִשִׂימֶהָ תֵּל־עוֹלָם ובתיו וגנזכיו וגבריא אלך
תְּלָתֵהֹון פהדה אלתלת תאואת מא ערפת מן כאלף פיהא ואמא
לשון בתים פקד אבתלף פיה ⁽L1:18v⁾ 540

II.L.1.9.3.

ואעלם אן אלטבראניין דכרו אן להם ריש לא יקראה גירהם
ואלקריב אן הו בלדהם יפעלה והו יגרי מגרי אלתו פי לשון
בתים עלי ראי בן נפתלי אלדי יגעלה הו מנזלה בין מנזלתין

II.L.1.9.4.

פאלריש ענדהם לה חרוף מכצוצה כמא לבְבָגְדְכְפָת חרוף אֹוֹיֹה̇
והי דֹזֹצֹתֹטֹס לֹן פהדה אלה̇ חרוף חרפאן מנהא תעמל קבל 545

and לֹן. Two of these eight letters operate both before the *resh*
and after it, namely לֹן, and the six other letters before the *resh*.
The eight letters affect the *resh* only when *shewa* is under it or
(when *shewa* is) under the eight letters that are specific to it.

II.L.1.9.5.

The light *resh* in their tradition is (in words) such as רְתֹם הַמֶּרְכָּבָה
'Harness the chariot!' (Micah 1.13), רְסִיסֵי לָיְלָה 'drops of the night'
(Cant. 5.2), בְּמִרְכֶּבֶת הַמִּשְׁנֶה 'in his second chariot' (Gen. 41.43).
Such cases and similar ones are their normal pronunciation of
the letter, for they consider it to be the light *resh*.

II.L.1.9.6.

The major *resh* in their tradition are cases such as הֲרְאִיתֶם 'Have
you seen?' (2 Kings 6.32), הַרְעִמָה 'to irritate her' (1 Sam. 1.6),
and the like.

II.L.1.9.7.

The grade between two grades (of the *resh*) where *dalet* precedes
it are cases such as דַּרְכֵי צִיֹּון 'the roads to Zion' (Lam. 1.4), דַּרְכֹּו
'his way' (Gen. 24.21), לִדְרָאֹון 'to contempt' (Dan. 12.2). Cases
with *zayin* are זַרְזִיף 'dripping' (Psa. 72.6), מִזַּרְעֹו לַמֹּלֶךְ 'any of his
offspring to Molech' (Lev. 20.2), יְזָרֶק 'He scatters' (Isa. 28.25).
Cases with *ṣade* are מַצְרֵף 'the crucible' (Prov. 17.3), כִּצְרֹף 'as
testing' (Zech. 13.9), עַד־צָרְפַת 'as far as Zarephath' (Obd. 1.20).
Cases of *tav* are תַּרְקִיעַ 'you spread out' (Job 37.18), וְתִרְאֲלָה 'and
Taralah' (Josh. 18.27), תַרְבִּיעַ 'you will (not) cause to breed' (Lev.
19.19). Cases of *ṭet* are כָּל־טַרְפֵּי צִמְחָהּ 'all the leaves of its
sprouting' (Ezek. 17.9), יִכְסֹוף לִטְרֹוף 'He is eager to tear' (Psa.
17.12), מִטְרֹות עֻזֹּו 'the rains of his strength' (Job 37.6). A case
with *samekh* is סַרְעַפֹּתָיו 'its boughs' (Ezek. 31.5). Cases with

אלריש ובעדה והמא לןْ ואלסתה חרוף מן קבל אלריש והדא

אלריש אלמדכור לא תותר פיה חרופה אלהֿ אלא אן יכון תחתה

שוא או תחת חרופה אלהֿ [אל]מכצוצה בה

II.L.1.9.5.

פאלריש אלכפיף אלדי להם מתל רَתם המרכבה רסיסי לילה

במרכבת המשנה פהדא ומא שאכלה מא כלאמהם עליהא לאן   550

הדא ענדהם הו אלריש אלכפיף

II.L.1.9.6.

ואלריש אלכביר ענדהם הו הראיתם הרעימה ואמתאלהֿמא

II.L.1.9.7.

ואלמנזלה בין מנזלתין ממא קבלה [אלד]אל כֿ דרכי ציון דרכו

לדראון ואלזאי זרזיף מזרעו למולך <יזרוק> אלצדי מַצְרֵף

[כ]צרוף עד צרפת אלתו תרקיע ותראלה תרביע טית כל טרפי   555

צמחה יכסוף לטרוף מטרות עזו אלסמאךֿ סרעפותיו אללמאד

---

554 יזרוק] יזרוק אל יסוד L1

lamed are לִרְחֹץ 'to wash' (Gen. 24.32), לִרְעוֹת 'to graze' (1 Sam. 17.15), לִרְצֹנְכֶם 'for your favour' (Lev. 19.5), לִרְצֹנוֹ 'for his favour' (Lev. 1.3). Cases with *nun* are סַרְנֵי 'rulers of' (Josh. 13.3), נִרְדִּי 'my nard' (Cant. 1.12). They call these cases and similar ones a grade (of *resh*) between two grades, namely (the grades of) *dagesh* and *rafe*. Whoever investigates this carefully (will see that) it is as they say, since the difference is clear between the *resh* of רְתָם and רְסִיסֵי and (the *resh*) that is adjacent to the eight letters (preceding it) when they have *shewa* under them or when *shewa* is under it. Its heaviness is clear compared to the lightness of the *resh* of רְתָם and the like.

II.L.1.9.8.

It has been stated previously that I do not know anything that I can report about the *zāy makrūkh*. I only mentioned it so that it be known that letters have different attributes and because speech is dependent on letters.

II.L.1.10. (Conjugations)

Take note that the people of the language made the conjugations of the language in four categories: from one root letter, such as הַכֵּה 'hit' and the like, from two letters, such as בְּנֵה 'build' and the like, from three letters, such as שְׁמֹר and the like and from four letters, such as כַּרְבֵּל 'wrap', and the like. A letter may also change position in a word with the result that its meaning changes. I shall mention here the phenomenon of change of position in one word as an example: עֶרֶב with three letters from 'becoming evening', עָרֵב לָאִישׁ 'sweet to a man' (Prov. 20.17) from the lexical class of 'delight', עָרֹב כָּבֵד 'heavy swarm' (Exod. 8.20) from the lexical class of 'mixing', עֹרֵב לְמִינוֹ '(every) raven according to its kind' (Lev. 11.15), a bird, אֶת־עֹרֵב וְאֶת־זְאֵב 'Oreb and Zeeb' (Jud. 7.25), the name of a man. When you

לרחוק לרעות לרצונכם לרצונו אלנון סרני נרדי פהדה

אלאמתאל ואשבאההא יסמונהא מנזלה בין מנזלתין והמא

אלדגש ואלרפי ומן תאמל דלך כאן כמא דכרו אד ^(L1:19r) אלפרק

טאהר בין ריש רְתם וריש רסיסי ללמגאור להדה אלח חרוף   560

אדא כאן תחתהא או תחתה שוא ותקלה טאהרא ענד כפה ריש

רתם ומא מאתלה

II.L.1.9.8.

וקד תקדם אלקול אן אלזאי אלמכרוך מא ערפת פיה שיא

אדכרה ואנמא דכרתה ליערף אן ללחרוף אחכאם ולאן

אלכלאם מתעלק באלחרוף   565

II.L.1.10.

ואעלם אן אהל אללגה געלו תצאריף אללגה עלי ארבעה ^(L3:8r)

אקסאם מן חרף ואחד אצלי מתל הַכֵּה ונחוה ומן חרפין מתל

בנה ונחוה ומן ג מתל שָׁמַר ונחוה ומן ד מתל כרבל ונחוה

ואלחרף איצא קד תתקלב פי אללפטה ותתגאיר מעאניהא

פאדכר מן גנס אלתקליב לפטה ואחדה לתכון נמודגא עֶרֶב ג   570

חרוף מן אלגרוב עָרֶב לאיש מן לגה אללדה ^(L3:8v) עָרֹב כבד מן

לגה אלאכתלאט עֶרֶב למינו טאיר עֶרֶב וזאב אסם רגל ואדא

change the position of their letters, they become בֶּרַע 'Bera' (Gen.
14.2), the name of a man, רֶבַע 'a quarter', בַּעַר 'stupidity' from
(the lexical class) of 'being stupid', from אִישׁ־בַּעַר לֹא יֵדָע 'The
stupid man does not know' (Psa. 92.7), כִּי יַבְעֶר־אִישׁ 'when (a
man) causes (a field or vineyard) to be grazed over' (Exod. 22.4)
from the lexical class of 'trampling, befouling with dung',
וַיַּבְעֶר־אֵשׁ 'He ignited fire' (Jud. 15.5) from the lexical class of
'kindling and setting fire', and וּבִעַרְתָּ הָרָע 'and you will remove
the evil' (Deut. 13.6, etc.) from the lexical class of 'removing'.

II.L.1.11. Chapter concerning the Occurrence of Letters for the Sake of Enhancement

II.L.1.11.1.

Take note that you do not find in the Bible a word that consists
of less than two letters, as, for example, אַךְ 'surely, but', כִּי 'for,
when', בּוֹ 'in it', מִן 'from', עַל 'upon', מִי 'who'. A word may
consist of three letters, for example, שְׁמֹר 'keep', זְכֹר 'remember',
עֲבֹר 'pass'. It may consist of four letters, for example כַּרְבֵּל 'wrap',
from וְדָוִיד מְכֻרְבָּל 'and David was wrapped' (1 Chron. 15.27).
Expressions may be constructed from five up to eleven letters.
We have not found more than that number. This is found in only
three words: וּבְתוֹעֲבוֹתֵיהֶן 'and in their abominations' (Ezek.
16.47), וְכַעֲלִילוֹתֵיכֶם 'according to your deeds' (Ezek. 20.44),
וְהָאֲחַשְׁדַּרְפְּנִים 'and the satraps' (Esther 9.3). It has been said that it
would have been possible for the people of the language to use
twelve letters in the expression וּמֵהַעֲצוּמוֹתֵיכֶם 'and from your
strength' (cf. וְתַעֲצֻמוֹת 'and strength' Psa. 68.35) and other
expressions according as the need may have arisen. As for words
of two letters, when you move the first to the (position of) the
last and the last to the (position of) the first, they turn out to be
a functional part of speech consisting of two parts, for example,

אקלבתהא גת בֶרֶע אסם רגל [ר]בֶּע רֶבע בֶּעֶר מן אלתגאהל מן

איש בער לא ידע כי יבער איש מן לגה אלתבאער ויבער אֵש מן

575   לגה אלאחראק ואלאשעאל ובערת הרע מן לגה אלנפי

II.L.1.11. באב פי מא יגי מן אלחרוף ללתפכים

II.L.1.11.1.
אעלם אן כלמה פי אלמקרא אקל מן חרפין לא תגד מתל אַך כִּי

בּוֹ מֶן עַל מִי ותכון מן ג̇ כֹּך שמר זכר עבֹר ותכון מן ד̇ כרבל מן

ודוד מכרבל ותנבני אלאלפאט̇ מן ה̇ ומא זאד אלי יֹא ומא וגדנא

580   אזיד מן דלך והו ג̇ אלפאט̇ פקט ובתועבותיהן וכעלילותיכם

והאחשדרפנים וקד קיל אן ימכן אן יסתעמלו אהל אללגה יֹב

חרפא פי לפט̇ה ומתעצומותיכם וגיר דלך ממא תדעוהם

אלחאגה אליה ומא כאן מן אלכלם מן חרפין אדא נקלת אלאול

אלי אלאכיר ואלאכיר אלי אלאול תכון עלי אלקסמין כלאמא

אָב 'father'—בָּא 'he came', כָּל 'he measured'—לְךָ 'to you', גַּד 'Gad'
—דָּג 'fish', חֹם 'heat'—מֹחַ 'brain', צַק 'pour'—קֵץ 'end', and similar
cases.

II.L.1.11.2.

An expression consisting of two or more letters may be
enhanced. Enhancement includes various different types. A noun
that is enhanced by *he*, as in עַצְמוֹן 'Azmon'—עַצְמוֹנָה 'to Azmon'
(Josh. 15.4), דְּבִיר 'Devir'—דְּבִרָה 'to Devir' (Josh. 10.38, etc.), בָּבֶל
'Babylon'—בָּבֶלָה 'to Babylon' (2 Kings 20.17, etc.) is one type. A
second type is where a feminine noun ending in *he* is enhanced
by *tav*, for example סוּפָה 'storm'—סוּפָתָה 'storm' (Hos. 8.7), עֵיפָה
'darkness'—עֵיפָתָה 'darkness' (Job 10.22), יְשׁוּעָה 'salvation'—
יְשׁוּעָתָה 'salvation' (Psa. 3.3, etc.), and similar cases. It may be
said that in מִצְרַיִם—מִצְרַיְמָה 'to Egypt' (Gen. 46.3, etc.) and יְרוּשָׁלַם
—יְרוּשָׁלַמָה 'to Jerusalem' (1 Kings 10.2, etc.) that the *he* at the
end of the word is in place of אֶל 'to'. A verb may also be
enhanced with *he*, as in סְלַח־נָא 'pardon' (Num. 14.19)—סְלָחָה
'pardon' (Dan. 9.19), שְׁמַע 'hear'—שְׁמָעָה 'hear' (Dan. 9.19), שׁוּב
'return'—שׁוּבָה 'return' (Num. 10.36, etc.), קוּם 'arise'—קוּמָה 'arise'
(Num. 10.35, etc.).

II.L.1.11.3.

Inflected nouns may be enhanced by *yod*, for example הַיֹּשְׁבִי 'the
one sitting' (Psa. 123.1), הַהֹפְכִי 'the one who changes' (Psa.
114.8), הַמַּגְבִּיהִי 'the one who makes high' (Psa. 113.5), הַמַּשְׁפִּילִי
'the one who makes low' (Psa. 113.6). Feminine nouns may also
be enhanced by *yod*, as in תַּחֲלֻאָיְכִי 'your diseases' (Psa. 103.3),
נְעוּרָיְכִי 'your youth' (Psa. 103.5), חַיָּיְכִי 'your life' (Psa. 103.4).
Nouns may also be enhanced by *vav*, for example בְּנוֹ בְעֹר 'the son

585 מסתעמלא (L3:10r) מתל אָב בָא כָל לָד גָד דָג חֹם מֹח צַק קֶץ

ואמתאל דלך

II.L.1.11.2.

פאללפט אלדי הו מן חרפין ומא זאד יפכם ואלתפכים עלי וגוה

פאלאסם אלדי יפכם באלהא מתל עצמון עצמונה דביר דבירה

בבל בבלה וגה ב̇ והו אדא כאן אלאסם מונת בהא קד יפכם

590 בתָ[ו] מתל סופה סופתה עיפה עיפתה ישועה ישועתה ואמתאל

דלך וקד יקאל אן מצרים מצרימה ירושלם ירושלמה אן אלהא

פי אכר אלאסם מקאם אָל ואלפעל יפכם באלהא איצֿא מתל

סלח נא סלְחָה שמַע שמְעָה שוב שובָה קום קומָה

II.L.1.11.3.

ואלאסמא אלמתצרפה פקד תפכם באליוד הישבי ההופכי

595 המגביהי המשפילי ואלאסמא אלמונתה קד תפכם איצֿא באליוד

מתל תחלואיכי נעוריכי חיָיֵכי ואלאסמא איצֿא תפכם בואו מתל

---

of Beor' (Num. 24.3, etc.), חַיְתוֹ־אֶרֶץ 'beasts of the earth' (Gen. 1.24), לְמַעְיְנוֹ־מָיִם 'into a spring of water' (Psa. 114.8).

II.L.1.11.4.

Functional particles may be enhanced by *yod*, for example עֲלֵי־עָשׂוֹר וַעֲלֵי־נָבֶל 'on a ten-stringed instrument and on a harp' (Psa. 92.4), עַד 'until'—עֲדֵי־ 'until'. Functional particles may also be enhanced by *mem* and *vav*, for example אֲאַמִּצְכֶם בְּמוֹ־פִי 'I strengthen you with my mouth' (Job 16.5), the virtual form of which is בְּפִי, וְאָנִיעָה עֲלֵיכֶם בְּמוֹ ראשִׁי 'and I shake my head at you' (Job 16.4), the virtual form of which is בְּראשִׁי, כִּי־תֵלֵךְ בְּמוֹ־אֵשׁ 'when you walk through fire' (Isa. 43.2), the virtual form of which is בָּאֵשׁ. The same is found in the middle of words, for example כְּמוֹהֶם 'like them'—כָּהֶם 'like them' (2 Kings 17.15).

II.L.1.11.5.

Take note that somebody who has discussed enhancement has stated that וּמִשִּׁירִי אֲהוֹדֶנּוּ 'and with my song I give thanks to him' (Psa. 28.7) is enhanced by *he*, and that if it was not enhanced, it would have been אוֹדֶנּוּ. Likewise he has stated יוֹשִׁיעַ 'he saves' is enhanced to יְהוֹשִׁיעַ 'he saves' (1 Sam. 17.47, etc.), and also יוֹדוּךְ 'they praise you'—יְהוֹדֻךָ 'they praise you' (Psa. 45.18). The situation is not, however, as he states, because the imperative forms are הוֹדֵה and הוֹשַׁע and it is the rule that the (prefixed) letter of the future is attached to the imperatives of active verbs, so in the forms אֲהוֹדֶנּוּ, יְהוֹשִׁיעַ and יְהוֹדֻךָ the *he* is part of the basic structure and it is not a *he* of enhancement. Since, however, the people of the language regarded this as heavy, they elided the *he*s in such forms, in order to make the word lighter. You will find this explained in the books of the grammarians.

בנו בעור חייתו ארץ למעינו מים

ותפכם אלכואדם באליוד מתל עלי עָשׁוּר וַעֲלֵי נָבֶל עַד עֲדֵי

ותפכים איצֿא אלכואדם במאם וואו מתל אאמצכם במו פי

תקדירה בפי ואניעה עליכם במו ראשי תקדירה בראשי כי תלך   600

במו אש תקדירה בָּאש ומתל דלך פי וסט אלכלאם כמוהם כהם

ואעלם אן מן תכלם פי אלתפכים קאל אן ומשירי (L3:10v) אהוֹדֶנוּ

הו מפכם בהא ולו לם יפכם כאן אוּדֶנוּ ומתלה קאל יושִׁיעַ יפכם

יהושִׁיעַ וכדלך יודוך יהודוך וליס אלאמר כמא דכר לאן אלאמר

הוֹדֶה הוּשֵׁע ומן חכם חרף אלאסתקבאל ידכל עלי אלאואמר   605

ממא יסמא פאעלה פאדא קאל אהודנו יהושיע יהודוך אלהא

קרת מקרהא פליס הי הא תפכים ואנמא למא אסתתקל דלך

אהל אללגה חדפו אלהאאת ממא מאתלהא אסתכפאפא

ללכלאם והדא תגדה פי כתב אללגויין מביינא

II.L.1.11.6.

Verbs may be enhanced by a *vav* at the end of the word, for example וְגֵרַשְׁתָּמוֹ מִפָּנֶיךָ 'and you will drive them out from before you' (Exod. 23.31), the virtual form of which is וְגֵרַשְׁתָּם. Similar examples are הֲנִיעֵמוֹ בְחֵילְךָ וְהוֹרִידֵמוֹ 'make them move by your power, and bring them down' (Psa. 59.12), כִּי־תִפְאֶרֶת עֻזָּמוֹ 'for (you are) the glory of their strength' (Psa. 89.18), and further cases.

II.L.1.12. Section

II.L.1.12.1.

One person who has discussed enhancement has said that identical successive letters are enhanced in (ways that fall into) two categories. The first category is (an enhancement) of a letter by another identical letter, whereby they become two letters. The second is (an enhancement) of two letters by two identical adjacent letters, whereby they become four.

II.L.1.12.2.

Examples of the first category include the following. *Bet*: עוֹד יְנוּבוּן 'They still bring forth fruit' (Psa. 92.15), which does not have successive letters, and יְנוֹבֵב בְּתֻלוֹת 'It will make the maidens flourish' (Zech. 9.17). *Gimel*: וְיָחֹגּוּ לִי 'that they may hold a feast for me' (Exod. 5.1), וְחֹגְגִים 'and celebrating' (1 Sam. 30.16). *Dalet*: וְלֹא תָנוּד 'and you should not waver' (Jer. 4.1), כִּי־מִדֵּי דְבָרֶיךָ בּוֹ תִּתְנוֹדָד 'whenever you spoke of him, you shook your head' (Jer. 48.27). *He*: וַתֵּכַהּ מִכַּעַשׂ '(My eye) has grown dim from anger' (Job 17.1), כָּהֹה תִכְהֶה '(Let his right eye) be utterly blinded' (Zech. 11.17). *Zayin*: בֹּזּוּ כֶסֶף 'Plunder the silver' (Nahum 2.10), וּבָזְזוּ אֶת־בֹּזְזֵיהֶם 'and they will plunder those who plunder them' (Ezek. 39.10). *Ḥet*: אָשִׂיחָה 'I will complain' (Job 7.11, etc.), אֲשׂוֹחֵחַ 'I muse' (Psa. 143.5). *Ṭet*: יִמּוֹטוּ 'are shaken' (Psa. 82.5), מוֹט

II.L.1.11.6.

610 וקד תפכם אלאפעאל פי אכר אלכלאם בואו כק וגרשתמו

מפניך תקדירה וגרשתם ומתלה הניעמו בחילך והורידמו כי

תפארת עזמו אלי גיר דלך

II.L.1.12. פצל

II.L.1.12.1.

קאל מן תכלם פי אלתפכים אן אלחרוף אלמתראדפה תפכם

615 עלי קסמין אלקסם אלואחד חרף לחרף מתמאתלין פיצירא

חרפאן אלב׳ חרפין לחרפין מתגאורה פיצירון ארבעה

II.L.1.12.2.

אלקסם אלאול אלבﬞَא עוד ינובון גיר מתראדף ינובב בתולות

מתראדף אלגמאל ויחגו לי וחוגגים   אלדאל ולא תנוד כי מדי

דבריך בו תתנודﬞَד אלהא ותֶﬞבֶה מכעס (L1:20v) כהה תכהה אלזאי

620 בזו כסף ובזזו את בזזיהם אלחית אשיחה אשוחה אלטית ימוטו

הִתְמוֹטְטָה 'is violently shaken' (Isa. 24.19); שׁוּט 'go through' (2 Sam. 24.2), שׁוֹטְטוּ 'go through' (Jer. 5.1). *Yod:* כִּתִּים 'Kittim' (Gen. 10.4, etc.), כְתִיִּם 'Kittim' (Jer. 2.10,. etc.). *Kaf:* כְּשֹׁךְ חֲמַת הַמֶּלֶךְ 'when the anger of the king had abated' (Esther 2.1), וַחֲמַת הַמֶּלֶךְ שָׁכָכָה 'The anger of the king abated' (Esther 7.10). *Lamed:* יִמַּל 'withers' (Job 18.16), יְמוֹלֵל 'withers' (Psa. 90.6). *Mem:* דוּמָה 'in silence' (Psa. 94.17), דוּמֶם 'in silence' (Isa. 47.5, etc.). *Nun:* וַהֲכִינוֹתִי 'and I will establish' (1 Chron. 17.11, etc.), וְכֹנַנְתִּי 'and I will establish' (2 Sam. 7.13). *Samekh:* לָרֹס 'to moisten' (Ezek. 46.14), רְסִיסֵי 'drops' (Cant. 5.2). *ʿAyin:* תְּרֹעֵם 'You shall break them' (Psa. 2.9), רֹעָה הִתְרֹעֲעָה 'is utterly broken' (Isa. 24.19). *Pe:* וְהֵנִיף יָדוֹ 'and he will wave his hand' (2 Kings 5.11, etc.), יְנֹפֵף יָדוֹ 'He will shake his hand' (Isa. 10.32). *Ṣade:* וַיַּחַץ 'and he divided' (Gen. 32.8, etc.), וּמִסְפַּר חֳדָשָׁיו חֻצָּצוּ 'while the number of his months have been cut in two' (Job 21.21). *Qof:* וּמָקוֹם לַזָּהָב יָזֹקּוּ 'and a place for gold that they refine' (Job 28.1), מְזֻקָּק 'refined' (1 Chron. 28.18, etc.). *Resh:* אוֹרוּ מֵרוֹז 'Curse Meroz' (Jud. 5.23), אֹרוּ אָרוֹר 'Curse bitterly' (Jud. 5.23). *Shin:* וַיָּחִילוּ עַד־בּוֹשׁ 'and they waited until they were disappointed' (Jud. 3.25), בֹשֵׁשׁ 'He disappointed (by delaying)' (Exod. 32.1); הִתְקוֹשְׁשׁוּ וָקוֹשּׁוּ 'Come together and hold assembly' (Zeph. 2.1). *Tav:* יֵחַתּוּ 'will be broken' (1 Sam 2.10, etc.), וְהַחְתַּתִּי 'and I will cause to be dismayed' (Jer. 49.37). These are examples of a letter being followed by another letter to form two (identical) letters.

II.L.1.12.3.

Now, the second category, in which two letters follow two letters, include cases such as וְנָפוֹץ הַכַּדִּים 'smashed the jars' (Jud. 7.19), וַיְפַצְפְּצֵנִי 'and he dashed me to pieces' (Job 16.12); אֲרֻזָה עֹרָה 'The cedar work has been laid bare' (Zeph. 2.14), עַרְעֵר תִּתְעַרְעָר

מוט התמוטטה שוט שוטטו אליוד כתים כתים אלכאף כשך חֹ

וחמת הֹמ שכבה אללמאד ימל ימֻלֵל אלמאם דומה דומם אלנון

והכינותי וכוננתי אלסמאך לרס רסִיסֵי אלעין תרועם רעה

התרועעה אלפא והניף ידו ינופף ידו אלצדי ויחץ מספר חדשיו

חֶצָצוּ אלקוף ומקום לזהב יזקו מזקק אלריש ארו מרוז ארו ארור   625

אלשין ויחילו עד בוש בושש התקוששו וקשו אלתו יחתו

והחתתי פהדה מן תראדף חרף לחרף פצאר חרפין

II.L.1.12.3.
והדא אלקסם אלבֹ והו מא יתראדף חרפין לחרפין ונפֵץ

‹הכדים› ויפצפצני ארזה ערה ‹ערער› תתערער אלי גיר דלך

---

629 הכדים] הכדים L1 | הבדים L3:1r | ערער] ערה L3:1r L1 ערה L1

'will be laid utterly bare' (Jer. 51.58), and other cases, which have been stated to be enhancement by a scholar who has discussed enhancement. Note, however, according to the *diqduq* scholars this is not enhancement. This is because the meaning (of a word) can be fully expressed without a letter of enhancement and also (a letter of enhancement) is not a fixed component of a conjugation. These scholars fall into two groups. Some of them consider it (i.e. the enhanced letter in the examples above) to be a root letter due to the fact that it is a fixed component of the conjugation. Others call it an auxiliary letter and do not consider that it should be called a root letter, since one may utter (inflections of) the lexical class without it, but not in the way that (inflections of) a lexical class are uttered without a letter that is for the purpose of enhancement.

II.L.1.13. Chapter on Contraction

Take note that *he* may occur for the sake of enhancement without expressing meaning and, conversely, it may be contracted, being indicated only by the grammar, and retain the meaning of *he*. It is contracted after *ʾalef*, as in וַיֵּדֶא 'He flew swiftly' (Psa. 18.11), the virtual form of which is יִדְאֶה, like כַּאֲשֶׁר יִדְאֶה 'as (the eagle) flies swiftly' (Deut. 28.49), its imperative being דְאֵה. *He* is contracted after *bet*, as in וְהָעוֹף יִרֶב 'and let the birds multiply' (Gen. 1.22), the virtual form of which is יִרְבֶּה, and after *gimel*, as in הַגָּג 'the roof', הַגָּגָה 'to the roof' (Josh. 2.6). *He* is contracted after *dalet*, as in תַּעְדֶּה כֵלֶיהָ 'She adorns herself with her jewels' (Isa. 61.10), וַתַּעַד נִזְמָהּ 'She decked herself with her ring' (Hos. 2.15). It is contracted after *he*: תִּכְהֶה 'will be blinded' (Zech. 11.17), וַתֵּכַהּ '(My eye) has grown dim' (Job 17.7). It is contracted after *vav*: וְיִתְאָו '(The king) will desire'

ממא קאלה מן תכלם פי אלתפכים אנה תפכים ואעלם אן   630

אלדקדוקיין ליס הדא ענדהם תפכים לאן חרף אלתפכים יתם

אלגרץ מן דונה ואיצֿא פלא יתבת פי תצריף והם עלי קסמין

מנהם מן יגעלה חרף אצלי לתבותה פי אלתצריף ומנהם מן

יסמיה מסתעמל [ולא ירי] אן יסמיה אצלי לאן קד יתכלם

באללגה מן דונה לא עלי אלוגה אלדי ^(L3:1v) יתכלם באללגה מן   635

דון אלחרף אלדי ללתפכים

II.L.1.13. באב פי אלאכתצאר

אעלם אן אלהא תגי ללתפכים ולא יטהר להא מעני ותגי בעכס

דלך והו אן תכתצר ותדל עליהא אללגה ויכון להא מעני אלהא

קד תכתצר בעד אלאלף כך וידא תקדירה וידאה מתל כאשר   640

ידאה אלאמר מנה דאֶה ויכתצר אלהא בעד אלבא מתל והעוף

ותקדירה יֶרְבַה ובעד גמאל [הג]ג הגגֶה ויכתצר אלהא בעד

אלדאל מתל תעדה כֶ[ליה] ותעד נזמה ויכתצר בעד אלהא

תכְהֶה ותֶּכַה ויכתצר בעד אלואו ויתאו ויתאוה ויכתצר בעד

(Psa. 45.12), וַיִּתְאַוֶּה 'and he longed' (2 Sam. 23.15). It is contracted after *zayin*: וַיִּבֶז עֵשָׂו 'and Esau despised' (Gen. 25.34), אֱלֹהִים לֹא תִבְזֶה 'God, you will not despise' (Psa. 51.19). It is contracted after *ḥet*: וַיִּמַח 'and he blotted out' (Gen. 7.23), תִּמְחֶה 'You will blot out' (Deut. 25.19). It is contracted after *ṭet*: וַיֵּט 'and he stretched' (Gen. 29.21, etc.), יַטֶּה יָדוֹ '(The Lord) stretches out his hand' (Isa. 31.3). It is contracted after *yod*: אֵי הֶבֶל אָחִיךָ 'Where is Abel your brother?' (Gen. 4.9), אַיֵּה | חֲסָדֶיךָ 'Where is your loving kindness?' (Psa. 89.50). It is contracted after *kaf*: וַתֵּבְךְּ וְלֹא תֹאכֵל 'and she wept before him' (Jud. 14.17), וַתִּבְכֶּה וְלֹא תֹאכַל 'and she wept and did not eat' (1 Sam. 1.17). It is contracted after *lamed*: וַיַּעַל נְשִׂאִים 'He made the mists rise' (Jer. 51.16), נְשִׂאִים 'and he made the mists rise' (Jer. 10.13). It is contracted after *mem*: מִצָּפוֹן וּמִיָּם 'from the north and from the south' (Psa. 107.3, etc.), יָמָּה וְצָפֹנָה 'westward and northward' (Deut. 3.27, etc.). It is contracted after *nun*: וַיִּבֶן אֶת־הַבַּיִת 'and he built the house' (1 Kings 6.9), וַיִּבְנֶה 'and he built' (Josh. 19.50). It is contracted after *samekh*: אֶעֱלֶה אֲכַסֶּה־אָרֶץ 'I will arise and cover the earth' (Jer. 46.8), וַיְכַס אֶת־עֵין כָּל־הָאָרֶץ 'and it covered the face of the whole land' (Exod. 10.15). It is contracted after *ʿayin*: וַיִּשַׁע יְהֹוָה אֶל־הֶבֶל וְאֶל־מִנְחָתוֹ 'and the Lord had regard for Abel and his offering' (Gen. 4.4), יִשְׁעֶה הָאָדָם 'man will regard' (Isa. 17.7). It is contracted after *pe*: אַל־תֶּרֶף יָדֶיךָ 'Do not release your hand' (Josh. 10.6), הַרְפֵּה 'release' (Jud. 11.37). It is contracted after *ṣade*: וְתֵרֶץ אָז תִּרְצֶה הָאָרֶץ אֶת־שַׁבְּתֹתֶיהָ 'Let it enjoy its sabbaths' (Lev. 26.43), 'Then the land will enjoy' (Lev. 26.34). It is contracted after *qof*: וַיַּשְׁק אֶת־בְּנֵי יִשְׂרָאֵל 'and he made the people of Israel drink' (Exod. 32.20), וָאַשְׁקֶה אֶת־כָּל־הַגּוֹיִם 'and I made all the nations drink' (Jer. 25.17). It is contracted after *resh*: אַל־תְּעַר נַפְשִׁי 'Do not pour out my soul' (Psa. 141.8), אֲשֶׁר הֶעֱרָה לַמָּוֶת נַפְשׁוֹ 'because he poured out his soul to death' (Isa. 53.12). It is contrated after *shin*: וַיֶּקֱשׁ דְּבַר־אִישׁ יְהוּדָה 'The words of the men of Judah were harder' (2

645   אלזאי ויבז עשו אלהים לא תבזה ויכתצר בעד אלחית וימח

תמחֶה ויכתצר בעד אלטית ויט יטה ידו ויכתצר בעד אליוד אי

הבל אחיך איה חסדיך ויכתצר בעד אלכאף ותֶבְךְ עליו ותבְכֶּה

ולא תאכֵל ויכתצר בעד אללמאד ויעל נשיאים ויעלה נשיאים

ויכתצר בעד אלמאם מצפון ומים ימה וצפונה ויכתצר בעד אלנון

650   ויבן את הבית ויבנה ויכתצר בעד אלסמאך אעלה אכסה ארץ

ויכס את עין כל הארץ ויכתצר בעד אלעין וישע ייי אל הבל ואל

מנחתו (L3:12r) ישעה האדם ויכתצר בעד אל[פ]א אל תרף ידי[ך]

הרפה ויכתצר בעד אל[צ]די ותרץ את שבתותיה אז תרצה

הארץ ויכתצר בעד אלקוף וישק את בני יש ואשקה את כל

655   הגוים ויכתצר בעד ריש אל תער אל תער נפשי אשר הערה למות

נפ[שו] ויכתצר בעד אלשין ויקש דבר איש יהודה לא יקשה

Sam. 19.44), לֹא־יִקְשֶׁה בְעֵינֶךָ 'It will not seem hard to you' (Deut. 15.18). It contracts after *tav*: הַעִירֹוֹתִי מִצָּפֹון וַיַּאת 'I stirred up (one) from the north and he has come' (Isa. 41.25), עָדֶיךָ תֵּאתֶה 'To you it will come' (Micah 4.8). (To these can be added) other examples of this type.

This is what needs to be said in the discourse on the letters. It is finished, much praise be to God.

בעיניך ויכתצר בעד אלתֻו העירותי מצפון ויֵאת עדיֵך תֵאתֵה אלי

גיר דלך מן הדא אלגנס

פהדא מא לאח אן ידכר פי מקאלה אלחרוף תמת ואלחמד ללה

660   כתירא

II.L.2.0.
THE SECOND DISCOURSE

II.L.2.1. (Preliminary Remarks on Vowels)

II.L.2.1.1.

Discussion concerning the 'kings'. If you wish, you may say concerning the 'melodies', and if you wish, you may say concerning the 'inflections'. The meaning of these is the same.[8] Four preliminary issues will be presented at the beginning of this section. Some of these have already been mentioned previously.

II.L.2.1.2.

The first is that speech cannot begin with a 'melody' (vowel), i.e. a 'king' (vowel). Rather it must begin with a letter. This is because when somebody begins speaking, the first component of his speech that is heard is one of the letters. He cannot begin with one of the vowels without putting a letter before it.

II.L.2.1.3.

The second is that when somebody begins (speech) with a letter, he must attach vocalic articulation (ʾiʿrāb) to this, since the letter cannot be deprived of this when it is the beginning (of speech).

II.L.2.1.4.

The third is that if somebody utters a word consisting of two letters that appear in speech,[9] a vowel must come between

---

[8] I.e. they refer to the vowels. | [9] I.e. letters that are consonants and not 'soft' vowel letters.

II.L.2.0.
אל מקאלה אלתאניה

II.L.2.1.
II.L.2.1.1.
אלכלאם פי אלמלוך ואן שית אן תקול פי אלנגמאת ואן שית

תקול פי אלאנחא פאלמעני פי דלך ואחד יקדם להדה

אלמקאלה ארבע מקדמאת ממא קד דכר טרף מנה פימא

תקדם 665

II.L.2.1.2.
אלאול אלנטק לא יכון אבתדאה ואולה נגמה אעני מלך ואנמא

יכון אולה חרף ודלך אן אלמבתדי באלכלאם אול מא יטהר

ללסמע מן נטקה אחד אלחרוף ולא ימכנה אן יבדא בשי מן

אלמלוך דון אן יקדם קבלה חרף

II.L.2.1.3.
ואלתאני הו ⁽ᴸ³:¹²ᵛ⁾ אן אדא אבתדא בחרף לא בד מן אן יתבעה 670

אעראב אד לא יגוז אן יערא אלחרף מן דלך אדא כאן אבתדא

II.L.2.1.4.
ואלתאלתה הו אנה אדא נטק בלפטה דאת חרפין טאהרין פי

אלנטק לא בד מן אן יתולד בינהמא מן אלנגמה אעני אחד

them, I mean one of the eight vowels, as in שָׁם, עָם, לְךָ, and as in וַיֵּלֶךְ,[10] and similar cases.

II.L.2.1.5.
The fourth is that the vowels always belong to the letters and the letters do not belong to vowels. This is because the vowels cannot function without letters. A letter may be deprived of a vowel but a vowel may not be deprived of a letter. This is because speech must consist of quiescent and mobile components and a mobile component is only made mobile by a vowel, whereas a quiescent component dispenses with this, as will be described in what follows.

II.L.2.2. Chapter concerning the Number of the Vowels and those of them that are 'High', those of them that are 'Level' and those of them that are 'Low', and what is Connected to this

II.L.2.2.1.
What is to be said concerning the vowels is manifest and clear, and not obscure, because it is through them that the purpose of a speaker is understood, and without them speech would be nonsense. Surely you see that in the original establishment (of language) by convention they were indispensable. This is because the origin of language was with Adam, peace be upon him. Either at the beginning the angels and he established language by mutual convention[11] or they taught him language. It is not possible that God, may He be exalted, established

---

[10] This word consists of two consonantal radicals, viz. ל and ך, the inflectional prefix being ignored. | [11] Literally: The angels established language by convention with him and he established it by convention with them.

אלתמאניה נגמאת מתל קו שם עם לך וכקו וילך ואמתאל דלך

ואלראבעה הו אן אלמלוך אבדא תאבעה ללחרוף וליס אלחרוף   675

תאבעה ללמלוך לאן לא תפיד אלמלוך מן דון אלחרוף ואלחרף

קד יערי מן נגמה ואלנגמה לא תערי מן חרף לאן אלנטק לא בד

לה מן סאכן ומתחרך פאלמתחרך לא יתחרך אלא בנגמה

ואלסאכן מסתגני ען דלך עלי מא יגי דכרה פי מא בעד

II.L.2.2. (L5:2r) **באב פי עדד אלנגמאת ומא מנהא רפע ומא**   680
מנהא נצב ומא מנהא כפץ ומא יתצל בדלך

אלכלאם פי אלמלוך טאהר (L5:2v) גלי גיר כפי לאן בהא יפהם ען

אלמתכלם גרצה ולולאהא לכאן אלכלאם עבתא אלי תרי אן פי

אצל אלמואצעה לא בד מנהא ודאך אן אצל אללגה מע אדם על

אלס אמא אן תכון אלמלאיכה ואצעתה אללגה וואצעהא   685

אבתדא או עלמתה אללגה תעלימא ואלמלאיכה לא יגוז אן

language by convention with the angels, because the establishment by convention requires the pointing to the thing for which language is conventionally established. Pointing can only be undertaken with a limb, but He, may He be exalted, transcends the need to have limbs. If somebody were to say that He could have created a limb with which to establish (language) just as He could have created an instrument for speech, with which He could speak, (the response would be): but He must have taught them language to some extent for the sake of His first speech, namely when He said to the angels יְהִי אוֹר 'Let there be light' (Gen. 1.3), and He caused this to happen after this speech and thereby obliged them to recognize that 'light' is the name of what came into being after the speech and they learnt this. Then other items (of language) followed a similar course. He would have helped them receive and retain (language) from the first instance.

II.L.2.2.2.

When He said יְהִי אוֹר, the *shewa* in it under the *yod* must of necessity have been pronounced mobile and the *hireq* must have been pronounced under the *he*, so that יְהִי was a future form. Similarly, when He said to Adam מִכֹּל עֵץ־הַגָּן אָכֹל תֹּאכֵל 'You may eat of every tree of the garden' (Gen. 2.16), if He had not pronounced *qames* under the *ʾalef* and *holem* over the *kaf*, it would not have been known that this is an infinitive. This is because the meaning of the letters in a case such as אכל changes with *patah*, resulting in the change of vowels into the form אָכַל. When *patah* occurs in the place of *holem*, it becomes a past verb. So with אֲכֹל, when *shewa* occurs in place of *qames*, it becomes an imperative. Likewise with אֹכֵל, when *holem* occurs on *ʾalef* and

יואצֿעהא אללה תﬠֿ לאן אלמואצֿעה לא בד להא מן אלאשארה

אלי אלשי אלמתואצֿﬠ עליה ואלאשארה לא תכון אלא בגֿארחה

והו תﬠ יתﬠאלי ﬠן אן יכון בדי גֿארחה (L5:3r) ואן כאן קד קאל

בעצֿהם אנה יגֿוז אן יכלק גֿארחה [יואצֿﬠ] בהא כמא יגֿוז אן   690

יכלק אלה ללכלאם ויתכלם בהא לכן ﬠלי אלקול אלאול יכון

ﬠלמהם אללגֿה ﬠלי וגֿה והו אן יכון קאל ללמלאיכה יהי אור

פחדת פי אלתאני מן קולה ואצֿטרהם אלי אן אור אלﬠ אלשי

אלחאדת מן בﬠד אלקול פﬠלמוה ומא כאן סואה גֿרי מגֿראה

ויכון קד אידהם באלקבול ואלחפטֿ מן אול מרה   695

II.L.2.2.2.

פלמא קאל יהי אור לם יכון בד מן חרכה אלשוא מנטוק בהא

תחת אליוד ואלחרק תחת אלהא (L5:3v) חתי יכון יהי מסתקבלא

וכדלך למא קאל לאדם מכל ﬠץ הגן אכל תאכל לולא מא אתי

בחרכה אלקמץ תחת אלאלף וחרכה אלחלם פוק אלכאף למא

ﬠלם אן דלך מצדר לאן מתל חרוף אכל יתגֿייר (L3:13v) באלפתחה   700

מﬠנאהא לאגֿל תגֿייר אלמלוך בקו אֲכָל למא צֿארת אלפתחה

ﬠוץֿ אלחלם צֿאר פﬠלא מאצֿיא וכדלך אֲכֹל למא צֿאר ﬠוץֿ

אלקמץ שוא צֿארת אמרא כדלך אֲכֵל למא צֿאר ﬠלי אלאלף

ṣere under the *kaf*, it becomes a participle. The changes in meaning of these three letters that you see, without themselves changing, are all due to the change of vowels, so without them none of what has been mentioned (with regard to changes of meaning) could have come about and no speech would have taken place. A similar case is עָשׂה, עָשָׂה, עֲשֵׂה, עֹשֶׂה, עֹשָׂה.

II.L.2.2.3.

So it is clear to you that the vowels are not innovations but rather the fourth of the obligatory requirements, in accordance with what has been discussed previously in the first discourse. A single letter may exist without a vowel. When a speaker wants to speak, he adds to the single letter another letter, and further letters, but he is in no circumstances able to add a second letter when the first letter is deprived of a vowel. A letter is an element (of speech), but communication between people can only be achieved by combining a letter with a vowel. A letter can stand without a (subsequent) vowel but a vowel can only stand with (a preceding) letter.

II.L.2.3. Section concerning what Corresponds to (Arabic) Inflectional Vowels

II.L.2.3.1.

In this regard it has been said that vowels are a basic component of speech and every language requires certain vowels so that speakers can make their intentions understood to one another.

II.L.2.3.2. Section

The Arabs have three inflectional vowels in their language. These are 'raising' (*rafᶜ*), i.e. the vowel *ḍamma*, which is written above; 'holding level' (*naṣb*), i.e. the vowel *fatḥa*, which is written above; and 'lowering' (*khafḍ*), i.e. the vowel *kasra*, which is written below. They also have vowelless inflection

חלם ותחת אלכאף צֶרי צַאר פאעל פמא תרי אלי מא צאַרת

705 אליה הדה אלתלתה אלחרוף מן תגייר אלמעאני והי מא תגיירת

פי דאתהא וכל דלך מן אגל תגייר אלנגמאת פלולאהא למא צח

מן גמיע מא דכר שיא ולא תם כלאם ומתל דלך עָשָׂה עָשָׂה

עָשֶׂה עָשֶׂה עָשָׂה

II.L.2.2.3.

פקד באן לך אן אלמלוך ליס הי מסתחדתה בל הי אלראבע מן

710 אלאפתקאראת עלי מא מצא אלכלאם פי אלמקאלה אלאולי

פאלחרף אלואחד ימכן וגודה עארי מן מלך פאדא אראד

אלמתכלם אן יתכלם זאד עלי אלחרף אלואחד חרף אכר ומא

זאד גיר אנה לא ימכן אן יזיד חרפא תאניא ואלאול עארי מן

מלך בתה פצאר אלחרף אצלא ולא יתם אלתכאטב (L3:2r) בה

715 ללאפאדה אלא באלמלך פחרף [ק]ד יכון בלא מלך ומלך לא

יכון אלא בחרף

II.L.2.3. **פצל [פי] מא גרי מגרי אלאעראב**

II.L.2.3.1.

ולהדא קיל אן אלמלוך אצלא תאבתא ללכלאם פלא בד לכל

לגה מן חרכאת מא ליפהמו בעצהם בעץ אגראצהם

II.L.2.3.2. **פצל**

720 ללערב פי לגתהם מן אלאעראב תלתה והי אלרפע והו אלצֶמה

מן פוק ואלנצב והו אלפתחה מן פוק ואלכפץ והי אלכסרה מן

אספל ולהם אלגזם אלדי יגזמו בה אלחרף אעני יסכנהו והי

(*jazm*), in which they cut short a letter, I mean they make it quiescent (without a vowel). This is a circle (sign) written over the letter that is made quiescent. 'Raising' (*rafʿ*) is a form such as *Zayd-u*, 'holding level' (*naṣb*) is *Zayd-a* and 'lowering' (*khafḍ*) is *Zayd-i*. They have given the agent *rafʿ* inflection due to its agency. They have given the patient *naṣb* inflection due to the occurrence of the action upon it. They have made the affixed particles *bi-*, *ka-* and *li-* govern *khafḍ* inflection and they say *dār li-Zayd-in* 'a house of Zayd', *marartu bi-Zayd-in* 'I passed by Zayd', *Zayd-u ka-Bakr-in* 'Zayd is like Bakr', and the same applies also to other particles that govern *khafḍ* inflection other than these three affixes, i.e. *min, ʿalā, ʿan, ʾilā, fawqa, ʾasfala, taḥta, quddāma,* and other *khafḍ*-governing particles. I have mentioned this to show that the Hebrew language has vowels corresponding to these inflectional vowels that are greater in number than those of the Arabic language. In this respect Hebrew exhibits its superiority over Arabic, as it does in other features that are not connected with the topic I have described.

II.L.2.4. Section on the Correspondence (of Hebrew Vowels) to Arabic Inflectional Vowels

(What corresponds to) Arabic inflectional vowels (*ʾiʿrāb*) in the Hebrew language consists of three categories: 'raising' (*rafʿ*), 'holding level' (*naṣb*) and 'lowering' (*khafḍ*). (What corresponds to Arabic) vowelless inflection (*jazm*) in Hebrew falls into two categories, one like the vowellessness of the Arabic language and the other is not found in it (i.e. in Arabic). For this reason I have said that the vowels of our language are greater in number than the inflectional vowels of Arabic. The last category (i.e. mobile *shewa*) is divided into three types. The first of these types corresponds to the three types of Arabic inflectional vowels. The second type corresponds to the 'holding level' (*naṣb*) only. The third type corresponds to the 'lowering' (*khafḍ*) only. What

דאירה עלי אלחרוף אלמגזום פאלרפע נחו זיד ואלנצב זידַא

ואלכפץֵ זידֵ פגעלו אלפאעל מרפוע בפעלה וגעלו אלמפעול

מנצובא בוקוע אלפעל עליה וגעלו אלבא ואלכאף ואללאם

אלזואיד תכפץֵ פיקולון דאר לזידֵ ומררת בזידֵ וזיד כבכרֵ מע

מא להם מן חרוף אלכפץֵ גיר אלגֵ זואיד והי מן ועלי ועַן ואלי

ופוק ואספל ותחת וקדאם אלי גיר דלך מן אלחרוף אלכאפצֵה

ואנמא אורדת דלך לאורי אן אללגה אלעבראניה להא ממא

יגרי מגרי אלאעראב אכתר ממא ללגה אלערביה פתטֹהר 730

פצֵילתהא פי הדא אללוגה מע מא להא עליהא סוא דלך ממא

ליס יתעלק בה אלכלאם פי מא קצדתה

II.L.2.4. (L3:2v) פצֵל [פי] מא יגרי מגרי אלאעראב

אלאעראב פי אללגה אלעבראניה תלת רפע ונצב וכפץֵ ואלגזם

פי אלעבראני עלי קסמין אלואחד מתל גזם אללגה אלערביה 735

ואלאכר ליס הו להא פלהדא קלת אן חרכאת לגתנא אכתר מן

אעראבהא והדא אלקסם אלאכיר ינקסם עלי גֵ אקסאם אלקסם

אלאול מן הדה ינוב עַן גֵ אקסאם אלאעראב ואלקסם אלבֵ ינוב

עַן אלנצב פקט ואלקסם אלגֵ ינוב עַן אלכפץֵ פקט אלרפע פי

corresponds in Hebrew to (the Arabic inflectional vowel) 'raising' (*rafʿ*) are two vowels, namely אֹ and אוּ. Three vowels correspond to (the Arabic inflectional vowel) 'holding level' (*naṣb*), namely 'big *fatḥa*', i.e. אָ, 'medium *fatḥa*', i.e. אַ, and 'small *fatḥa*', i.e. אֱ. Two vowels correspond to (the Arabic inflectional vowel) 'lowering' (*khafḍ*), namely אֶ and אִי. The vowelless inflection (*jazm*) is the quiescent *shewa*. This is the vowellessness of Arabic. The other *jazm* is the mobile *shewa*. This, as I have mentioned, is divided into three types. The *shewa* requires special discussion and this will come in its appropriate place, with the help of God.

II.L.2.5. Section (on *Rafʿ*)

Take note that one category of 'raising' (*rafʿ*) in the Hebrew language is used in the active participle in certain conjugations, for example בּוֹנֶה, קוֹנֶה, and other examples with this pattern, שׁוֹמֵר, אוֹכֵל, and other examples with this pattern, פָּתַח, שָׁמַע, and other examples with this pattern. To these should be added forms that are used for the imperative and the past such as שׂוֹרֵף 'be burnt', שׂוֹרַף 'was burnt', and other examples of this pattern; those that are used for the imperative in the conjugaton כּוֹנֵן such as סֹב 'turn', חֹן 'be gracious'; those that are used for the past in the conjugation שִׁירוֹ, such as נוֹדַע 'be known', נוֹשַׁע 'be saved'; those that are used for unconjugated nouns designating bodies and abstractions, such as אֹהֶל 'tent', בֹּהֶן 'thumb', אֹפֶן 'circumstance', אוֹצָר 'store', and similar cases, and the abstractions רוֹגֶז 'anger', חֹרֶב 'desolation', אֹמֶר 'speech', and so forth. This vowel is not found in (forms expressing) a patient. This category (of *rafʿ*) is used for agents, just as the Arabs use [their] *rafʿ* for agents. The Hebrews use it for forms other than those designating agents by extension, just as the Arabs use their *rafʿ* for forms other than those designating agents by extension, such as

740 לגה אלעבראני דכל תחתה נגמתאן והמא אֹוֹ וֹאוֹ וֹאלנצב ידכל

תחתה גֹ נגמאת אלפתחה אלכברי והי אַ ואלפתחה אלוסטי והי

אֶ ואלפתחה אלצגרי והי אִ ואלכפץֹ ידכל תחתה נגמתאן והמא

אֵי אִי ואלגזם הו אלשוֹא אלסאכן והו אלגזם אלדי ללערבי

ואלגזם אלאכר הו אלשוֹא אלמתחרך והו אלדי דכרת אנה

745 ינקסם גֹ אקסאם וללשוֹא כלאם מפיד פיגי פי מוֹצֹעה בעון אללה

פצל II.L.2.5.

אעלם אן אלקסם אלואחד מן אלרפע פי אללגה אלעבראניה

אסתעמלוה פי תצאריף מכצוֹצה פי אלפאעל נחו בונֶה קונֶה

וזנהמא ואוֹכֵל ושוֹמֵר וזנהמא ^(L3:11v) ושֶמֵע ופתַח וזנהמא אלי

750 גיר דלך ממא קד אסתעמל פי אלאמר ואלעבר מתל שוֹרֵף

שוֹרֵף וזנהמא ואסתעמל פי אלאמר מן תצריף כוֹנֵן נחו סֹב חֹן

ואסתעמל פי אלעבר מן תצריף שירו נחו נוֹדַע נוֹשַע ואסתעמל

פי אלאסמא אלגיר מתצרפה פי אלאגסאם ואלאעראץֹ כקֹו פי

אלאגסאם אהֶל בהֶן אופֶן אוֹצֵר ואמתאל דלך ואלאעראץֹ רוֹגֶז

755 חֹרֶב אמֶר אלי גיר דלך ולא יוגד הדא אלמלך פי מפעול פקד

צאר הדא אלקסם אלואחד יסתעמל פי אלפאעלין כמא

אסתעמלו אלערב רפע[הם פ]י אלפאעלין ואסתעמלו

אלעבראניין פי גיר אלפאעלין תוסעא כמא אסתעמלו אלערב

רפעהם פי ג[יר] אלפאעלין תוסעא מן נחו אלאבתדא

topicalization, interrogative constructions, and so forth. Nobody can object to my statement that this category of *rafᶜ* is not used in (a form expressing) a patient by saying that מִזְרָה הָרֶשֶׁת 'the net is spread' (Prov. 1.17) is a patient and that it has been made a patient by *rafᶜ*, i.e. אוֹ. This is because my statement refers only to cases where this type of *rafᶜ* occurs at the beginning of a word with the first letter but the *mem* in מִזְרָה has been placed before the *rafᶜ*, and it is for this reason that I have stated that this category of *rafᶜ* is not found in a patient.

II.L.2.6. Section on the Second *Rafᶜ*

As for א, the Hebrews use this in the imperative of (conjugations in the category) שׁוּעַל, as in שׁוּב, קוּם, and the like. They use it in a verb whose agent is not named (i.e. a passive verb), for example סֻפַּר, קֻבַּר, and the like. They use it in concrete and abstract nouns and in the names of people. An example of a personal name is וּפֻרָה נַעַרְךָ 'and Purah, your servant' (Jud. 7.10). A concrete noun is פּוּרָה | דָּרַכְתִּי 'I have trodden the wine press' (Isa. 63.3). An abstract noun is דוּמֶה (Psa. 94.17, etc.), דֻמִיָּה (Psa. 22.3, etc.) 'silence'. To these can be added further examples.

II.L.2.7. Section on *Naṣb*

II.L.2.7.1.

The small *naṣb*, which is *qameṣ*, like *naṣb* in the language of the Arabs, is used in (forms expressing) the patient, for example שָׁמוּר 'guarded', שָׁבוּר 'broken', זָכוּר 'remembered', בָּנוּי 'built', and the like. It is used in the 'absolute patient', i.e the infinitive, as in שָׁמוֹר 'guarding', זָכוֹר 'remembering', בָּנֹה 'building', עָשֹׂה 'doing', and the like. It is used in past verbs, such as שָׁמָר 'he built', בָּנָה 'he built', and the like. It is used in the form that expresses both the past and the active participle such as שָׁם, קָם and words with this pattern.

ואלאסתפהאם וגיר דלך וליס למעתרץׁ אן יעתרץׁ מא קלתה אן   760

לא יוגד הדא אלרפע פי מפעול באן יקול אן מזוֹרה הרשת

מפעולה ובאלרפע צארת מפעולה והו או לאן אנמא כלאמי פי

מא כאן הדא אלרפע פי אול לפטׄה מע אלחרף אלאול ואלמאם

פי מזוֹרה קד תקדם [אל]רפ[ע פלדל]ךׄ קלת אנה לא יוגד פי

מפעול מן הד[א אלקס[ם   765

II.L.2.6. פצל [פי] אלרפע אלתׄאני

אׅ אסתעמלוה אלעבראניין פי אלאמר מן שועֹל נחו שוב   (L3:11r)

קום ואמתאל דלך ואסתעמלוה פי אלפעל אלדׄי לם יסם פאעלה

מתׄל סֶפֿֿר קֻבַר ונחוהמא ואסתעמלוה פי אלאסמא אלגׄאמדה

ואלאעראץׁ ואסמא אלנאס פאסם אנסאן מתׄל ופוּרה נערך   770

ואלגׄמאד פוּרה דרכתי ואלערץׁ דוּמָה דומיה אלי גיר דלך

II.L.2.7. פצל פי אלנצב

II.L.2.7.1.

אלנצב אלצֹגיר והו אלקאמצה תגרי מגרי אלנצב פי לגה אלערב

יסתעמל פי אלמפעול כֹך שָׁמוֹר שָׁבוּר זָכֹור בָּנוּי [ואמ]תׄאלה

ואסתעמל פי אלמפעול אלמטלק והו אלמצדר נחו שָׁמֹר זָכֹר   775

בָּנֹה עָשֹה ואמתאל דלך יסתעמל פי אלאפעאל אלמאצׁיה נחו

שָׁמַר בָּנָה ואמתאלהמא ויסתעמל פי אללפׄטׄה אלואחדה

ללעבר ולאסם אלפאעל מתׄל שָׁם קָם ואוזאנהמא

II.L.2.7.2.

The 'big *naṣb*' is used in imperatives from (conjugations in the category) גַּנִּי, such as הַכֵּה 'hit', הַטֵּה 'incline', הַאֲכֵל 'feed', הַעֲמֵד 'cause to stand', and the like. It is used in 'transposed infinitives', such as דַּבֵּר 'speak', קַוֵּה לְשָׁלוֹם '(we) look for peace' (Jer. 8.15, etc.), and other forms expressed by this category of *naṣb*.

II.L.2.7.3.

The third (category of) *naṣb*, i.e. *segol*, is used in imperative forms such as הֶרֶף מִמֶּנִּי 'leave me alone' (Deut. 9.14), הֶרֶב כַּבְּסֵנִי 'wash me thoroughly' (Psa. 51.4). They use it in past forms such as הֶאֱכִיל 'he fed', הֶחֱזִיק 'he made strong', הֶחֱשׁוּ 'they were silent', and so forth.

II.L.2.8. Section on *Khafḍ*

II.L.2.8.1.

The *khafḍ* vowel אֵי is used in past forms such as הֵקִים 'he caused to rise', הֵעִיד 'he bore witness'. It is used in a noun of agent (active participle) such as מֵקִים 'causing to rise', מֵעִיד 'bearing witness'. It is used in imperative forms substituting for the other category of *khafḍ* (i.e. *ḥireq*) when it is followed by one of the letters אהחע, as in הֵעָלוּ 'remove yourselves' (Num. 16.24), הֵרֹמּוּ מִתּוֹךְ 'remove yourselves from the midst' (Num. 17.10), and the like.

II.L.2.8.2.

The second category of *khafḍ*, i.e. אִי, is used in the past of all conjugations from the category גַּנִּי, for example הִכָּה 'he hit', הִצִּיל 'he saved', הִגַּשׁ 'he approached', הִנַּח 'he placed', גִּלָּה 'he revealed', הִגְלָה 'he exiled', דִּבֶּר 'he spoke', בִּלַּע 'he swallowed', זִבַּח

II.L.2.7.2.

אלנצב אלכביר יסתעמלוה פי אלאואמר מן גֵנִי נחו הכה הטֶה

780 הָאֹכֶל הָעֲמֵד ונחו דלך ואסתעמלוה פי אלמצֹאדר אלמסתעארה

נחו דבֵר קֻוֵה לשלום אלי גיר דלך ממא יפידה הדא אלנצב

II.L.2.7.3.

אלנצב אלתאלת והו אלסגֹול אסתעמלוה (L5:19r) פי אלאמר נחו

הֶרֶף ממני הֶרֶב כבסני (L3:7r) ואסתעמלוה פי אלעבר נחו הֶאָכִיל

הַחֲזִיק הַחֲשׁוּ אלי גיר דלך

II.L.2.8. פצֹל פי אלכפץֹ 785

II.L.2.8.1.

אלמלך אלדי ללכפץֹ אי אסתעמלוה פי אלעבר נחו הֵקִים הֵעִיד

ואסתעמלוה פי אסם אלפאעל נחו מֵקִים מֵעִיד ואסתעמלוה פי

אלאמר נאיבא ען אלכפץֹ אלאכר אדא כאן בעדה חרף מן חרוף

אֹהֹחֹע נחו הֵעֲלוּ הֵרֹמוּ מתוד אלי גיר דלך

II.L.2.8.2.

790 אלכפץֹ אלב הו אי אסתעמלוה פי אלעבר מן גֵנִי פי גֹמיע

תצֹאריפהא נחו הכה הצֹיל הגֹש הנח ⟨גֹלה⟩ הגֹלה דבֵר בלֵע

---

786 אֵי [אֵ L5:19r   790 אֵי [אֵ L5:19r   791 גֹלה] גֹלה L3

'he sacrificed', נִחַם 'he comforted', הִשְׁלִיךְ 'he threw', הִשְׁלִיךְ 'he threw', הִפְצַר 'he pushed', הִשְׂבִּיעַ 'he sated', בִּקְשָׁה 'he sought', הִדְרְכָה 'he bent (bow)', כִּרְבֵּל 'he mantled', תִּעְתֵּעַ 'he mocked', הִשְׂמְאִיל 'he turned left'. It is used in the imperative of all conjugations in the category of שִׁירָה, for example שִׂים 'place', שִׂיחַ 'tell', הִכּוֹן 'be prepared', הִסּוֹעַ '?', הִמַּק 'decay', הִבּוֹךְ 'be confused'. It is used in the imperative, the past and the active participle of most conjugations of the category מֵסַב, for example הִתְהַלֵּךְ, מִתְהַלֵּךְ, הִתְהַלֵּךְ. These and others are examples of the use of *khafḍ*, *naṣb* and *rafʿ* in the Hebrew language.

II.L.2.9. Section (Preliminary Remarks on the *Shewa*)

(What corresponds to Arabic) vowellessness (*jazm*) in the Hebrew language is the quiescent *shewa*. This is because the *shewa* falls into two categories, quiescent and mobile. The quiescent *shewa* is what deprives a letter of a vowel so that it is not mobile. The mobile *shewa* is additional to the (inventory of) vowels of the Arabic language, (the treatment of which) has various subsections.

II.L.2.10. Section concerning the *Shewa*

II.L.2.10.1.

The *shewa* is divided into two categories, quiescent and mobile. There is no third category. The quiescent *shewa* has features by which it is distinguished from the mobile *shewa*. The mobile *shewa* has two features by which it is distinguished from the quiescent *shewa*.

II.L.2.10.2.

A feature of the quiescent *shewa* is that it makes a letter under which it occurs quiescent and makes it part of the preceding

זְבַח נְחַם הַשְלִיך הַשְלֵיך הַפְצַר הַשְבִיעַ בְּקִשָה הַדְרָכָה <כְרבֵל>

תַעְתַע הַשְמְאִיל ואסתעמלוה פי אלאמר מן שירה פי גֹמיע

תצאריפהא נחו שִים ושִיחַ והָכֹון והֹסוע והֹמק והֹבוך

795 ואסתעמלוה פי אלאמר ואלעבר ואלפאעל מן עלאמה מֵסַב פי

אכתר תצאריפהא נחו התהלֵך התהלֵך מתהלֵך אלי גיר דלך

ממא אסתעמל אלכפִץ ואלנצב ואלרפע פי לגה אלעבראניה

II.L.2.9. ^(L5:20r) **פצל**

אלגֹזם פי לגה אלעבראני הו אלשוא אלסאכן לאן אלשוא עלי

800 קסמין סאכן ומתחרך פאלסאכן הו אלדי יגֹזם אלחרף לילא

יתחרך ואלמתחרך הו אלזאיד ען אנחא אללֹגֹה אלערביה ולה

פנון עדה

II.L.2.10. **פצל פי אלשוא**

II.L.2.10.1.

אלשוא ינקסם קסמין סאכן ומתחרך ולא קסם תאלת להמא

805 פאלסאכן עלאמאת יתמיז בהא מן אלמתחרך וללמתחרך

עלאמתין יתמיז בהא מן ^(L5:20v) אלסאכן

II.L.2.10.2.

מן עלאמה אלסאכן אנה יסכן אלחרף אלדי הו תחתה ויגֹעלה

(syllabic) group, for example יִשְׂרָאֵל 'Israel', יֶחְדְּיָהוּ 'Jehdeiah', זִמְרִי 'Zimri', לְמִשְׁעִי 'for cleansing' (Ezek. 16.4), וּפִסְלִי וְנִסְכִּי 'my graven image and my molten image' (Isa. 48.5). So the letter under which the (quiescent) *shewa* occurs becomes quiescent. Whatever letter it occurs under is not mobile at all and it (the quiescent *shewa*) cuts it off from what is after it and conjoins it to what is before it.

II.L.2.10.3.

Another of it features is that it divides a word into (units) that have the status of words. This is because every letter at the end of a word is quiescent when it is deprived of an accompanying vowel and this letter that is deprived of a vowel is the stopping point of the word and its place of division, as in בְּרֵאשִׁית, in which the *tav* is the stopping point of the word, and אוֹר, in which the *resh* is the stopping point of the word, and so forth. A quiescent *shewa* in the middle of a word has the same status, for it is in a sense a stopping point on account of its quiescence, for example וְהָאֲחַשְׁדַּרְפְּנִים 'and the satraps' (Esther 9.3), הַמְצַפְצְפִים 'those who chirp' (Isa. 8.19). Each of these two expressions has the status of three words on account of the quiescent *shewa*. If it were absent, this division would not be admissible.

II.L.2.10.4.

Another of its features is that it indicates the feminine gender in many cases, for example, רָחַצְתְּ כָּחַלְתְּ 'you (fs.) washed and you painted (fs.) (your eyes)' (Ezek. 23.40), and similar cases. Forms such as דֶּרֶךְ and מֶלֶךְ are not counterevidence, since I did not say that it occurred at the end of a word only to express the feminine gender, but that it indicates feminine gender in many cases.

פי חזב מא תקדמה נחו יִשְׂרָאֵל יַחְדָּיְהו זִמְרִי לְמִשְׁעִי וּפִסְלִי וּנְסָכְּי

פצאר אלחרף אלדי תחתה אלשוא סאכנא לא יתחרך בתה

מהמא הוא תחתה ופצלה ממא בעדה ואצّאפה אלי מא קבלה   810

II.L.2.10.3.

ומן עלאמאתה איצّא אנה יקסם אללפטה מתאבה כלם לאן כל
חרף פי אכר כלמה הו סאכן אדא ערי מן מלך יכון מעה פיכון
דלך אלחרף אלעארי מן (L4:4r) מלך הו מחט אלכלמה ומקטעהא
נחו בְּרֵאשִׁית אלדי אלתו מחט אלכלמה ונחו אור אלדי אלריש
מחט אלכלמה אלי גיר דלך פאלשוא אלסאכן פי וסט אלכלמה   815
יגרי הדא אלמגרי לאנה קד צאר מחט עלי וגה לסכונה מתל
והאחשדרפנים המצפצפים צארת כל לפטה מן האתין
אללפטתין במתאבה תלת כלם לאגל אלשוא אלסאכן ולו
אנעדם לם תצח אלקסמה פיהא

II.L.2.10.4.

(L4:4v) ומן עלאמאתה איצّא אנה ינבה עלי אלתאנית פי כתיר מן   820
אלמואצّע נחו רָחַצְתְּ כָּחַלְתְּ ומא מאתל דלך ולא יעתרץ דלך
דֶּרֶךְ מֶלֶךְ לאני מא קלת אנה לא יכון פי אכר כלמה אלא
ללתאנית ואנמא קלת אנה ינבה עלי אלתאנית פי כתיר מן
אלמואצّע

II.L.2.11. Section (on the Nature of Mobile *Shewa*)

II.L.2.11.1.

A feature of mobile *shewa* is that when it occurs under a letter, the letter is not in any way static or at rest. If a speaker wished to make it quiescent, he would never speak, just as if a speaker wanted to always make a quiescent *shewa* mobile, ….

GAP

II.L.2.11.2.

Another of its features is that it does not make the letter following it quiescent but rather only makes the third letter after it quiescent. This statement is valid since it (the mobile *shewa*) itself is not removed from under its letter but rather its letter is made mobile and the letter after it is made light (i.e. *rafe*). Quiescence may occur in the third letter or one greater (in number) than that. Examples of the occurrence of quiescence on the third letter are בְּיִשְׂרָאֵל 'in Israel', בְּיִזְרְעֶאל 'in Jezreel', לְיִרְמְיָה 'to Jeremiah' (Neh. 12.12, etc.). Examples (of quiescence) in a later syllable are בְּרֵאשִׁית 'in the beginning', בְּאֶרֶץ 'in the land (of)', בְּחֶרֶב 'with a sword', and similar cases.

II.L.2.11.3.

And if somebody were to say 'What are the full facts concerning the two of them, I mean the quiescent and the mobile *shewa*?', the response would be as follows. As for the quiescent *shewa*, I do not know any more of its distinctive features than those that I have already mentioned. With regard to the mobile *shewa*, it must be treated in various subsections. All the following subsections, therefore, concern the mobile *shewa* rather than

II.L.2.11. **פצל** 825

II.L.2.11.1.

מן עלאמה אלמתחרך אנה אדא כאן תחת חרף לא יסתקר דלך
אלחרף ולא יסכן בתה עלי וגה מן אלוגוה ולו ראם אלמתכלם אן
יסכנה למא תכלם אבדא כמא אנה לו ראם אלמתכלם אן יחרך
אלסאכן דאימא

GAP

II.L.2.11.2.

(L5:4r) ומן עלאמאתה איצֹא אנה מא יסכן עלי אלחרף אלתאני 830

מנה בל לא יסכן אלא עלי אלחרף אלתאלת הדא אלקול הו

תגֹז לאנה הו בעינה לא יברח מן תחת חרפה ואנמא יתחרך

חרפה ויכף אלחרף אלדי בעדה פקד יקע אלסכון פי אלתאלת

וקד יקע פי מא זאד ען דלך פתקול פימא וקע אלסכון פי

אלתאלת בְּיִשְׂרָאֵל בְּיִזְרְעֶאל לְיִרְמְיָה ומא זאד ען דלך מתל 835

בְּרֵאשִׁית בְּאֶרֶץ בְּחֶרֶב ואמתאל דלך

II.L.2.11.3.

(L5:4v) פאן קאל פמא מחצֹה אלפאידה בהמא אעני אלסאכן

ואלמתחרך קיל לה אמא אלסאכן פמא ערפת לה מן אלחטֹ

אלא מא דכרתה מן עלאמאתה ואמא אלמתחרך פהו אלמפנן

באלפנון פגֹמיע מא בעד מן אלפנון פהי ללמתחרך דון אלסאכן 840

the quiescent *shewa*. It is not necessary to mention the corresponding quiescent *shewa* in each place, since it is sufficient to say that the quiescent *shewa* does not have any more features than those that have been mentioned. I shall present below the various subsections concerning the mobile *shewa*.

II.L.2.12. Chapter concerning the Mobile *Shewa* and what is Related to this

Take note that the inventory (of letters) consists of twenty-two basic letters, in addition to which there are the 'straight' letters, the letters with *rafe* and the letters 'between two grades', as has been stated previously. The discussion here relates only to basic features and not to secondary features.

II.L.2.12.1. The First Subsection

II.L.2.12.1.1.

This is its influence by the four letters אהחע. When these four letters are preceded by a letter that is not one of them and under this letter there is *shewa*, the *shewa* is pronounced as a shortened vowel like the vowel that is under one of the four letters. Now, if it is appropriate for *gaʿya* to occur on it, it is pronounced equal to the vowel (following it). For example, וְאִם־כְּכָה 'and if thus' (Num. 11.15), in which *shewa* is under *vav* and the *vav* is pronounced with *hireq* like that which is under the *ʾalef*, but shortened since it it does not have *gaʿya*. Surely you see that when it is appropriate for it to have *gaʿya*, it is pronounced with the (vowel) pronounced on the letter equally, without any difference, for example וְאִם־יִוָּתֵר 'and if there remains' (Exod. 29.34). Similar to the preceding examples are

פלא חאגה אלי דכר סאכן אלמתחרך פי כל מוצׄע אדׄ קד גנית

בקולי אן מא ללסאכן פאידה גיר מא דכר מן עלאמאתה פאדכר

מא יתגה מן פנון אלמתחרך

II.L.2.12. באב פי (L5:5r) אלשוא אלמתחרך ומא יתצל בדלך

אעלם אן אלקבאלה אתנין עשרין חרפא אצׄולא מא סוי 845
אלפשוטות ואלחרוף אלמרפיה ואלחרוף אלמנזלה בין מנזלתין
כמא תקדם אלקול פיה ואלכלאם האהנא אנמא יתעלק
באלאצׄול דון אלפרוע

II.L.2.12.1.
II.L.2.12.1.1.
אלפן אלאול הוא מא יחצל לה מן אלתאתיר פי ארבע חרוף

אֹהֹחֹעֹ פאן הדה אלארבע חרוף אדא כאן קבל אחדהא חרף מן 850
סואהא תחתה שוא כרגׄ דלך אלשוא בכרוגׄ (L5:5v) דלך אלמלך
אלדי תחת אלארבעה חרוף מכפפא אלאן אן יחסן מעה דכול
אלגעיה כרגׄ בכרוגׄ אלמלך סוא נחו וְאִם כָּכָה אלשוא תחת
אלואו כרגׄ אלואו בחרק מתל מא תחת אלאלף מכפפא למא לם
תכון מעה אלגעיה אלי תרי אן למא חסן מעה דכול אלגעיה כרגׄ 855
בכרוגׄ אלחרף סוא מן גיר פרק כקו וְאִם יָוָתֵּר ומתל אלדי תקדם

וְאֶת־תַּעְנַךְ 'and Taanach' (Jud. 1.27), וְאֶת־מְגִדּוֹ וְאֶת־גָּזֶר 'Megiddo and Gezer' (1 Kings 9.15), in which the *shewa* is pronounced as a shortened *segol*. When, however, you say וְאֶת־בָּנָיו 'and his sons' (Gen. 9.1, etc.), the *shewa* is pronounced with a *segol* of full length on account of the *gaʿya*, and so also other cases where *shewa* is pronounced with the pointing of the *ʾalef*.

II.L.2.12.1.2.

As for *he*, a *shewa* before it is pronounced with the vowel of the *he*, for example in וְהָיָה the *shewa* is pronounced as a short *qameṣ* on account of the absence of *gaʿya*. When *gaʿya* is appropriate, the *shewa* is pronounced with the *qameṣ* of the *he* with its full length, for example וְהָיָה. In יְהוּדָה the *shewa* is pronounced with a shortened *qibbuṣ*, due to the absence of *gaʿya*, and other cases where *shewa* is pronounced like the pointing of the *he*.

II.L.2.12.1.3.

Ḥet: Examples of *shewa* before *ḥet* are רְחוֹקָה־הִיא 'it is far' (Jdg 18.28), כִּי קוֹל כְּחוֹלָה 'for (I heard) the voice of a woman in travail' (Jer. 4.31), וְחָלָה חֶרֶב 'and the sword will rage' (Hosea 11.6), וְחֵשֶׁב אֲפֻדָּתוֹ 'and the skilfully woven band' (Exod. 28.8, etc.), וְחִכֵּךְ כְּיֵין הַטּוֹב 'and your palate is the best of wine' (Cant. 7.10), and other cases.

II.L.2.12.1.4.

ʿAyin: Examples of *shewa* before *ʿayin* are בָּרוּךְ יְהוָה לְעוֹלָם 'blessed be the Lord for ever' (Psa. 89.53), in which the *lamed* of לְעוֹלָם is pronounced with a *holem* like the *ʿayin* but shortened. When it is appropriate for it to have *gaʿya*, there is no difference between the *shewa* and the *holem*, for example יְהִי שְׁמוֹ לְעוֹלָם 'may his

‹וְאֶת› תַּעֲנָךְ וְאֶת מְגִדּוֹ וְאֶת גֶּזֶר כרג אלשוא בתלת נקט
מכפפא ואדא קלת וְאֶת בָּנָיו כרג אל ^(L4:1r) שוא בתלת נקט
מסתופאה לאגל אלגעיה אלי גיר דלך ממא יכרג אלשוא בנקט
אלאלף   860

II.L.2.12.1.2.

אלהא יכרג אלשוא אדא כאן קבלה באלמלך אלדי יתחרך
אלהא כקו וְהָיָה כרג אלשוא בקמצה כפיפה לעדם אלגעיה
ואדא חסנת אלגעיה כרג אלשוא בקאמצה אלהא מסתופאה
כקו וְהָיָה ‹וִיהוּדָה› כרג אלשוא באלזֶג מכפפא לעדם אלגעיה
אלי גיר דלך ממא [כ]רג אלשוא בנקט אלהא   865

II.L.2.12.1.3.

אלחית אלשוא קבל אלחית כקו רָחוֹקָה הִיא כִי קוֹ[ל כ]חולה
וְחָלָה חרב וְחֵשַׁב אפדתו וְחֲכֵך כיין הטוב אלי גיר דלך ^(L4:1v)

II.L.2.12.1.4.

אלעין אלשוא קבל אלעין ברוך יְיָ לְעוֹלָם כרג אללמאד מן
לְעוֹלָם [ב]חלם מתל אלעין מכפפא ולמא חסן מעה דכול
אלגעיה לם יכון בין אלשוא ואלחלם פרק נחו יְהִי שְׁמוֹ לְעוֹלָם   870

---

857 וְאֶת¹] אֶת L5   864 וִיהוּדָה] וְיהוּדה L4

name be for ever' (Psa. 72.17). Similar cases are וְאִם רַע בְּעֵינֵיכֶם 'and if it is bad in your eyes' (Josh. 24.15), בְּעֵינֵי אֱלֹהִים 'in the eyes of God' (Prov. 3.4), וְאָדָם 'and a man' (Gen. 2.5, etc.), וְעָלָה הַגְּבוּל 'and the boundary goes up' (Josh. 15.6, etc.), וְעֶפְרוֹן יֹשֵׁב 'and Ephron was sitting' (Gen. 23.10), וְעָרֵי מִבְצָר 'and the fortified cities' (Josh. 19.35), and other cases.

II.L.2.12.1.5.

Now this rule applies to *shewa* with the four letters when *shewa* is under a letter that is not one of the four.

II.L.2.12.1.6.

When it is of one of the four, the rule does not apply, for example יִמְחֲאוּ־כָף 'let them clap their hands' (Psa. 98.8, etc.), אֱלָהֲהֹם דִּי '(the house of) their God which' (Ezra 7.16). If it is said 'Why is it that these four letters differ in this way from the other letters when they come before (another of the four letters) and have *shewa*, and why does the rule not apply to all (letters)?', the response to him would be as follows. Since the letter (i.e. one of the אהחע letters) that is before the four letters requires a vowel together with *shewa* (i.e. a vowel represented by a *ḥaṭef* sign), the vowel (of the *ḥaṭef*) is dominant, so the *shewa* does not have any influence and the *ḥet* of יִמְחֲאוּ is pronounced with *pataḥ* and the *he* of אֱלָהֲהֹם is also pronounced with it. Moreover יִמְחֲאוּ cannot be pronounced with *pataḥ* and *shureq* and it is also not possible for it be pronounced with *shureq* and not *pataḥ*, for if it were pronounced with *shureq*, I mean *qibbuṣ*, there would be no reason for *pataḥ* to occur. Since these two situations are impossible, it must be pronounced with *pataḥ*, due to its natural association with it. What has been said concerning יִמְחֲאוּ־כָף applies equally to אֱלָהֲהֹם. If somebody says 'Why are the other

וּמִתָּלֵה וְאִם רַע בְּעֵינֵיכֶם בְּעֵינֵי אלהים וְאָדָם וְעָלָה הגבול וְעֶפְרוֹן

יוֹשֵׁב וְעָרֵי מבצר אלי גיר דלך

II.L.2.12.1.5.
אלאן הדא אלשרט לאזם פי אלשוא מע אלארבע חרוף מתי
כאן אלשוא תחת חרף מן סוי אל ^(L4:2r) ארבעה

II.L.2.12.1.6.
875 פאמא אן כאן מן אלארבעה בטל הדא אלשרט נחו קוֹ יִמְחָאוּ

כַּף <אֲלָהְהוֹם די> פאן קיל ולם כאלפת הדה אלארבעה חרוף

אדא כאנת קבל ותחתהא שוא לסאיר אלחרוף פי מא הדא

סבילה ולם לא כאנת אלעלה סאירה פי אלכל קיל לה למא כאן

אלחרף אלדי קבל אלארבעה מנהא אחתאג אלי מלך מע

880 אלשוא פאלחכם ללמלך פלדלך לם יותר אלשוא אתרא פכרג

חית יִמְחָאוּ באלפאתחה וכרג הֵא אלהֹהוֹם בהَא איצֿא ^(L4:2v)

ואסתחאל כרוג ימחאו באלפתחה ואלשרק ואמתנע איצֿא

כרוגה באלשרק מן דון אלפתחה אד לו כרג באלשרק אעני

באלזֵّג לכאן לא פאידה פי מגי אלפתחה ולמא אמתנעא

885 אלקסמאן וגב כרוגה באלפתחה לאכתצאצהא בה ואלכלאם פי

אלההום כאלכלאם פי ימחאו כף סוא פאן קיל ולם לא כאן חכם

---

876 אֲלָהְהוֹם די] די אַלָהְהוֹם L4

letters not like these four letters when they are before the aforementioned (four letters), especially when every *shewa* under a letter must be pronounced as a vowel when …

GAP

II.L.2.12.2. (The Second Subsection)

II.L.2.12.2.1.

…. because *shewa* has not changed form but rather is adjacent to it, just as *qameṣ* is adjacent to *pataḥ* and other vowels. This is demonstrated by the fact that *mem* in לְיִרְמְיָה 'to Jeremiah' has *shewa* under it and the *yod* after it has *qameṣ* under it, but the *shewa* is not pronounced like *qameṣ* but rather is pronounced like *ḥireq*, unlike the four letters. The *shewa* of the four letters is restricted by what is before it, but the *shewa* of *yod* is not restricted by what is after it. The difference, therefore, is clear between the two subsections.

II.L.2.12.2.2.

If somebody were to say 'What is the value of us knowing this?', the response to him would be as follows. When *shewa* comes before *yod*, in most cases this is an indication of the indefinite. If a vowel were to occur in place of it, this would be an indication of the definite, for example בְּיוֹם זִבְחֲכֶם 'on the day of your sacrifice' (Lev. 19.6), (which is) indefinite, and בַּיּוֹם הַהוּא כֶּרֶם 'on that day, a vineyard' (Isa. 27.2), (which is) definite, הָפַךְ יָם לְיַבָּשָׁה | 'He turned the sea into dry land' (Psa. 66.6), (which is) indefinite, בַּיַּבָּשָׁה עָבַר יִשְׂרָאֵל 'Israel passed on the dry land' (Josh. 4.22), (which is) definite, and so forth.

בקיה אלחרוף כחכם הדה אלארבעה אדא כאנת קבל הדה

אלמדכורה ולא סימא אן כל שוא תחת חרף יגב אן יכרג במלך

מתי

GAP

II.L.2.12.2.

II.L.2.12.2.1.

890 ⁽L3:3r⁾ ....לאן אלשוא מא גייר חכם בל גאורה כמא יגאור אלקמץ

ללפאתחה וסואהא מן אלמלוך יביין דלך אן אלמאם מן לירמְיָה

תחתה שוא ואליוד בעדה תחתה קמץ ולם יכרג אלשוא

באלקאמצה בל כרג בחרק מכאלפא ללארבעה חרוף פשוא

אלדֹ חרוף מקצור עלי מא קבלה ושוא אליוד גיר מקצור עלי מא

895 בעדה פאלפרק טאהר בין אלפנין

II.L.2.12.2.2.

פאן קאל ומא אלפאידה פי מערפתנא דלך קיל לה אן אלשוא

אדא כאן קבל אליוד פי אכתר אלמואצֹע יכון דלאלה עלי

אלמנכר ולו כאן עוצֹה מלך לכאן דלאלה עלי אלמְיָדֹע כק בְיֶום

זִבְחֲכֶם מִנֶּכָּר בְּיֶום הַהוּא כרם מְיָדֹע הָפַךֹ יָם לְיַבָּשָה מִנֶכָּר

900 בַּיַבָּשָה עָבַר יִשְׂרָאֵל מְיוּדֹע ואמתאל דלך

II.L.2.12.3. The Third Subsection

II.L.2.12.3.1.

The remainder of the inventory of letters amounts to seventeen letters. If *yod* (which has been discussed above) is added to them, they come to eighteen letters. *Shewa* under these eighteen letters is pronounced as a short *pataḥ*. Examples of cases in which it is not appropriate for *gaʿya* to occur include בְּרָב־עָם 'in a multitude of people' (Prov. 14.28), גְּרֻשֹׁתֵיכֶם 'your evictions' (Ezek. 45.9), דְּרָכָיו רָאִיתִי 'I have seen his ways' (Isa. 57.18), וְרֹאשׁ־עֹרֵב 'and the head of Oreb' (Jud. 7.25), זְכוֹר־יְהוָה 'remember, oh Lord' (Psa. 132.1), טְמֵאַת הַשֵּׁם 'unclean of name' (Ezek. 22.5), יְראוּ אֶת־יְהוָה 'fear the Lord' (Jos. 24.14), and other cases with these eighteen letters. If one were to say 'Tell me about the *shewa* that is pronounced as *pataḥ* under these eighteen letters. Is it substituting for another (pronunciation), or is it alone the pronunciation that is the rule under the letters to the exclusion of any other, or is this pronunciation together with another the rule under them, or what is the situation concerning this?', the response to him would be as follows. These letters are pronounced as *pataḥ*. It is a feature of this *pataḥ* that it is only pronounced short. *Shewa* is the only way to represent this shortness. Since according to their principles *shewa* is not combined with a vowel under these eighteen letters, they marked the *shewa* alone. It was not possible for them to mark the *pataḥ* by itself, since it would have been pronounced as a full vowel.

II.L.2.12.3.2.

If one were to say 'According to this statement, when a *shewa* occurs under these eighteen letters it is only pronounced as short *pataḥ*, but we seen a contradiction of this in cases such as כְּשִׂמְחָתְךָ לְנַחֲלַת בֵּית־יִשְׂרָאֵל 'As you rejoiced over the inheritance of

II.L.2.12.3. פנא תאלתא

II.L.2.12.3.1.

אלבאקי מן חרוף אלקבאלה יֹז חרף ותעוד אליהא אליוד תציר

יֹח חרפא [פֹה]דא יֹח חרפא יכרג אלשוא תחתהא בפאתחה

[כפיפה] ומא לא יחסן מעהא דכול גَעיה כֹ בְּרָב עָם

[גרש]וּתיכם דְּרָכֶיו ראיתי וְראֹש עָרֵב וּזְאֵב זְכוֹר יֹיֵי טְמֵאת הַשֵּׁם 905

יִרְאוּ את יֹיֵי אלי גיר דלך מן הדה (L3:3v) אליֹח חרפא פאן קאל

כברני ען אלשוא אלדי יכרג בפאתחה תחת הדה אלחרוף אליֹח

הו נאיב ען גירה אם הו וחדה באלואגב תחת הדה אלחרוף דון

גירה אם הו וגירה באלואגב תחתהא אם כיף אלחאל פי דלך

קיל לה אן הדה אלחרוף נטקהא אלפאתחה ומן חכם הדה 910

אלפאתחה אלמדכורה לא תכון אלא כפיפה ולא וגה לכפתהא

גיר אלשוא ולמא לם יכון אלשוא פי אצולהם יגתמע מע מלך

תחת הדה אליֹח חרפא גَעלו אלשוא פקט ולם ימכן אן יגעלו

אלפאתחה (L4:5r) וחדהא לאנהא תגّי מסתופאה

II.L.2.12.3.2.

פאן קאל אן עלי הדא אלקול אן הדה אליֹח חרפא מתי כאן 915

תחתהא שוא לא יכרג אלא בפאתחה כפיפה ונחן נרי כלאף

דלך כקוֹ כְּשִׂמְחָתְךָ לְנַחֲלַת בית ישראל אלדי אללמאד מן

the house of Israel' (Ezek. 35.15), in which the *lamed* of לְנַחְלַת is 'heavy', the response to him would be that what makes the *lamed* heavy is the *gaʿya*, for this is the only thing that can change the form of the vocalic pronunciation of the *shewa*.[12] If he says '(Why) have they not marked a *pataḥ* where the *gaʿya* occurs to express heaviness and a *shewa* where there is shortness?', the response to him would be as follows. It is not permissible to mark a *pataḥ* where (the *shewa* is pronounced with) heaviness, because the rule regarding the marking of *shewa* and *pataḥ* on these eighteen letters is that the *pataḥ* alone does not indicate *shewa* but *shewa* alone indicates *pataḥ*. Furthermore if they marked *pataḥ* where there is heaviness, that would make it unclear as to whether the following letter had *dagesh* or not, since one of the features of *pataḥ* is that in many places it is followed by *dagesh* to express definiteness, for example הַנֹּגֵעַ בָּאִישׁ הַזֶּה 'whoever touches this man' (Gen. 26.11), בַּיּוֹם הַהוּא 'on that day', and so forth. A mobile *shewa* can never be followed by *dagesh* in the reading of Scripture, except in שְׁתַּיִם and שְׁתֵּי. In the discussion concerning these below, however, I shall explain that the *shewa* in these two words is quiescent and not mobile.

II.L.2.12.3.3.

Furthermore, *gaʿya* is not obligatory under a letter as a vowel and *shewa* are obligatory, because *gaʿya* is only an exhalation of air in speech, and its elision is possible. The reader chooses in his reading (whether to pronounce it or not). There are some places, however, in which the speaker does not have a choice,

---

[12] The extant model manuscripts L, A and C do not have *gaʿya* on the *shewa* here: L לְנַחְלַת; A, C לְנַחֲלַת. Moreover in the available manuscripts of *Hidāyat al-Qāriʾ* a *gaʿya* sign is not marked.

לנחלת תקיל קיל לה אן אלדי תקל ללמאד אלגעיה אד ליס תם

שי יגייר חכם תחריך אלשוא סואהא פאן קאל והלא געלו מוצע

אלגעיה אלתי תגי ללתתקיל פאתחה ומוצע אלתכפיף שוא קיל

לה לא ^(L4:5v) יגוז אן יכון מוצע אלתתקיל פאתחה לאן אלואגב   920

ללחרף מן הדה אליّה אלשוא ואלפאתחה פאלפאתחה וחדהא

לא תדל עלי אלשוא ואלשוא וחדה ידל עלי אלפאתחה ואיצَא

פאן לו געלו אלפאתחה מוצע אלתתקיל לאשכל דלך פי אן

אלחרף אלתאני מנה מדגוש או גיר מדגוש לאן מן בעَץ אחכאם   925

אלפאתחה פי כתיר מן אלמואצע אן יגי בעדהא אלדגש

ללתעריף כקו הַנּוֹגֵעַ בּﭏ הֵז בַּיּﬡֹם ההוא ואמתאלהמא ^(L4:6r)

ואלשוא אלמתחרך לא יכון בעדה דגש אבדא פי אלמקרא אלא

שֻׁתַים וَעَלי מא יגי אלכלאם עליהמא פי מא בעד ואביّן אן

אלשוא פיהמא הו סאכן וליס הו מתחרך   930

II.L.2.12.3.3.

ואיצَא פאן אלגעיה ליסת הי באלואגב תחת אלחרוף כמא יגב

ללמלך ואלשוא לאן אלגעיה אנמא הי תנפס פי אלכלאם

פחדפהא ממכן ואלקאר מכייר פי קראתהא אלא פי מואצע ליס

for example כִּי לָא יִשְׁנוּ אִם־לָא יָרֵעוּ 'for they do not sleep unless they do wrong' (Prov. 4.16), because the *gaʿya* makes it into the lexical class of 'slumber and sleep'. If it were lacking, it would be from the lexical class of repeating, as in שְׁנוּ וַיִּשְׁנוּ '"Do it a second time" and they did it a second time' (1 Kings 18.34). This applies also to the lexical classes of 'fearing' and 'seeing'. The lexical class of 'fearing' has *gaʿya*, for example יִרְאוּ מֵיהוָה 'Let them fear the Lord' (Psa. 33.8). Although here it has two *yods*, there is potential doubt in cases such as יִרְאוּ גוֹיִם וְיֵבֹשׁוּ 'The nations will see and be ashamed' (Micah 7.16). If this is the case, the occurrence of *gaʿya* in the lexical class of 'fearing' prevents it. To these can be added further examples in which the reader does not have a choice. Cases in which the reader does have a choice include וְהָיְתָה—וְהָיָה, וְהָיְתָה—וְהָיָה, and the like. Such cases do not attain the status of the vowels and the *shewa*, because the construction of a word is based on the vowels. Its construction is not based on the *gaʿya*. For this reason the scholars of language in this discipline say 'The *gaʿya* has no principle'. For these reasons, when there is a need for lengthening, you mark a *gaʿya* with *shewa* and you do not mark *pataḥ* by itself. This is the appropriate response to the question.

II.L.2.12.4. The Fourth Subsection

II.L.2.12.4.1.

When *shewa* is under a letter, it is not possible for any of the disjunctive or conjunctive accents to be under this letter, so long as *shewa* is under it, since it is a principle of *shewa* that it does not combine with an accent on a letter in any circumstances. If

אלקאר פיהא מכייר נחו כי לא יֵשְׁנוּ אִם לא יָרֵעוּ לאן אלגעיה

935 גّעלתהא מן לגה אלסנה ואלנום ולّולאהא לצّארת מן לגה (L4:6v)

אלתתניה כקّו שנו וישנו ומתל דלך לגה אלכשיה ואלנّטّר אלّדי

לגה אלכשיה בגّעיה כקّו > יֵּראו < מייّ ואן כאנת ביّודّין פלא

יומן מן חّצّול אלّאלתבאס פי מתל יראו גّוים ויבّשّו פאן וקע כאן

תّבّות אלّגّעיה פי לגה אלכשיה תّמנّע מנה אלّי גّיר דّלך ממّא לא

940 יّמّכן אלّקّאר אלכّיّאّר פّיّה וّמّמّא יّמּכّן אלّקّאר אלכّיّאّر פّיّה וְהָיָה

וְהָיָה וְהָיְתָה וְהָיְתָה ואמّתّאّל ד̇ פّמّא כّאّן הّדّא סّבّיّלّה לا יّבّלّג

מבّלّג (L5:6r) אّלّמّלّוّך ואّלّשّוّא לّאّן בّנّיّה אّלّכّלّאّם עّלّי אّلّחّرّכّاّת

וّلّيّس בّנّيّתّه עّلّي אّלّגّعّيّه וّلّدّلّך יّקّوّلّוّن אّهّل אّلّلّגّה אّلّדّي לّהّדّا

אّלّعّلّם אّيّن אّב לّلّغّعّيّه פّמّن אّغّل הّدّه אّלّوّגّوّه אّدّا אّحّتّيّגّ אّلّي

945 אّلّתّתّקّيّل גّעّلّת אّلّגّعّيّה מّע אّלّשّוّا וّلّا תّגّעّل פّאّתّحّه וّحّدّهّا

והّدّא אّלّדّي לّاّح פّي גّوّاّب הّדّه אّلّمّסّلّה

II.L.2.12.4. **פנא ד̇**

II.L.2.12.4.1.

אלّשّוّא אّדّא כّאّنّت תّחّת חّрّف אّמّתّنّע אّن יّכّוّن תّחّت דّلّך אّلّحّرّف

שّيّא מّن אّלّاّלّחّاّن וّاّلّכّدّاّם מّהّمّا אّلّשّوّا תّחّתּה לّאّن מّن חّכّם

950 אّلّשّوّا אّלّا יّגّתّמّע הّו וّטّעّم (L5:6v) פّي חّرّف בّתّה פّאّن קّאّל וّلّם

---

somebody says: 'Why is that, when you have not denied that the
combination of a *shewa* and an accent on the same letter is
possible, although we do not find them combined?', the
response to him would be as follows. Even if the *shewa* of both
categories, i.e. quiescent and mobile, were to combine (with an
accent), the combination of an accent with quiescent *shewa*
could not take place, since it is the principle of the quiescent
shewa that it makes the letter quiescent and does not move at
all, as is the case with the *resh* in כַּרְמִי, the *mem* in זְמְרִי and the
bet in עַבְדִּי. A disjunctive accent and a conjunctive accent by
their nature cause the letter to move (with a vowel) and
introduce a melody or melodies in it. A quiescent letter cannot
have a melody at all. A melody is movement, so how can a
quiescent *shewa* be also mobile at the same time? Is this not a
contradiction? So this is impossible.

II.L.2.12.4.2.

If somebody were to say 'Although the combination of an accent
with a quiescent *shewa* is impossible, it would be permissible for
one to be combined with mobile *shewa*, because there is no
contradiction', the response to him would be as follows. The
statement that an accent moves a letter with a vowel does not
imply that its movement is like that of *shewa*. This is because
shewa makes a letter mobile, but causes its articulation to be
quick, so that one cannot tarry on the letter, like the *bet* in
בְּרֵאשִׁית 'in the beginning', since it is not permissible to hold onto
it when the speaker wishes to express his intention. Likewise
dalet in דְּרוֹר 'liberty', and the *ṣade* in צְרוֹר 'bundle', in which the
shewa causes the letter to move quickly with a speed that does
not allow tarrying on it. This is not the case with an accent,
which, rather, causes the letter to have a vowel and introduces
melodies into it. The letter is given a vowel in its place without
moving back or forward so long as it is given a melody. Surely

דלך ומא אנכרת אן אגתמאע אלשוא ואלטעם פי חרף ואחד
יצח ואן כאן לא נראהמא מגתמעין קיל לה לו אגתמע אלשוא
מן אלקסמין אלמדכורין והמא אלסאכן ואלמתחרך פאגתמאעה
מע אלסאכן לא יתם לאן אלסאכן מן חכמה אן יסכן אלחרף ולא
יצטרב בתה כאלריש מן כרﬞמי ואלמאם מן זמﬞרי ואלבא מן עﬞבﬞדי
955 ואללחן ואלכאדם מן שאנהמא ⁽L5:7r⁾ אן יחרכא אלחרף ויגעלא
פיה נגמה ונגמאת ואלחרף אלסאכן לא יצח פיה נגמה בתה
ואלנגמה הי אלחרכה פכיﬞף יכון אלסאכן מתחרכא פי חﬞאל
ואחד פאליס הﬞדא מנאקﬞצﬞה פקד אסתחאל דלך

פאן קאל אדﬞא כאן קד אסתחאל אגתמאע אללחן מע אלשוא
960 אלסאכן פיגוז אגתמאעה מע אלשוא אלמתחרך לאן מא תﬞם
מנאקﬞצﬞה קיל לה ליס אלקול באן אללחן יחרך אלחרף יקתצﬞי אן
תכון חרכתה כחרכה ⁽L5:7v⁾ אלשוא ודﬞאך אן אלשוא יחרך
אלחרף ויסרע בנטקה חתﬞי לא ימכן אחד אן ילבﬞת בדﬞלך אלחרף
965 כאלבא מן בראשית אדﬞי לא יצח מסכה וללמתכלם גרצﬞא פי
אלכלאם וכﬞדﬞלך אלדﬞאל מן דרור ואלצﬞאד מן צרור פאלשוא
יסרע באלחרף סרעה לא ימכן אלתﬞבאת מעהא וליס כﬞדﬞלך
אללחן בל הו יחרך אלחרף ויגעל פיה נגמאת ואלחרף פי מוצﬞעה
יתחרך לא ירגﬞע אלי כלﬞף ולא אלי קﬞדﬞאם מהמא אלחרף ינגם

you see how it (the accent) gives the *resh* a melody in וַֽיְמַהֲרֹוּ 'they made haste' (Josh. 8.14) and the letter does not move from its place. The accent has given it a melody, or two or more. One does not tarry on the *dalet* in דְּרֹור and the like (with *shewa*) in the way one tarries on the *resh* or the *kaf* in וַֽיְמַהֲרֹוּ וַיַּשְׁכִּ֫ימוּ 'They made haste and rose early' (Josh. 8.14). The *shewa* moves quickly forwards whereas an accent causes vocalic movement within its place. If these were to combine there would be a logical contradiction. It is, therefore, clear from this that *shewa* and an accent cannot combine together in a single letter.

II.L.2.12.5. The Fifth Subsection

A mobile *shewa* is not followed by a letter with *dagesh*, for example כְּכַלֹּות 'on finishing' (Deut. 31.24, etc.), בְּבֹאָם 'when they enter' (Exod. 28.43, etc.), פְּנֹות אֶל־הַמִּנְחָה 'regarding the offering' (Mal. 2.13), בְּכָל 'in all', and the like. This is not contradicted by שְׁתַּיִם and שְׁתֵּי. For if there is an added ʾalef and you say [ʔeʃˈtʰaːjim] and [ʔeʃˈtʰeː], the *shewa* becomes quiescent. I shall discuss this at greater length in the section concerning *yetiv* with the help of God and His good will. If one were to say 'Why is *shewa* not followed by a letter with *dagesh*?', the response to him would be as follows. The principle of *dagesh* is to make a letter heavy and give it a kind of quiescence. A mobile *shewa* is not dwelt upon and so the letter that is after it must be light. When the letter that is after it is heavy, it is not possible to give it the mobility to the extent that I have mentioned.

II.L.2.12.6. The Sixth Subsection

Mobile *shewa* does not combine with a vowel on a letter of the alphabet with the exception of the four letters אהחע, for example אֲנִי יְהֹוֶה הֹוּא שְׁמִי 'I am the Lord, that is my name' (Isa. 42.8), הֲלֹא

אלי תרי כיף ינגם אלריש (L5:8r) מן וַיְמַהֲרוֹ ואלחרף מן מוצעה 970

מא ברח וקד חרכה נגמה ותנתין ומא זאד ואלדאל מן דרור ומא

מאתלה לא ילבתה לבת אלריש ואלכאף פי וַיְמַהֲרוֹ וַיִשְׁבִּימוֹ

פצאר אלשוא יתחרך בסרעה אלי קדאם ואללחן יחרך פי

אלמוצע בעינה פלו אגמתע לכאן דלך מתנאקצֹא פבאן מן דלך

אן שוא ולחן לא יגתמעא פי חרף ואחד מעא 975

II.L.2.12.5. פנא הֹ

אלשוא אלמתחרך לא יכון בעדה חרף דגש כקו כְּבֹלוֹת בְּבֹואָם

פְנות אל המנחה (L5:8v) בְכָל ואמתאל דלך ולא יעתרץֹ דלך

שְתַים ושְתֵי פאן תם אלף מסתעאר פאדא קלת שְתַים שְתֵי צאר

אלשוא סאכן ואנא אסתופי אלכלאם פיה פי לחן אליתיב בעון 980

אללה ומשיתה פאן קאל לם לא יכון בעד אלשוא חרף דגש קיל

לה אן מן חכם אלדגש אן יתקל אלאחרף ויגעל פיה צֹרבא מן

אלתסכין ואלשוא אלמתחרך פלא ילבת פיחתאגֹ אן יכון אלאחרף

אלדי בעדה כפיפא פמתי כאן אלאחרף אלדי בעדה תקיל לם

ימכן תחריכה עלי אלחד אלדי דכרתה 985

II.L.2.12.6. (L5:9r) פנא וֹ

אלשוא אלמתחרך לא יגתמע מע מלך פי חרף מן חרוף אלף

בית אלא פי ארבע חרוף אֹהֹחֹע כקו אֲנִי יײ הוא שמי הֲלֹא הוּא

הוּא 'did he not?' (Gen. 20.5), וַחֲנֵה 'and encamp' (2 Sam. 12.28), עֲלוּ־אֵלַי וְעִזְרֻנִי 'Come up to me and help me' (Josh. 10.4), and similar cases. If one were to say 'Is not *shewa* combined with *qameṣ* under the *dalet* of מָרְדְּכַי, under the *qof* with *qameṣ* in קֳדָם 'before', קֳדָמֵיהוֹן 'before them', under the *mem* with *qameṣ* in מָשְׁכוּ אוֹתָהּ 'drag her!' (Ezek. 32.20) and under the *bet* with *segol* in דִּי־אֲנָה בֱנַיְתַהּ 'which I built' (Dan. 4.27)?', the response to him would be as follows. This does not contradict what I stated. This is because the people responsible for this matter have agreed on the rule of combining *shewa* and a vowel only under the four letters. It is said, however, that some scribes wanted to remove uncertainty from places that may lead to error and have combined a vowel with *shewa* in this way, because they thought that people would err in the reading of מָרְדְּכַי. When some people saw *shewa* without *qameṣ* in מָרְדְּכַי, they read it as *pataḥ*. If they saw *qameṣ* alone, they were at risk of giving the *qameṣ* its full length. So, the scribes decided to combine them so that this degree of uncertainty be removed. This applied also to similar cases (cited above). This is an exception to their customary practice. What supports the claim that this is the view of only some of them with regard to letters not belonging to the group of the four (אהחע) is that in most codices one does not find what has been presented as counterevidence, but all codices are uniform in the combination of *shewa* with a vowel under the four letters.

II.L.2.12.7. The Seventh Subsection

When *shewa* is combined with a vowel in a letter, the vowel is deprived of its full length, as in חֳרֵם וּבֵית־עֲנָת 'Horem and Betanath' (Josh. 19.38), in which the *ḥet* is pronounced with a short vowel on account of the *shewa* that is with the *qameṣ*. The same applies to גַּם כָּל־חֳלִי 'also every sickness' (Deut. 28.61), in which *shewa* is combined with the vowel and the vowel has

וַחֲנֵה עֲלֵי אלי ועז ואם דלך פאן קאל אליס קד אגׄתמע אלשוא

990 ואלקמץ תחת אלדאל מן מָרְדֳכִי ותחת אלקוף מע אלקמץ מן

קֳדָם קֳדֳמֵיהון ותחת אלמאם מע אלקמץ מן מֶשְכו אותה ותחת

אלבא פי די אַנָה בֳנֵיתָה מע אלסגׄולה קיל לה ליס דלך בנאקׄ

למא דכרתה ודלך אן אהל הדא אלשאן אצטלחו אן לא יגׄמעו

אלשוא ואלמלך אלא תחת הדה אלארבעה חרוף ואנמא (L5:9v)

995 קיל אן בעץׄ אלסופרים אראד אן ירפע אלאשכאל מן אלמואצׄע

אלמגׄלטה פגׄמע אלמלך מע אלשוא להדא אלוגׄה לאנה ראי

אלנאס יגׄלטו פי קראה מרדכי פמנהם מן אדא ראי אלשוא בלא

קאמצה קראהא מפתוחה ואן ראי אלקאמצה וחדהא לם יאמן

אן יסתופי אלקאמצה פראי אן יגׄמעהמא חתי ירפע הדא

1000 אלקדר מן אלאשכאל וכדלך מא מאתלה והדא כארגׄ ען סננהם

ואלדי יקוי אן (L5:10r) הדא ראי אלבעץׄ מנהם פי גיר אלארבעה

חרוף הו אן אכתר אלמצאחף לא יוגד פיהא מא אעתרץׄ בה

אלמעתרץׄ ואלמצאחף כלהא מטבקה עלי גׄמע אלשוא ואלמלך

תחת הדה אלדׄ חרוף

II.L.2.12.7. פׁנא זׁ

1005 אלשוא אדא אגׄתמע מע מלך מע מלך פי חרף סלב אלמלך חטה מן אן

יסתופא כקו חֳרֶם ובית עֳנָת גׄא אלחית כפיפא לאגׄל אלשוא

אלדי מע אלקאמצה וכדלך גֶם כָל חֳלִי גׄא אלשוא מע אלמלך

become short. If it were said 'Why is it that when *shewa* is combined with a vowel under a letter, the vowel is deprived of its full quantity?' the response would be as follows. This is because when there is mobile *shewa*, it is not permissible to slow down on or dwell on the letter. This is a principle that cannot be avoided. When they both occur under a letter, its principle holds, namely moving forward quickly, and so it is not possible for the vowel to be given its full quantity. This is determined by the principle of the *shewa*. If somebody were to say 'Just as the *shewa* has an unavoidable principle, likewise a vowel has an indissoluble feature, namely slowness and steadiness, so why is the vowel not more worthy of fulfilling its principle than something else?', the response to him would be as follows. If they wanted to maintain the principle of the vowel, they would not have combined it with *shewa*, since that would be nonsense. Rather they combined them in order for the principle of the vowel to be eliminated. The combination of the two principles is impossible, just as is the elimination of the two principles. It is necessary to maintain one of them, and this is the principle of the *shewa*. If somebody were to say 'With how many vowels does *shewa* combine?', the response would be: with three, *qameṣ*, *pataḥ* and *segol*. If he said 'Why is it combined specifically with these three and not the others?', the response would be: because with these three vowels it is permissible to melodize, pause and read quickly, whereas this is not possible with the other vowels.

כאן אלמלך כפיפא פאן קאל ולם כאן אדא (L5:10v) אגתמע
אלשוא מע מלך תחת חרף סלב דלך אלמלך חטֹה קיל לה לאן 1010
אלשוא אלמתחרך לא יצח פיה אלתבאטי ואללבת פי אלחרף
והדה עלה לא יצח אנפכאכה מנהא פאדא חצלא גמיעא תחת
חרף תבתת עלתה והי אלנהוץ בסרעה פלא ימכן אלמלך אן
יסתופי חטה פיכון דלך מקצֹא לעלה אלשוא פאן קיל כמא אן
ללשוא עלה לא תפארקה כדלך ללמלך עלה לא תפארקה והי 1015
אלתבאטי ואלתבאת פלם לא כאן אלמלך (L5:11r) באסתיפא
עלתה אולי מן סואה קיל לה לו אראדו אן יתבתו עלה אלמלך
לם יגמעו מעה אלשוא אד כאן דלך עבת ואנמא גמעוהא לתזול
עלה אלמלך ואגתמאע אלעלתין מסתחיל ואנתפא אלעלתין
כדלך פלא בד מן תבות אחדהמא והי עלה אלשוא פאן קיל 1020
פמע כם מן אלמלוך תגתמע אלשוא קיל לה מע תלאת
אלקאמצה ואלפאתחה ואלסגולה פאן קאל ולם אכתץ בהדה
אלתלתה דון סואהא קיל לה לאן הדה (L5:11v) אלתלתה יצח
פיהא פי אלתנגים אלתוקף ואלסרעה ומא סואהם לא יתם פיה
דלך 1025

II.L.2.12.8. The Eighth Subsection

II.L.2.12.8.1.

When *shewa* is at the beginning of a word, it is always mobile, for example דְּבַר־מִי יָקוּם 'the word of whom will stand' (Jer. 44.28), לְעֶת־יוֹם בְּיוֹם 'from day to day' (1 Chron. 12.23), כִּרְשִׁיוֹן כּוֹרֶשׁ 'according to the permission of Cyrus' (Ezra 3.7), כְּחֹם הַיּוֹם 'in the heat of the day' (Gen. 18.1), and similar cases. If somebody were to say 'Why have you claimed that quiescent *shewa* never occurs at the beginning of a word?', the response would be that a quiescent *shewa* is the stopping point of what precedes it, and the beginning of a word has nothing before it, as the *ʾalef* in אִישׁ הָיָה בְאֶרֶץ־עוּץ 'There was a man in the land of Uz' (Job 1.1) and the *shin* in שָׁמַיִם לָרוּם וָאָרֶץ לָעֹמֶק 'the heavens for height, and the earth for depth' (Prov. 25.3), and similar cases. And if somebody said 'Do you not say that every *shewa* beginning a word is mobile, but we find a mobile *shewa* that is not word-initial, for example וְהַמְאַסֵּף 'and the rear guard' (Josh. 6.9, etc.), וְסָגַר פֻּם 'He has shut the mouth' (Dan. 6.23), וַיִּשְׁמְעוּ 'and they heard', וַיִּשְׁכְּבוּ 'and they lay down'?', the response to him would be as follows. When I said that every *shewa* at the beginning of a word is mobile, this does not oblige me to claim that a mobile *shewa* is found only in word-initial position. Indeed a mobile *shewa* may be in the middle of a word. This claim would, however, be contradicted if a *shewa* that is not mobile is found in word-initial position. Yet in the examples that I have adduced, and others like them, they are in initial position in the sense that they are preceded by quiescence and a stopping point.

II.L.2.12.8. פנא ח

II.L.2.12.8.1.

אלשוא אדא כאן פי אול אלכלאם אבדא יכון מתחרך כקו דְּבַר

מִי יָקוּם לְעֵת יוֹם בְּיוֹם כִּרְשְׁיוֹן כּוֹרֶש כְּחֹם הַיוֹם אלי גיר דלך פאן

קאל ולם זעמת אן אלשוא אלסאכן לא יכון פי אואיל אלכלם

אבדא קיל לה אן אלסאכן הו מחט למא תקדמה ואבתדא 1030

אלכלאם לא יכון קבלה שי כאלאלף מן איש היה בארץ עוץ

ואלשין מן שמים (L5:12r) לָרוּם וָאָרֶץ לָעוֹמֶק אלי גיר דלך פאן

קאל אליס תקול אן כל מבתדא מתחרך ונחן נגד אלמתחרך פי

גיר אלמבתדא כקו וְהַמְאַסֵף וסגר פֶם וַיִּשְׁמְעוּ וַיִּשְׁכְּבוּ קיל לה

ליס אדא קלת אן כל שוא פי בדו אלכלאם מתחרך ילזמני אלא 1035

יכון מתחרך אלא פי אלאבתדי בל קד יכון פי אלתוסט מתחרך

ואנמא כאן יעתרץ דלך לו וגד שוא פי אלאבתדא גיר מתחרך

ומע דלך אן אלמואצֻע אלדי דכרתהא ומא מאתלהא פהי כדלך

מבתדאה עלי (L5:12v) וגה מן חית אן קבלהא סכון ומחט

II.L.2.12.8.2.

If somebody were to say 'So do you say that a letter by itself can
have the status of a word and have mobility and quiescence, but
this is a contradiction with regard to a single letter, so according
to this וּסְגַר could not have a mobile *shewa* until the *shewa*
becomes mobile after quiescence, as you say?', the response
would be as follows. The stopping point may be a quiescent
shewa after a mobile letter, as in וַיִּשְׁמְעוּ, and the like. It may also
be what is analagous to it and may be called a stopping point,
namely the introduction of heaviness to a letter. This may cause
(the following *shewa*) to be mobile, as in וּשֲׁבֵה שֶׁבְיְךָ 'and capture
your captives!' (Jud. 5.12), in which the heaviness of the *vav*
has the status of a word with two letters, so the *shewa* is mobile
on account of this. The heaviness of the letter corresponds to
quiescence of a *shewa* and becomes a stopping point, as in הֵם
הַמְדַבְּרִים 'the ones who speak' (Exod. 6.27), and similar cases, as
will be explained in the discussion about *he* and *mem* below.

II.L.2.12.9. The Ninth Subsection

A mobile *shewa* is followed by quiescence only in a letter that is
not less than the third letter after it. Quiescence in a letter that
is greater (in number than the third) is possible, but the
minimum for quiescence is the third (letter after the mobile
shewa), as in לְיָשְׁבְּקָשָׁה 'to Joshbekashah' (1 Chron 25.24), לִיקָמְעָם
'to Jokmeam' (1 Kings 4.12), and the like. Examples of
quiescence in a letter that is greater than the third (after the
mobile *shewa*) are אֱלֹהִים 'God', בְּרוֹשִׁים 'cypresses', and the like. If
somebody were to say 'Do not שָׁמְרָה נַפְשִׁי וְהַצִּילֵנִי 'Guard my life
and deliver me' (Psa. 25.20), מָשְׁכוּ אוֹתָהּ 'Draw her down' (Ezek.

II.L.2.12.8.2.

פאן קאל אפתקול אן אלחרף וחדה יקום מקאם לפטֹה פיכון   1040

פיה אלתחריך ואלסכון והדה מנאקצֹה פי אלחרף אלואחד פלא

יגֹז על הדא אן יכון וסֵגֵר ‹מתחרד› חתי יתחרך אלשוא בעד

אלסכון עלי קולך קיל לה אן אלמחט קד יכון סאכן בעד מתחרך

מתל קו וישמעו ונחוה וקד יכון מא יגֹרי מגֹראה יסמי מחט והו

אלתתקיל פי חרף ואחד פאנה קד יחרך כקו וְשֻׁבֶה שָׁבְיֵךְ פצאר   1045

אלתתקיל פי ^(L5:13r) אלואו ינוב מנאב לפטֹה פיהא חרפין

פיתחרך אלשוא לדלך אלתתקיל מן דלך אלחרף לסכן אלשוא

וצאר מחט מתל הֵם הַמְדברים ונחוה עלי מא יגֹי אלכלאם פי

הֵא ומאם משרוחא מן בעד

II.L.2.12.9. פנֵא טֹ   1050

אלשוא אלמתחרך לא יכון בעדה סכון אלי אקל מן אלחרף

אלתאלת ומא זאד ען דלך ממכן לכן אקל מא יכון מן אלסכון

עלי אלתאלת כקו לְיָשבקָשָה לְיָקמעֻם ונחוה ואמא מא זאד על

אלתאלת פי אלסכון מתל אלהֹים בְרוֹשים ונחוההמא ^(L5:13v) פאן

קאל אליס שָמְרָה נפשי והצילני ומשכו אותה ומא גֹרי   1055

1042 מתחרד] מתחרד סאכן L5

32.20) and analogous cases refute the principle that you have formulated?', the response to him would be as follows. I spoke only about *shewa* that is present under a letter. Cases of shortness and lightness that have been transmitted by teaching from the people of the language are not relevant for this argument.

II.L.2.12.10. The Tenth Subsection

Mobile *shewa* does not occur adjacent to another mobile *shewa* at the beginning, middle or end of a word, for if they were adjacent, the word would be defective. This is because a word must consist of a letter with a vowel and what is attached to the letter with a vowel by way of an initial mobile *shewa* is of a lesser vowel movement than the following vowel. These two may be followed by a quiescent consonant. This structure cannot be broken. Therefore, two mobile *shewas* are not linked together, as two quiescent *shewas* are.

II.L.2.12.11. The Eleventh Subsection

Two quiescent *shewas* cannot follow one another at the beginning of a word or in the middle of it. If somebody were to say 'Why is this so?', the response to him would be: because the first *shewa* is quiescent on account of it being the stopping point of what precedes it. The second *shewa*, however, is not preceded by a letter with a vowel, for which the second *shewa* would be a stopping point. For this reason, two quiescent *shewas* are not linked together in the places mentioned.

II.L.2.12.12. The Twelfth Subsection

When there are two *shewas* following one another, a sequence in which the first is mobile and the second quiescent is not permissible, rather the first must be made quiescent and the

מגّראהמא קד ינקّץ מא בניתה מן הדא אלאצّל קיל לה אנמא
תכלמת פי אלשוא אלחאצّר תחת אלחרף ואמא מא תסלם
כטפה וכפתה מן אהל אללגה תלקינא לם יכון פי הדא אלכלאם
פי שי

II.L.2.12.10. **פנא י** 1060
שוא מתחרך לא יגّאור שוא מתחרך לא פי אול אלכלאם ולא פי
וסטה ולא פי אכרה לאן לו תגّאורא לאנפסד אלכלאם ודאך אן
אלכלאם אנמא יכון מתחרך (L5:14r) ומא ילחק אלמתחרך פהו
אקל חרכה מן אלמתחרך אדא אבתדאה באלשוא ואלסאכן קד
יתבעّהמא והדה בניה לא יגّוז נקצّהא פלדלך לם יכתרנא 1065
מתחרכין כמא יכתרנא אלסאכנין

II.L.2.12.11. **פנא יّא**
שׁוׇאֵין סאכנין לא יגّוז תראדפّהמא לא פי אול אלכלאם ולא פי
וסטה פאן קאל ולם כאן דלך קיל לה לאן אלשוא אלאול אנמא
סכן לכונה מחט למא תקדמה ואלתאני פّלם יתקדמה חרף 1070
מתחרך פّיכון אלתّאני מחט לה פّלדלך לם (L5:14v) יכתרנא
אלסאכנין פי אלמוצّעין אלמדכורין

II.L.2.12.12. **פנא יّב**
שׁוׇאֵין מתראדפّין אלّאול מתחרך ואלתّאני סאכן לא יגّוז
תראדפّהמא אלّא אן יכון אלّאול ללסאכן ואלתّאני ללמתחרך 1075

second mobile. If somebody were to say 'Why is that?', the response to him would be as follows. When the first *shewa* is mobile, it is not permissible for it to be followed by a quiescent letter, because if that were the case, the mobile *shewa* would not have scope to spring forward quickly. It has been stated previously that quiescence cannot occur on less than the third letter after a mobile *shewa*. Furthermore it is not possible to pronounce a mobile *shewa* followed by a quiescent *shewa* for the reason just mentioned, whereas a pronunciation of a quiescent *shewa* in the first letter and a mobile *shewa* on the second letter is acceptable, as in וַיִּקְבְּצוּ 'and they gathered', and the like. Take note that *shewa* may be construed as a successive sequence (of two) even though only one is written. This applies to cases such as מִזְּעֹק 'from crying' (1 Sam. 7.8), מְזַבְּחִים 'sacrificing', מְחַלְלִים 'playing the pipe' (1 Kings 1.40, etc.), מִמְּלֹךְ 'from being king' (1 Sam. 8.7, etc.). The *shewa* here is pronounced mobile. The reason for this is that the letter is pronounced as two letters. This is the custom of Hebrew, namely that every letter with strengthening, I mean with *dagesh*, in the middle of a word, where it does not have the status of beginning (a word or syllable), under which there is *shewa*, is pronounced as two letters. This is shown by הַכְּמוֹת נָבָל 'Is it like a fool?' (2 Sam. 3.33) in that the *kaf* in הַכְּמוֹת is pronounced as two *kafs*, and so in other cases. The *dagesh* on the letter, therefore, is in place of the quiescent *shewa* and the *shewa* that is present under the letter is mobile, and so it is pronounced as two letters.

II.L.2.12.13. The Thirteenth Subsection

A *shewa* at the end of a word can only be quiescent, as in דֶּרֶךְ 'way', מֶלֶךְ 'king', and the like.

פאן קיל ולם דלך קיל לה אדא כאן אלשוא אלאול מתחרך לא

יגוז יכון בעדה חרפא סאכנא לאנה אן כאן דלך לא יציב

אלמתחרך פסחה ללנהוץ וקד תקדם אלכלאם אן לא יכון בעד

אלשוא אלמתחרך סכון פי אקל מן אלחרף (L5:15r) אלתאלת

ואיצא פאן אלמתחרך ובעדה אלסאכן לא יצח אלנטק בהמא 1080

עלי אלוגה אלמדכור בל אלנטק באלסאכן פי אלאול ואלמתחרך

פי אלתאני מפהומא מתל ויקָבצו ונחוה ואעלם אן תם שוא

בניתה עלי אלתראדף ואן כאן ליס אלא ואחד מכתוב והו נחו קֹ

מִזְעֹק מזבחים מחלְלים ממלוך פאן אלשוא כרג כאלמתחרך

ואלסבב פי דלך לאן אלחרף כרג בחרפין פהדה סירה פי 1085

אלעבראני והו אן אן כל חרף משדד (L5:15v) אעני מדגוש פי וסט

כלמה בחית לא יגרי מגרי אבתדא ותחתה שוא יכרג בחרפין

יביין דלך קֹ הכְמֹת נָבָל והו אן אלכאף פי הכמות כרג בכאפין

אלי גיר דלך פיכון אלדגש פי אלחרף מקאם אלשוא אלסאכן

ויכון אלשוא אלאחצّר תחת אלחרף מתחרך ולדלך כרג בחרפין 1090

II.L.2.12.13. פנא יֹג

אלשוא פי אכר אלכלאם לא יכון אלא סאכנא נחו דרך מלך

ואמתאלהמא

II.L.2.12.14. The Fourteenth Subsection

Two successive silent *shewa*s occur only at the end of a word, as in יֹשַׁבְתְּ בַּלְּבָנוֹן מְקֻנַּנְתְּ בָּאֲרָזִים 'inhabitant of Lebanon, nested among the cedars' (Jer. 22.23), חֻתָּלְתְּ 'you were swathed in bands' (Ezek. 16.4), כָּחַלְתְּ 'you painted (your eyes)' (Ezek. 23.40), and similar examples. A *shewa* at the end of a word indicates feminine gender in many cases, both when following (another *shewa*) and also when not in such a sequence. In some cases *shewa* does not indicate feminine gender but rather pause, as in וַיִּשְׁבְּ | מִמֶּנּוּ 'and he took captives from him' (Num. 21.1), וְיֵרְדְּ מִיַּעֲקֹב 'and out of Jacob shall one have dominion' (Num. 24.19). If somebody were to say 'What is the value of the two successive *shewa*s at the end of a word?', the response would be as follows. One is a stopping point, namely the first one, as in וְיָשַׁבְתְּ עַל־מִטָּה כְבוּדָּה 'and you sat on a stately couch' (Ezek. 23.41). The *bet* in וְיָשַׁבְתְּ is the end of a word expressing the masculine singular. The second *shewa* under the *tav* indicates the feminine gender. You will find this practice in many places.

II.L.2.13. Section (concerning Uncertainty regarding the Reading of the *Shewa*)

II.L.2.13.1.

The *shewa* may be the cause of uncertainty for the reader in some places as to whether it is mobile or quiescent. (This applies to) הַמְ. It has been stated previously that in words containing not more than five letters the *shewa* is mobile, as in הַמְסֻכָּן תְּרוּמָה 'he who is impoverished in respect to offering' (Isa. 40.20), הַמְדַבֵּר 'the one speaking' (Gen. 45.12, etc.), except for one case, namely הַמְשֻׁגָּע הַזֶּה 'this madman' (2 Kings 9.11). The reason why it is not mobile is that there is no heaviness in the *he*. If you were to give heaviness to the *he*, the *shewa* would be

II.L.2.12.14. **פנא יד**

1095 שְׁוָאֵין מתראדפין סאכנין לא יכונא אלא פי אכר אלכלאם כקו

יוֹשֶׁבְתְּ ^(L5:16r) בלבנון מְקֻנֶנְתְּ בארזים חֲתָלְתְּ כָחַלְתְּ ואמתאל ד

ואלשוא פי אכר אלכלאם קד ידל עלי אלמונת פי אכתר

אלמואצֵע פי אלתראדף וגיר אלתראדף ותם שוא לא ידל עלי

אלמונת בל עלי קטע כקו וַיְשָׁב ממנו וַיֵרֶד מיֵע פאן קאל ומא

1100 אלפאידה פי אלשואין אלמתראדפין פי אכר אלכלאם קיל לה

אלואחד מחט והו אלאול כקו וַיֵשַׁבְתְּ על מטה כבודה פאלבא

מן וַיֵשָׁב הו נהאיה כלמה ללמדכר ואלשוא אלבֿ אלדי תחת

אלתו דאל עלי אל אל ^(L5:16v) תאנית והדה אלסירה תגדהא פי כתיר

מן אלמואצֵע

II.L.2.13. **פצל** 1105

II.L.2.13.1.

אלשוא קד ישכל פי מואצֵע עלי אלקאר הל הו מתחרך אם הו

סאכן הֵם וקד תקדם אלקול אן מא כאן מן אלכלם אלדי עדד

חרופהא כמסה לא אזיד פאן אלשוא יכון מתחרך נחו המֵסְכָן

תרומה הַמֵדַבֵר מא סוי מוצֵע ואחד והו הַמֵשְׁגָע הזה ואלסבב פי

1110 אנהא לם תתחרך אן ליס פי אלהא תתקיל ולו תקלת אלהא

made mobile. As for words beginning with *he* and *mem* that have more than five letters, the rule concerning these is that if the accent is on the fifth letter or later, the *shewa* is silent, for example הַמְדַבְּרִים 'those who speak' (Exod. 6.27), הַמְאָרֲרִים 'those who curse' (Num. 5.19), apart from some exceptions that deviate from this rule, for example הַמְבַקְשִׁים 'those who seek' (Exod. 4.19, etc.), and the like. When the accent is on the fourth letter, the *shewa* is mobile, for example, הַמְחַכִּים 'those who wait' (Job 3.21), הַמְנַדִּים 'those who remove' (Amos 6.3), and the like.

II.L.2.13.2.

As for a series of two successive identical letters in the middle of a word that one may be uncertain about, this has been discussed above. The (reading of the *shewa*) is determined by heaviness in it, for example וּלְלַמְּדָם סֵפֶר 'and to teach them the writing' (Dan. 1.4). If the heaviness was removed from the *vav*, the *shewa* would not be pronounced like *pataḥ*. There are six words that deviate from this rule, namely אָז יִקְרָאֻנְנִי 'Then they will call upon me' (Prov. 1.28), יְשַׁחֲרֻנְנִי וְלֹא יִמְצָאֻנְנִי 'They will seek me diligently but will not find me' (Prov. 1.28), בַּצַּר לָהֶם יְשַׁחֲרֻנְנִי 'and in their distress they seek me' (Hos. 5.15), וּמְשַׁחֲרַי יִמְצָאֻנְנִי 'and those who seek me diligently find me' (Prov. 8.17), זֹבֵחַ תּוֹדָה יְכַבְּדָנְנִי 'He who brings thanksgiving as his sacrifice honours me' (Psa. 50.23).

II.L.2.13.3.

As for what can cause uncertainty in forms such as וְזָהָב 'and the gold of' (Gen. 2.12), וְסָגַר 'and he closed' (Dan. 6.23), it may be said concerning cases that are linked to what follows by the accent, such as וְדָמֵה-לְךָ לִצְבִי 'and resemble a gazelle' (Cant. 8.14), that since *maqqef* occurs on וְדָמֵה, the *shewa* is quiescent, but if

לתחרך אלשוא ואמא מא יזיד ען כמסה חרוף מן אלכלם (L2:6r)

אלתי אולהא הֵא ומֵאם פאלשרט פי דלך הו אן אן כאן אללחן

עלי אלחרף אלהֹ ומא זאד כאן אלשוא סאכן מתל הַמְדַבְּרִים

הַמְאָרְרִים אלא שואד כארג ען דלך מתל הַמְבַקְשִׁים ונחוה

1115   ואדא כאן אללחן עלי אלחרף אלֹד כאן אלשוא מתחרך (L7:1v)

מתל הַמְחַכִּים הַמְנַדִּים ונחוהמא

II.L.2.13.2.

ואמא מא ילתבס מן אלחרפין אלמתראדפין פי וסט אלכלאם

פקד תקדם אלקול פיה איצֹא והו אן אלתתקיל שרט פיה כקֹו

וּלֵלַמְדָם סֵפֶר ולו זאל אלתתקיל מן אלואו לם יפתח אלשוא

1120   ואלדי כרג ען דלך סת לפטֹאת והי אז יִקְרָאוּנְנִי יְשַׁחֲרֻנְנִי ולא

יִמְצָאֻנְנִי בצר להם יְשַׁחֲרוּנְנִי ומשח[רי י]מְצָאֻנְנִי זבח תודה

יְכַבְּדָנְנִי

II.L.2.13.3.

ואמא מא > ילתבס וישכל < מן גנס וְזֶהַב וְסֻגַר אן קד יקאל פי

מא אתצל במא בעדה באללחן מתל וְדָמֶה לְךֹ לצבי אן למא

1125   חצל אלמקף פי ודמה סכן אלשוא ואן לו כאן פיה טעם תחרך

_____

there were an accent on it, the *shewa* would be mobile, as in וְשֵׁבֵה שֶׁבְיְךָ בֶּן־אֲבִינֹעַם 'Capture your captives, son of Abinoam' (Jud. 5.12). As for what is separated (by the accent), like וְסַגַּר 'and he closed' (Dan. 6.23), the heaviness has caused the *shewa* to be mobile. There are also some cases that are only learnt by listening.

GAP

II.L.2.14. (Section on the Names of the Vowels)

[...] the teeth make a squeaking sound with it.

The seventh is *shureq* [ ] three dots (written) obliquely. It may be replaced by one dot in the middle of *vav*, whose name is *shureq*, which is derived from לִשְׁמֹעַ שְׁרִקוֹת עֲדָרִים 'to hear the whistlings of the flocks' (Jud. 5.16), which is a whistling, because it gathers the lips together.

II.L.2.15. Section on their Place of Articulation
II.L.2.15.1.
The place of articulation of *holem* is the root of the tongue and the place of swallowing, which is the place of articulation of אהחע, and it moves over the surface of the entire mouth. Take note that if somebody were to investigate carefully their places of articulation, he would have something like the knowledge necessary as to what is first in position and what is last.

אלשוא (L2:6v) מתל קולה וּשֶׁבֵּה שְׁבִיַךְ בן אבי נעם ואמא מא כאן

מנפרדא מתל קולה וּסְגַר פאלתתקיל סבב פי אלתחריך ותם

מא לא יוכד אלא סמאעא

GAP

II.L.2.14.

תצר בהא אלאסנאן צרא (L8:101r)

1130 ואלסאבע שרק [ ] תלתה נקט מוארבה וקד יכון עוצֿהא נקטה

[ואחדה] פי קלב אלואו אסמוהא שרק ואשתקוה מן שריקות

עדרים והו אלצפיר לאנהא תגֿמע אלשפתין

II.L.2.15. **פצל פי מחלהא**

II.L.2.15.1.

[מחל] אלחלם עקר הלשון ובית הבליעה [והו מחל] אֹהֹחֹעֹ

1135 ומסירה עלי סטח אלפם כלה ואעלם [מן] תאמל מחאלהא

צארת לה כאלעלם אלצֿרורי לה מן דלך אי מא הו אלמתקדם

מנהא ואי מ[א הו] אלמתאכר

II.L.2.15.2.

The second place of articulation is the place of articulation of *qameṣ*. It is slightly above the root of the tongue, this being the (first) third of the tongue, and its movement is to above the palate.

II.L.2.15.3.

The third place of articulation is the place of articulation of *pataḥ*, which is the surface of the tongue at the bottom (of the mouth).

II.L.2.15.4.

The fourth place of articulation is the place of articulation of *segol*, which is the sides of the mouth, and its movement is upon the lower surface of the mouth.

II.L.2.15.5.

The fifth place of articulation is the place of articulation of *ṣere*, which is the teeth, without closure, because it breaks through them.

II.L.2.15.6.

The sixth place of articulation is the place of articulation of *ḥireq*, which is the closure of the teeth with force.

II.L.2.15.7.

The seventh place of articulation is the place of articulation of *shureq*, which is the lips gathered together (as if for) whistling.

II.L.2.15.2.

אלתאני מחל אלקאמצה והו פוק אצל אללסאן קלילא והו תלת

אללסאן וחרכתהא אלי פוק אלחנך

II.L.2.15.3.

ואלמחל אלתאלת מחל אלפאתחה והו סטח אללסאן מן (L6:1r) 1140

אספל

II.L.2.15.4.

ואלמחל אלראבע הו מחל אלסגולה והו אגנאב אלפם

וחרכתהא עלי סטח אלפם אלספלאני

II.L.2.15.5.

ואלמחל אלכאמס הו מחל אלצירי והו אלאסנאן בלא אטבאק

לאנה ישק בינהא שקא 1145

II.L.2.15.6.

ואלמחל אלסאדס מחל אלחרק והו אטבאק אלאסנאן בקוה

II.L.2.15.7.

אלמחל אלסאבע מחל אלשרק והו אלשפתין מצֿמומתין

כאלצפיר

_____

II.L.2.16. Section concerning Combinations of them (i.e. the Vowels) to Form Basic Nouns and Combinations of them to Form Abstractions

For example, אוֹנוֹ 'Ono (place name)' (1 Chron. 8.12, etc.), a basic noun (combining) *holem* with *holem* and the abstraction אוֹרוֹ 'his light' (Job 36.30, etc.). *Holem* with *qames*: the abstraction טוֹבָה 'good deed' (1 Sam. 24.19, etc.). *Holem* with *patah*: the basic noun רֹמַח 'spear' (Num. 25.7, etc.) and the abstraction הוֹדַע 'he made known' (Lev. 4.23, etc.). *Holem* with *segol*: the basic noun אֹהֶל 'tent' and the abstraction וַיֹּאמֶר. *Holem* with *sere*: the basic noun בּוֹצֵץ 'Bozez (name of a crag)' (1 Sam. 14.4) and the abstraction יוֹצֵא 'goes out'. *Holem* with *hireq*: basic noun דֹּפִי 'fault' (Psa. 50.20) and the abstraction עוֹשִׂים 'doing (mpl.)'. *Holem* with *shureq*: the basic noun תֹהוּ 'confusion' and the abstraction טוֹבוּ 'they are good' (cf. Num. 24.5, etc.). To these can be added further examples of this type of (arrangement of vowels), the seven with the seven.

II.L.2.17. Chapter concerning the Descending of the Vowels from One to the Other according to the Order of their Places of Articulation

Holem descends to *qames* with the attachment of a pronoun and the plural, for example כֹּפֶר 'ransom'—כָּפְרוֹ 'his ransom', עֹשֶׁר 'wealth'—עָשְׁרוֹ 'his wealth', קֹדֶשׁ 'holiness'—קָדְשׁוֹ 'his holiness', גֹּבַה 'height'—גָּבְהוֹ 'his height'. If you form a plural, you say קָדָשִׁים 'holinesses'. From *qames* to *patah*: חָדָשׁ 'new'—חֲדָשִׁים 'new (pl.) in every morning' (Lam. 3.23), לַבְּקָרִים עָנָן 'cloud'—עֲנָנִים 'clouds'. From *patah* to *segol*: they say אֶמְצָאֲךָ בַחוּץ 'I meet you outside' (Cant. 8.1)—כִּי לֹא יִמְצָאֶכָּה 'that he does not find you' (1 Kings 18.10). From *segol* to *sere* in a conjoined form, for example

II.L.2.16. פצל אלדי יתלף מנהא אסאס ואלדי יתלף מנהא ערף

1150 מת אונו אסאס חלם מע חלם וערף אורו חלם מע קאמצה ערף

טובה אלחלם מע פאתחה אסאס <רוֹמַח> וערף הוֹדַע אלחֹלם

מע אלסגולה אסאס אהל וערף ויאמֶר אלחֹלם מע אלצרי אסאס

בוֹצֶץ וערף יוֹצֵא אלחלם מע אלחרק אסאס דוֹפִי <וערף>

עוֹשִׂים אלחלם מע אלשרק אסאס תהו וערף טובו אלי גיר דלך

1155 מן צֹרבהא סבעה פי סבעה

II.L.2.17. באב פי אנחדאר אלמלוך בעצֹהא אלי בעץ עלי תרתיב מחאלהא

אלחלם ינחדר אלי אלקמץ ענד אתצאל אלצֹמיר ואלגמע נחו

כֹּפֶר כָּפְרוֹ עֹשֶׂר עָשְׂרוּ קֹדֶשׁ קָדְשׁוֹ גָּבַהּ גָּבְהוּ ואן גמעת קלת

1160 קָדְשִׁים מן קאמצה אלי פאתחה חָדָשׁ חֲדָשִׁים לבקרים עָנָן עֲנָנִים

ומן פאתחה אלי סגולה קאלו אַמְצָאֶךָ בחוץ כי לא יִמְצָאֶךָ ומן

סגולה (L6:1v) אלי צֵרִי פי אלסמוך מתל ק שֶׁבֶר תחת על שֶׁבֶר

1151 רוֹמַח] L8:101v   1153 רוֹמַה L6:1r   1153 וערף וערף[²] L6

שֶׁבֶר תַּחַת 'fracture for (fracture)' (Lev. 24.20)—עַל־שֶׁבֶר יוֹסֵף 'over the ruin of Joseph' (Amos 6.6). To these can be added other cases of vowels descending from one to the other in this way.

II.L.2.18. (On the Origin of the Vowels)

If somebody were to ask 'With regard to the form of these vowels, what is the origin of their formation? Do you say that the scribes established their form?' The response would be as follows. If the scribes were the source of this, it would be permissible for somebody who was not satisfied with it to come and create different forms. This would be permissible for every single scribe. There would be no limit or end to their forms. If one were to say 'Is not the *qameṣ* of the people of Iraq a superscribed half *ʾalef*, and so forth with regard to the shape of their vowels?', the response would be as follows. What should be relied upon in this regard is (the shape of vowels) in the Holy Land. It is not implausible that when the people of the exile moved away from the Holy Land they made a record of their reading and created shapes (of vowels) when they had moved away from the Holy Land for fear that they would forget the reading. The (original) shapes (of the vowels) of the Holy Land, however, remained. If somebody were to say 'So who formed them?', the response to him would be as follows. It is possible that the people of the language formed the shapes of the vowels just as they formed the shapes of the letters. It is also possible that the people of the language used to use them in conversation without their knowing any (written) form for them until the time of Habakkuk, peace be upon him, when God said to him כְּתוֹב חָזוֹן וּבָאֵר עַל־הַלֻּחוֹת 'Write the vision; make it plain upon tablets' (Hab. 2.2). He indicated the reason for this, namely לְמַעַן

יוֹסֵף אלי גיר דלך ממא תנחדר מן בעץ אלי בעץ עלי הדא
אלוגה

II.L.2.18.

פאן קאל אשכאל הדה אלמלוך כיף כאן אצל תשאכילהא   1165
אתקולון אן אלסופרים וצעו אשכאלהא קיל לה לו כאן
אלסופרים הם אלאצל פי דלך לכאן יגוז אן יגי מן לם ירץْ בדלך
וישכל אשכאלא סואהא וכאן יצח הדא מן כל סופר וסופר פלא
כאן יכון לאשכאלהא לא חד ולא אנקצّא פאן קאל אליס אהל
אלעראק קאמצתהם נצף אלף מן פוק אלי גיר ד מן אשכאל   1170
אנחאיהם קיל לה אן אלמעול פי דלך עלי ארץ הקדושה ומא
ימתנע אן למא בעדו אהל אלגולה ען ארץ הקדושה צבטו
קראתהם פגעלו להם אשכאל למא בעדו ען ארץ ישראל כוף מן
אן ינסו אלקראה ובקית אשכאל ארץ הק פאן קאל פמן שכלהא
קיל לה אן יגוז אן <אהל> אללגה כמא שכלו אשכאל אלחרוף   1175
שכלו ללמלוך איצّא אשכאל ויגוז איצّא אן אהל אללגה כאנו
יתכאטבו בהא מן גיר שכל יערפוה להא אלי זמאן חבקוק עׄ אׄ
פקאל לה אללה כתוב חָזוֹן ובָאֵר על הלוחות ואורא אלעלה פי
דלך והו למען ירוץ קורא בו ולא שך אן מן אכד מצחאפא

יְרוּץ קוֹרֵא בוֹ 'so that one who reads it can run' (Hab. 2.2). Indeed, there is no doubt that when somebody takes a simple codex without accents or pointing, he stumbles in the reading and does not 'run', apart from a few exceptional people that are found in some generations, such as Ben Asher and Ben Naftali in their time and those like them. If a reader has a codex in which the cantillation and pointing are clearly indicated, he can run and not stumble.

This is what needs to be said, but God knows best. The discourse is finished.

סאדגא בגיר לחן ולא <נקט> אנה יִכַּשֵׁל פי אלקראה ולא יָרוּץ 1180

אלא אחאד שואד קלאיל יוגדו פי בעץ אלאגיאל כאבן אֲשֶׁר

ואבן נפתָלִי (L6:2r) פי זמאנהמא ומן גרי מגראההמא ואדא כאן

ללקאר מצחף טאהר אללחן <ואלנקט> הו יָרוּץ ולא יִכַּשֵׁל

הדא מא לאח ואללה אעלם ותמת אלמקאלה

1180 נקט] נטק L6   1183 ואלנקט] L8:57r אלנטק L6

II.L.3.0.
THE THIRD DISCOURSE: ON THE ACCENTS
(SELECTED PASSAGES)

II.L.3.1. (On the *Gaʿya*)

If somebody were to say 'So, what do you say concerning the *gaʿya*?', the response to him would be as follows. The *gaʿya* does not have a definite status in the reading of Scripture. One reader may omit it and another reader may sustain it. There are some places, however, in which it may not be omitted, since it affects the meaning. This applies to the lexical class of 'fearing', and so they have said 'Every (form from) the lexical class of 'fearing' has *gaʿya*'. Likewise one says תֵּישָׁנוּ 'you sleep', יֵישְׁנוּ 'they sleep', with *gaʿya*, from the lexical class of 'sleeping', כִּי לֹא יֵישְׁנוּ אִם־לֹא יָרֵעוּ 'for they cannot sleep unless they have done wrong' (Prov. 4.16). If it is without *gaʿya*, it is from (the lexical class) of 'repeating', as in אִם־תִּשְׁנוּ יָד אֶשְׁלַח בְּכֶם 'If you do so again, I will lay hands on you' (Neh. 13.21). If somebody were to say 'So do you consider it to be one of the conjunctive accents or disjunctive accents?', the response to him would be as follows. It should not be considered to belong either with the disjunctive accents or the conjunctive accents, since it is only an exhalation in speech, which carries the words forward, and joins and binds them with one another, as in לְבִלְתִּי הַשְׁחִית הַכֹּל 'not destroying them all' (Isa. 65.8), אִם־לָמֹד יִלְמְדוּ אֶת־דַּרְכֵי עַמִּי 'if they will diligently learn the ways of my people' (Jer. 12.16). Its distinctive property is the extension of the melody so that joy is diffused in the heart, in order to conduct the reading along, animating the reader and moving him to read more. An expert of this discipline has said: If you wish to know whether *gaʿya* is correct, look at the place of the *gaʿya*. If it is permissible to put

II.L.3.0.

אלמקאלה אלתאלתה פי אלאלחאן

II.L.3.1.

(L1:35r) פאן קאל קאיל פמא תקולון פי אלגעיה קיל לה אן

אלגעיה ליס להא שיעור פי אלמקרא פקאר יחדפהא וקאר

יתבתהא ותם מואצע לא ימכן חדפהא לאן להא תאתיר פי

אלמעני פי לשון יראה וכדא קאלו כל לשון דחילה געי ומתלה

תָּשְׁנוּ יְשְׁנוּ פהי באלגעיה מן אלנום כי לא יְשְׁנוּ אם לא ירעו 1190

ואדא כאן בלא געיה מן אלתתניה בך אם תשנו יד אשלח בכם

פאן קאל פהל תחסבוהא מן אלאלחאן או מן אלכדאם קיל לה

מא תחסב לא מע אלאלחאן ולא מע אלכדאם לאנהא אנמא הי

תנפס פי אלכלאם ותסוק אלכלם ותוצלהא ותגמעהא בעצّהא

מע בעץ בך לבלתי השחית הכל אם למד ילמדו את דַרְכֵי עמי 1195

וכאציתה אלאמדאד באלנגם לינתשר אלסרור פי אלקלב ולזף

אלקראה ולתנשיט אלקאר להא ולתחרכה אלי אלתזייד וקד

קאל בעץ עלמא הדא אלעלם אדא ארדת אן תנטّר צחה

אלגעיה פאנטّר מוצע אלגעיה פאן צלח טעם אלכלמה עלי מוצע

the accent of the word on the place of the *gaʿya*, then the *gaʿya* is in order. If it does not come in the place of the accent, then return it to the place (of the accent).[13] He has said that by this principle one may distinguish a correct *gaʿya* from one that is incorrect. He then retracted this and said that this principle applies only to certain places. The first statement is the correct one.

II.L.3.2. Chapter concerning Cases whose Rule is not at all Dependent on an Accent and Cases whose Rule is Dependent on an Unspecified Accent.

II.L.3.2.1.

This includes מֶרְכָּבָה. If somebody were to ask, why is the form מֶרְכָּבָה sometimes pointed with *segol* and sometimes pointed with *pataḥ*, the response would be as follows. When the form is singular, *segol* occurs under the *mem*. Examples of the singular are כַּאֲשֶׁר הָפַּד־אִישׁ מֵעַל מֶרְכַּבְתּוֹ 'when the man turned from his chariot' (2 Kings 5.26), מֶרְכָּבָה וְסֻסִים 'a chariot and horses' (2 Sam. 15.1). In the plural you say מַדּוּעַ אֶחֱרוּ פַּעֲמֵי מַרְכְּבוֹתָיו 'Why tarry the hoofbeats of his chariots?' (Jud. 5.28), מַרְכְּבֹת פַּרְעֹה וְחֵילוֹ 'the chariots of Pharaoh and his army' (Exod. 15.4), and the like. There is one exception to this, in that it does not have *segol* (in the singular) but *ḥireq*, namely בְּמִרְכֶּבֶת הַמִּשְׁנֶה 'in his second chariot' (Gen. 41.43).

---

[13] The corrected reading פארדהא is a form IV imperative of the root *r-d-d*, which in medieval Judaeo-Arabic is often used with the sense of the form I (Blau 2006, 245).

אלגעיה פאלגעיה מסתויה ואן כאן לא תגי מוצע אלטעם

<פארדהא> עלי אלמוצע וקאל אן הדא אלאצל בה יועלם צחה

אלגעיה מן פסאדהא ורגע ען דלך פקאל אן הדא אלאצל יצח פי

בעץ אלמואצע ואלקול אלאול הו אלצחיח

II.L.3.2. (L1:35v) באב פי מא לם יכון שרטה מעלק בלחן בתה
ומא שרטה מעלק בלחן גיר מעיין

II.L.3.2.1.

מן דלך לשון מַרְכָּבָה אן סאל סאיל לם כאן לשון מֶרְכבה תארה

תנקט בתלת נקט ותארה בפאתחה אלגואב הוא אן מא כאן

מנהא לשון יחיד כאן תחת אלמאם תלת נקט בך פי אליחיד

כאשר הפך איש מעל מֶרְכבתו מֶרכבה וסוסים ותקול פי

אלרבים מדוע אחרו פעמי מַרְכבוֹתָיו מַרכבות פרעה וֹח ומֹת מא

סוי ואחדה פאנהא לא בתלת נקט אלא נקטה ואחדה והי

בְּמִרכבת המשנה

II.L.3.2.2.

Likewise people may ask concerning מַה and מֶה why their pointing varies and what is their rule. The response is as follows. When it is followed by *dagesh*, it has *pataḥ*, for example מַה־תֹּאמַר נַפְשֶׁךָ 'whatever your soul says' (1 Sam. 20.4), מַה־נְּדַבֵּר וּמַה־נִּצְטַדָּק 'What shall we speak? And how can we show ourselves to be just?' (Gen. 44.16). When it is followed by *rafe*, it has *segol*, for example מֶה לִֽידִידִ֫י 'What has my beloved?' (Jer. 11.15), מֶה לַעֲשֹׂות לָךְ הֲיֵשׁ לְדַבֶּר־לָךְ 'What is to be done for you? Would you have a word spoken on your behalf?' (2 Kings 4.13), and similar cases.

II.L.3.2.3.

People may ask concerning לָמָה what the rule is relating to the fact that it is sometimes with *dagesh* and sometimes *rafe*. The response relates to two factors. One is that it is because of the accent, namely when the accent is on the *mem* of למה, it is *rafe* and when the accent is on the *lamed*, it has *dagesh*, for example לָמָה הֲרֵעֹתָה֙ לָעָם הַזֶּה לָמָּה זֶּה 'Why have you done evil to this people? Why (did you ever send me)?' (Exod. 5.22). All of the reading of Scripture follows this rule except for one case in Job, for the accent is on the *lamed*, but it is *rafe*, namely לָמָה שַׂמְתַּנִי לְמִפְגָּע 'Why have you made me your mark?' (Job 7.20). The second response is that it is on account of the letter. This rule is superior to the first, since למה may be without an accent but rather have *maqqef*, for example לָמָּה־זֶּה מְחִיר בְּיַד־כְּסִיל 'Why should a fool have a price in his hand' (Prov. 17.16), and similar cases. The rule concerning this is that whenever למה are linked prosodically to three letters, namely *ʾalef*, *he* and *ʿayin*, it is *rafe*, for example וְלָמָה אַתָּה מִתְנַקֵּשׁ 'Why are you laying a snare?' (1 Sam. 28.9), לָמָה יְהוָה֙ יֶחֱרֶ֤ה אַפְּךָ֙ 'Why, oh Lord, does your anger

II.L.3.2.2.

וכדלך קד יסל אלנאס ען מַה ומֶה לם יכתלף נקטהמא ומא

שרטהמא אלגّואב הו אן אדא ‹תבעה› דגש כאנת בפאתחה

כֹּך מַה־תֹּאמַר נַפְשֶׁךּ מַה־נְּדַבֵּר וּמַה־נִּצְטַדָּק ומא תבעה רפֶّי כאן

בסגّולה כֹּך מֶה לִידִידִי מֶה לַעֲשֹוֹת לֹךְ הֲיֵשׁ לְדַבֵּר לֹךְ וּמֹתֹ

II.L.3.2.3.

וקד יסל אלנאס ען לָמֶה מא אלשרט פי כונה תארה מדגוש

ותארה רפّי אלגّואב פיה עלי וגהין אלّואחד מן אגّל אלטעם והו

אן אדא כאן אלטעם עלי ^(L1:36r) אלّמאם מן למה כאן רפّי ואדא

כאן אלטעם עלי אלّלמאד כאן דגש כֹּך למֶה הָרֵעֹֽתָ֙ לָעָ֣ם הַזֶּ֔ה

למה זה וכל אלמקרא עלי הדא אלّא ואחד פי איّוב פאן אלטעם

עלי אלّלמאד והו רפّי והו לָ֣מָה שַׂמְתַּ֣נִי לְמִפְּ֑ ואלגّואב אלֹב מן

אגّל אלחרף והדא אלשרט הו אבלג מן אלّאוّל לאן קד יכّון למה

בגיר אלטעם בל במקף כֹּך למה זה מָחִ֣יר בְּיַד־כְּסִ֑יל וּמֹתֹ

ואלשרט פי דלך הו אן אן כלמא אסתנד למה אלי תלת חרّוף והן

אלף הא עין כאן רפّי כֹּך וּלָ֤מֶה אַתָּה֙ מִתְנַקֵּ֔שׁ לָֽמָה יְיָ֭ יֶחֱרֶ֣ה אפֹּ֫

---

burn?' (Exod. 32.11), לָמָה הֲרֵעֹתָ 'Why have you dealt ill?' (Num. 11.11), לָמָה עֲלִיתֶם עָלֵינוּ 'Why have you come up against us?' (Jud. 15.10), and the like. There are five cases that are exceptions to this rule, since they are linked prosodically to אהע but have *dagesh*. These are לָמָה הִרְגַּזְתַּנִי 'Why have you vexed me?' (1 Sam. 28.15), לָמָה הִצִּיתוּ עֲבָדֶךָ 'Why have your servants set on fire?' (2 Sam. 14.31), לָמָה אִירָא בִּימֵי רָע 'Why should I fear in times of trouble?' (Psa. 49.6), לָמָה הָיָה כְאֵבִי נֶצַח 'Why is my pain unceasing?' (Jer. 15.18), לָמָה אַכֶּכָה אַרְצָה 'Why should I smite you to the ground?' (2 Sam. 2.22). Their mnemonic combination is 'The slave has vexed me; I have feared pain; I have killed him'. If you like, you may say 'The servant has vexed me; I have feared illness; I have smitten him.' Every למה that is prosodically bound to the other letters of the inventory, namely בֹּגֹדֹזֹוֹטֹיֹכֹלֹמֹנֹסֹפֹצֹקֹרֹשֹׁת, has *dagesh*, except for three cases, which are prosodically bound to *shin* and *zayin*, namely לָמָה שְׁכַחְתָּנִי 'Why have you forgotten me?' (Psa. 42.10), לָמָה זְנַחְתָּנִי 'Why have you rejected me?' (Psa. 43.2), לָמָה שַׂמְתַּנִי 'Why have you made me (your mark)?' (Job 7.20). Their mnemonic combination is: 'You made me forgotten and rejected'.

II.L.3.2.4.

People may ask concerning הֵן and הֶן, שֵׁשׁ and שֶׁשׁ, עֵת and עֶת, לֵב and לֶב, כֵּן and כֶּן, שֵׁן and שֶׁן why these sometimes occur with *ṣere* and sometimes with *segol*. The response concerning this is as follows. When the accent is on the first letter of the word following these words, they have *segol* so long as they have *maqqef*, for example הֶן־תָּוִי 'Here is my signature' (Job 31.35), הֶן־הוּא 'Behold it (is the joy of his way)' (Job 8.19). You say

למֶה הרעוֹת למה עליתם עלינו ומתֿ ואלדי כרג ען דלך כמסה

מואצֿע פאנהא מסתנדה אלי אֹהֹעֿ והי מדגושה והי למה

הרגזתַני למה הצחתו עבדיך למה אירא בימי רע למה היה כאבי

נצח למה אככה ארצה ורבאטהא אקלקני אלעבד כשית אלוגע 1230

קתלתה ואן ארדת תקול <הרגיזני> העבד ייראתי החולי הביתיו

וכל למה אסתנד אלי חרוף אלקבאלה אלאכר הם בֿגֿדֿוֹזֿטֿיֹבֿ

לֹמֹנֹסֹפֿצֿקֿרֹשֹׁתֿ יכון דגש מא סוי תלתה פאנהא תסתנד אלי שין

וזאי והן למה שכחתני למה זנחתני למה שמתני ורבאטהא

שִׂמַתַּנִי מָשְׁכָח מָזֻנָח 1235

II.L.3.2.4.

וקד יסל אלנאס ען הֵן והֵן ושֵׁש ושֵׁש ועֵת ועֵת ולֵב ולֵב וכֵן וכֵן

ושֵׁן ושֵׁן לם כאן הדה אלמדכוראת תגי תאַרה בצרי ותאַרה

בסגולה (L1:36v) ואלג'ואב פי דלך הו אן אדא כאן אלטעם פי אול

חרף מן אלכלמה אלתאניה להדה אלכלם צארת בסגולה מהמא

הי במקף בכ הֵן־תָוֹי הֵן הוא ותקול שֵׁש הֵנָה שֵׁש השעורים 1240

1231 הרגיזני] L2:2r הרגיני L1   1232 אסתנד...אלאכר] אסתנד אלי
בקיה חרוף אלקבאלה L2:2r

שֵׁשׁ־הֵנָּה 'They are six' (Prov. 6.16) and שֵׁשׁ־הַשְּׂעֹרִים 'six (measures) of barley' (Ruth 3.17). You say לֹא עֶת־בֹּא 'it is not the time of coming' (Haggai 1.2), כִּי לְעֶת־יֹום בְּיֹום 'for from day to day' (1 Chron. 12.23). An exception to the (expected form) עֵת is בְּלֹא עֶת־נִדָּתָהּ 'not at the time of her impurity' (Lev. 15.25), for the accent is not on the first letter but it has *segol*. You say פַּלְגֵי־מַיִם לֶב־מֶלֶךְ 'The king's heart is a stream of water' (Prov. 21.1), אֲשֶׁר יַעֲלֶה עַל לֶב־אִישׁ 'that comes into a man's heart' (2 Kings 12.5). You say כְדִבְרֵיכֶם כֶּן־הוּא 'Let it be as you say' (Gen. 44.10, etc.). You say עַל־שֶׁן־סֶּלַע 'in the crag of rock' (Job 39.28). The phrase שֵׁן־הַסֶּלַע 'a crag of rock' (1 Sam. 14.4) has *ṣere* since the accent occurs on the second letter.

II.L.3.2.5.

People may ask concerning אֶת and אֵת which of them has the accent and which has *maqqef*. The response is as follows. They say that every אֶת with *segol* in the reading of Scripture is always without an accent and has *maqqef*, except for three cases, namely בְּהַצּוֹתוֹ | אֶת אֲרַם 'when he strove with Aram(naharaim)' (Psa. 60.2), אֶת גְּאֹון יַעֲקֹב 'the pride of Jacob' (Psa. 47.5), כִּי אֶת אֲשֶׁר יֶאֱהַב 'for him whom he loves' (Prov. 3.12). Every אֵת with *ṣere* must have an accent and never has *maqqef*, except for one case, namely אֶת־כָּל־גָּבֹהַּ 'everything that is high' (Job 41.26).

II.L.3.2.6.

People may ask also concerning כָּל and כֹּל why it is with *qameṣ* and with *ḥolem*. The response is as follows. They have said that whenever it has *maqqef* it occurs only with *qameṣ*, except for

ותקול לא עֵת בָּא כִּי לעֵת ⟨יום⟩ ביום ואלדי יכרג ען ⟨עת⟩ קֹ

בלא עֵת נדתה פאן אלטעם ליס הו עלי אול חרף וקד גא בתלת

נקט ותקול פלגי מים לֵב מלך אשר יעלה על לֵב אישׁ ותקול

כדבריכם כֵן הוא ותקול על שֵׁן סלע שֵׁן הסֵלע צאר בצירי למא

צאר אלטעם מע אלחרף אלתאני   1245

II.L.3.2.5.

וקד יסל אלנאס ען אֵת ואֵת מא מנהא בטעם ומא מנהא במקף

אלגואב קאלו אן כל אֵת פי אלמקרא בסגולה לא יכון פיהא

טעם אלבתה בל במקף אלא גׄ והי בהצותו אֵת ארם אֵת גאון יׄעׄ

כי אֵת אשר יאהב וכל אֵת בצרי לא בד לה מן טעם ולא ידכלה

מקף בתה אלא וֹא והו אֵת־כל גבוה   1250

II.L.3.2.6.

וקד יסל אלנאס איצׄא ען כָּל וכֹל לם כאן בקאמצה ובחלם

אלגואב קאלו אן כל מא כאן במקף לא יכון ⟨אלא⟩ מקמוצא

─────────

1241 יום] יום יום L1 | עת] L2:2v L1 *omitted*   1252 אלא]
L1 *omitted*

two cases in the reading of Scripture: כָּל־עַצְמֹותָי 'all my bones'
(Psa. 22.15), כָּל אֲחֵי־רָשׁ 'all the brothers of a poor man' (Prov.
19.7), and also וְכָל בַּשָּׁלִשׁ 'and has measured in a third (measure)'
(Isa. 40.12), although they interpreted it as being from the
lexical class of 'measuring'. Whenever it occurs with *holem*, it
does not have *maqqef* but rather has an accent, for example כֹּל
הַנִּקְרָא בִשְׁמִי 'everyone who is called by my name' (Isa. 43.7), כֹּל
אֲשֶׁר תִּמְצָא יָדְךָ 'whatever your hand finds' (Ecc. 9.10).

II.L.3.2.7.

They may also ask concerning the lexical class of 'blessing' why
the *shewa* under the *resh* is sometimes quiescent and sometimes
mobile. The response is as follows. They have said that
whenever the accent is under the *bet* of the lexical class of
'blessing', the *shewa* is quiescent, for example בָּרְכוּ־נָא אֶת־יְהוָה
אֱלֹהֵיכֶם 'Bless the Lord your God' (1 Chron. 29.20). When the
accent is on the *kaf*, the *shewa* is mobile, for example בָּרֲכוּ יְהוָה
מַלְאָכָיו 'Bless the Lord, (you) his angels' (Psa. 103.20), בַּעֲבוּר
תְּבָרֲכַנִּי נַפְשֶׁךָ 'in order that your soul blesses me' (Gen. 27.19),
except one case, in which the accent is on the *kaf* but the *shewa*
is quiescent, namely וּלְעִלָּאָה בָּרְכֵת 'I blessed the Most High' (Dan.
4.31). It may be said that this last case has broken the rule since
it is in the Aramaic language. If, however, there is a case that
breaks the rule in Hebrew, then it must be וּמִבִּרְכָתְךָ יְבֹרַךְ בֵּית־עַבְדְּךָ
'with your blessing will the house of your servant be blessed' (2
Sam. 7.29), because the accent in this is on the *kaf* and the
shewa is silent, unless it be said that in this word there are two
accents. The most plausible statement is that it is a case that
breaks the rule because וַאֲבָרֲכָה מְבָרֲכֶיךָ 'I will bless those that
bless you' (Gen. 12.3) has two accents and the *shewa* is mobile.
Likewise in בִּרְכֹת אָבִיךָ 'the blessings of your father' (Gen. 49.26)
the accent is on the *kaf* and the *shewa* is quiescent, and this is
also a case that breaks the rule.

מא סוי תנתין פי אלמקרא כָּל־עצמותי כָּל אחי רש וּכָל בשליש

ואן כאן יפסרוהא מן אלמכיאל וכל מא כאן בחלם (L1:37r) לא

1255 ידכלה מקף בל יכון בטעם כק כֹל הנקרָא בשמי כל אשר תמצָא

ידֶךָ

II.L.3.2.7.

ויסל איצֿא ען לשון בְרָכָה לם כאן אלשוא אלדי תחת אלריש

תארה סאכן ותארה מתחרך ואלגֿואב קאלו אן כלמא אלטעם

תחת אלבא מן לשון ברכה כאן אלשוא סאכן כק בָּרְכוּ נָא את

1260 ייי אלהיכם ואדא כאן אלטעם עלי אלכאף כאן אלשוא מתחרך

כק ברכו ייָ מלאכיו בעבור תברכֵנִי נפשך אלא ואחדה פאן

אלטעם עלי אלכאף ואלשוא סאכן והי ולעָלְאָה בָרכֵת וקד ימכן

אן יקאל אנהא אנמא כסרת אלשרט לכונהא מן לגה אלכסדאני

גיר אן כאן כאסרה מן אלעבראני פינבגי אן תכון וּמִבִּרְכָתְךָֿ יברד

1265 בית עבדך לאן אלטעם פיהא עלי אלכאף ואלשוא סאכן אלא אן

יקאל אן פי הדה אלכלמה טעמין ואלקריב אנהא כאסרה לאן

ואברכה מברְכֶיךָֿ פיהא טעמין ואלשוא מתחרך וכדלך ברכות

אביך אלטעם עלי אלכאף ואלשוא סאכן פתכון איצֿא כאסרה

עלי אלשרט

HIDĀYAT AL-QĀRIʾ (SHORT VERSION)

II.S.0.0. (INTRODUCTION)

GAP

II.S.0.1.

This is the book of the abbreviated version of *The Guide for the Reader*, known as *The Book of Essential Requirements*.[1]

II.S.0.2.

Its author begins and says: You, may God support you, asked me to abbreviate for you *The Book of Rules*, which is generally known as *The Guide for the Reader*, in which I mention its essential requirements. So, I am here responding to this request of yours, asking God to grant me success in this, possibly including where necessary what was not mentioned in *The Guide for the Reader*. From Him, may He be exalted, I seek help.

II.S.0.3.

If somebody were to ask what the need is for knowledge of the rules of biblical recitation, the response should be: because the accents change meanings, for example קוּמִי אוֹרִי 'Arise! Shine!' (Isa. 60.1), which are two feminine singular imperatives, since the accent is on the first letter, but לְיֹום קוּמִי לְעֵד 'for the day when I arise as a witness' (Zeph. 3.8), יְהֹוָה | אוֹרִי וְיִשְׁעִי 'The Lord is my light and my salvation' (Psa. 27.1), which are two masculine nouns, since the accent is at the end and not the beginning of the word. Other examples are שָׁבוּ עַל־עֲוֺנֺת אֲבוֹתָם 'They have turned back to the iniquities of their forefathers' (Jer. 11.10), which denotes 'returning' since the accent is on the first letter,

---

[1] Literally: the book of the lifeblood.

https://doi.org/10.11647/OBP.0194.03

הדאיה אלקאר

II.S.0.0.

GAP

II.S.0.1.

(S20:1r) הדא כתאב מכתצר הדאיה אלקאר יוערף בכתאב
אלמהגה

II.S.0.2.

אבתדי מצנפה וקאל סאלתם איידכם אללה אן אכתצר לכם
כתאב אלשרוט אלמלקב בההדאיה אלקאר בחית אדכר מוהגה

וְהא אנא מגיב לכם אלי דלך סאילא ללה תופיקי פיה מע מא 5
עסאה אן ינצّאף אליה ממא לם ידכר פי הדאיה אלקאר ובה תע
אסתעין

II.S.0.3.

אן קאל קאיל מא אלחאגה אלי עלם אלשרוט פי אלמקרא קיל

לה לאן אלחאן מגיירה ללמעאני מתל קֻֽמֹי אֽוֹרֹי אמרין למונת

מן חית אן אלטעם עלי אול חרף מתל ליום קומי לעד ייי אורי 10

וישעי אסמין למדכר למא תאכר אללחן ען אול אלכלמה (S9:1r)

ומתל שבו על עונות אבותם מן אלרגוע לאן אלטעם עלי אול

but שָׁבוּ וַיָּבֹזּוּ 'they captured and made their prey' (Gen. 34.29), which denotes 'capturing' since the accent is placed not on the beginning of the word but on its end.

II.S.0.4.

A further reason is that this reading, which is now current in the Land of Israel, is the reading of Ezra, peace be upon him, and his generation, because the nation was not cut off from the Land of Israel from the time of Ezra, peace be upon him, in the Second Temple, until now, except from Jerusalem during the reign of Edom over the land. Israel taught this reading to their children until now, generation after generation. Another reason is that if somebody were to read the twenty-one books with the accents of the three books or the three books with the accents of the twenty-one books, this would be rejected. Likewise, if somebody read *merkha* in place of *darga* or *darga* in place of *merkha*, the congregation would declare him to be in error in this regard.

II.S.0.5.

So, if there are rules for the accents, there is a need to know them.

חרף שבו ויבוזו מן אלסבי לתאכר אללחן ען אול כלמה אלי
אכרהא

II.S.0.4.

15 ולאן הדה אלקראה אלדי פי ארץ ישראל אלאן הי קראה עזרא
עֹה וגילה לאן מא אנקטעת אלאמה מן ארץ ישראל מן זמאן
עזרא עֹה פי בית שני אלי אלאן אלא מן ירושלם פקט פי זמאן
מלך אדום ללארץֹ וישראל יעלמון אולאדהם אלי אלאן גיל בעד
גיל הדה אלקראה ולאן לו קרא אלאנסאן אלבֹא ספר בלחן אלגֹ
20 אספאר או אלגֹ אספאר בלחן אלבֹא ספר לרד דלך עליה וכדא
לו קרא מוצֹע סלסלה מארכה או מוצֹע מארכה סלסלה לגלטה
אלגמע פי דלך

II.S.0.5.

(S9:1v) ואדא כאן ללאלחאן שרוט פקד דעת אלחאגה אלא
עלמהא

II.S.1.0.

SECTION CONCERNING THE PLACE OF ARTICULATION OF THE LETTERS

II.S.1.1.
The letters consist of twenty-two basic letters. They fall into five groups in five places of articulation, namely אהֿחֿעֿ, גֿיֿכֿרֿקֿ, דֿטֿלֿנֿתֿ, זֿסֿצֿשֿ and בֿוֿמֿףֿ.

II.S.1.2.
Take note that the place of articulation of אהֿחֿעֿ is the root of the tongue and the place of swallowing, that is the throat and the base of the tongue. For this reason they are the lightest of the letters and never take *dagesh*. It may be thought that *he* and *'alef* take *dagesh*, but this is not the case. This is because the dot in the *he* at the end of a word indicates the (consonantal) property of the *he*. Surely you see that the property of the *he* at the beginning and in the middle of a word appears without a dot. As for (the dot in) *'alef* in the four places (where it is found), namely וַיָּבֵיאוּ לֹו 'and they brought him' (Gen. 43.26), תָּבֵיאוּ 'you shall bring' (Lev. 23.17), וַיָּבֵיאוּ לָנוּ 'and they brought to us' (Ezra 8.18), לֹא רֻאֻוּ 'were not seen' (Job 33.21), this reflects a strong effort to pronounce the letter by the reader and is not *dagesh*.

II.S.1.0.

פצל פי מחל אלחרוף

II.S.1.1.

אלחרוף כّב חרפא אצّולא ^(S20:2r) תגׄי כמס אקסאם פי כמסה
מ[חאל והי] אֹהֹחֹע גׄיכֹרֹק דֹטֹלֹנֹת זֹסֹצֹשׁ בֹוֹמֹף

II.S.1.2.

אעלם אן אֹהֹחֹע מחלהא עיקר הלשון ובית הבליעה והו
אלחלקום ואצّל אללّסאן ולדّלך כّאנת אכّף אלחרוף לא ידّכלהא
דגש בّתה ואלהי ואלّאלّף קד יّוצّן אן ידّכלהא דגש וליס אלחّאל
כّדّלך לّאן אלנקטה פי אלהי פי אכّר אלכّלאם תّטّהר טעם אלהّי
אלّי תّרّי אן טעם אלהّי פי אّוّל אלכّלאם ופי וסטה יّטّהר מן דّון
אלנקטה ואלّאלّף פי אלّארّבّעה מّואّצّע אלّתّי הّי ויّביאו לّו תّביאו
ויّביאו לّנّו לّא רّאּו פّהّו תّכّלّף יّתّכّלّפّה אלّקّאּר פّי כّّרّוּגّה שّّדّّידّא
פّّלّّّّّّّّّّ

פّליס הّדّّا דّגש 35

---

27 מ[חאל והי]] מחאל והי S8:1r | אֹהֹחֹע...בֹוֹמֹף] אֹהֹחֹע גׄיכֹק דֹטֹלֹנֹת
זֹסֹצֹרֹשׁ בֹוֹמֹף S9:1v | זֹסֹצֹשׁ] זֹסֹשׂ S8:1r 30 בّתה] אלבّתה S9:1v
ואלהי] אלהא et passim S8:1r | יّוצّן] יّטّן S8:1r 33 אלّארّבّעה] ארבّע
S8:1r

II.S.1.3.

The place of articulation of גִיכְרֹק is the middle of the tongue, in its wide part. The place of articulation of גִ pronounced *rafe* is the third of the tongue adjacent ot the throat.

II.S.1.4.

The place of articulation of דְטֹלְנֹת is the extremity of the tongue in combination with the flesh of the teeth. When the letters דֹת are pronounced *rafe*, the extremity of the tongue is pressed gently onto the flesh of the teeth.

II.S.1.5.

The place of articulation of זֹסְצֹשׁ is the teeth.

II.S.1.6.

The place of articulation of בֹוֹמֹף is the lips. When בֹף are *rafe*, the lips are closed gently while they are pronounced.

II.S.1.7.

It is said that the letters interchange with one another, as in בִּזַּר 'he scattered' (Psa. 68.31) and פִּזַּר 'he has distributed' (Psa. 112.9), יַעֲלֹס 'he will (not) rejoice' (Job 20.18), יַעֲלְץ 'it exults' (1 Chron. 16.32), and similar forms. There are cases of enhancement and reduction. It is preferable, however, not to call it 'interchanging', for it is possible that this takes place for a reason, either to express multiplicity or paucity, or for some

II.S.1.3.

גִّוֹבְרֹק מחלהא וסט אללסאן בערצّה ומחל גַّ אלמורפיין תלת

אללסאן ממא ילי אלחלקום

II.S.1.4.

דֹّטֹלٰנֹתֹ מחלהא טרף אל[לסאן ולח[ם אלאסנאן ודֹתֹ אלמורפیין

[ילצק טרף] אללסאן בלחם אלאסנאן ברפק ^(S20:2v)

II.S.1.5.

40 זֹסֹצֹשֹ מחלהא אלאסנאן

II.S.1.6.

בֹוֹמֹﬞ מחלהא אלשפתין בﬞﬞ אלמרפيין תטבק אלשפתין בהמא

ברפק

II.S.1.7.

אלחרוף יקאל אנהא תנבדל בעﬞ בבעﬞ מתל בَزَر פَّزَر יَعלֹוס

יَעלֹוﬞ ונחו דלך ותﬞי זואיד ונואקﬞ ואלאולא אן לא יקאל דלך

45 לאן ימכן אלתבדיל אדא כאן עלי וגה אמא לכתרה או לקלה או

---

36 גִّוֹבְרٔק [גִّוֹבְרٔק S15:1r   38 אל[לסאן ולח[ם] אללסאן ולחם S8:1v

39 [ילצק טרף[[ילצק טרף S8:1v   40 זֹסֹצٔשٔ [זֹסٔצٔשٔ S15:1r

44 ואלאולא [אלאולא S21:1v

other reason. They give the form *bet* to express one sense and for another sense they give it *pe*. Likewise with יַעֲלֹס, when the joy has a particular sense, they give it *samekh* and for another sense they give it *zayin*, and so forth concerning what I initially said were cases of interchange and inversion.

לוגה מן אלוגוה יגעלוהא בבי ועלי וגה גירה יגעלוהא בפי וכדלך
יעלוס אדא כאן אלמרח עלי וגה יגעלוהא בסמאך ועלי וגה אכר
יגעלוהא בזאי אלי גיר דלך ממא קד כנת פי אלאול אקול אנה
ינבדל וינקלב

---

46 יגעלוהא[¹ יגעלוה S21:1v | בבי] בבא S21:1v | גירה] אכר
S21:1v | יגעלוה[² יגעלוהא S21:1v | בפי] בפא S21:1v
47 יגעלוה [יגעלוהא S21:1v

II.S.2.0.

SECTION CONCERNING אֹוֹיֹהֹ AND בֹּגֹדֹכֹפֹת

II.S.2.1.

When one of these four letters, I mean אֹוֹיֹהֹ, is at the end of a word and the word is conjoined to what follows it by a (conjunctive) accent, and when the second word begins with one these six letters, I mean בֹּגֹדֹכֹפֹת, this letter is pronounced *rafe*, for example כִּי בְאַפָּם הָרְגוּ 'for in their anger they have slain' (Gen. 49.6), וַיְהִי דְבַר־יְהוָה 'and the word of the Lord was' (1 Kings 17.2, etc.), in וְאֶקְחָה פַת־לֶחֶם 'and I shall fetch a morsel of bread' (Gen. 18.5), and similar cases.

II.S.2.2.

There are nine types of cases that break the rule I have just mentioned. These are *'oghera, di-fsiq, di-dhḥiq, 'athe me-raḥiq, mappiq he, mappiq vav, mappiq yod*, two identical letters, *bet* and *pe*.

II.S.2.3.

As for *'oghera*, this is the 'collection' of only seven words. Four of these are in the song וַיּוֹשַׁע (Exod. 14.30, 'the Song of the Sea'). These are גָּאֹה גָּאָה 'he has triumphed gloriously' (Exod. 15.1) and the other case of this (Exod. 15.21), יִדְמוּ כָּאָבֶן 'they are as still as a stone' (Exod. 15.16), מִי כָּמֹכָה נֶאְדָּר בַּקֹּדֶשׁ 'Who is like you, majestic in holiness?' (Exod. 15.11). In the book of Isaiah

פצל פי חרוף אّוّיّה ובّגّדّכّפّתّ

II.S.2.1.

הדה אלארבעה חרוף אעני אّوّيّه אדא כאן אחדהא פי אכר
כלמה וכאנת אלכלמה מّצّאפה אלי מא בעדהא באללחן וכאנת
אלכלמה אלתّאניה אّولّהא אחד הדה אלסתה חרוף אעני בّגّ
כّפّתّ כרّג דלך אלחّרّף מרפّי כّפّיّף כّקّולّה כי באפّם (S20:3r) הרّגّו
ויהי דבר ייי ואקחה פת לחם ואمתאל דלך

II.S.2.2.

ואלדי כרّג ען מא דכרّת תّסّעّה כّואסّר הם אّוّזّיّرّה ودّفّסّיّק
ودّدّחّיّק وّאّתّّא מרّحّיّק ومّفّיّק הי ومّفّיّק ואו ومّفّيّק יוד וحّרّפّין
מתّראّדّفّין وّבّّי وّפّّי

II.S.2.3.

אّوّגّיّرّה גّאّمّעّה לّסّبّعّה כّלّם פّקّט פّקّט ארבעה מّנّהّא פّי שّيّرّה ويّوّשّע

וّהّיّ גّّאّה גّّّаّه וّحّбّيّرّو ידّמّו כّّّّّّّّّّّّّבּּّّّّّّّّّّّّّّّّّّّّ מی כّמّوّכّה נّّّّّّّّّّّّّّّّّّّّّّّّّّّّ ַ

---

there is וְשַׂמְתִּי כַּדְכֹד 'and I shall make (your pinnacles) of agate'
(Isa. 54.12). In the book of Jeremiah there is וְנִלְאֵיתִי כַּלְכֵל וְלֹא אוּכָל
'and I am weary of holding it in and I cannot' (Jer. 20.9). In the
book of Daniel there is וְחָכְמָה כְּחָכְמַת־אֱלָהִין 'and wisdom like
wisdom of the gods' (Dan. 5.11). I do not know any disagreements concerning these seven. In other cases, concerning which
there are disagreements, the reader should choose which of the
variants he wants to read in his reading and nobody can reject
this.

II.S.2.4.

As for *di-fsiq*, whenever *paseq* comes between one of the letters
אוּיה and the letters בֹגֹדֹכֹפֹת, the letters אוּיה have no influence, for
example, יוֹסֵף יְהוָה עַל־עַמּוֹ ׀ כָּהֶם 'May the Lord add to his people (a
hundred times as many) as them' (1 Chron. 21.3), עָשׂוּ ׀ כָּלָה 'they
have done completely' (Gen. 18.21), and similar cases. There is
no exception to this type of case that breaks the rule.

II.S.2.5.

Di-dhḥiq: The meaning of *di-dhḥiq* (literally: what is compressed)
is that between the accent that is in the word containing one of
the אוּיה letters and a בֹגֹדֹכֹפֹת letter there is a vowel and this
vowel is not dwelt upon or prolonged in pronunciation. On
account of this compressed vowel the rule of the אוּיה is broken,
as in וְאָעִידָה בָּם 'that I may call to witness against them' (Deut.
31.28), וְהָגִיתָ בּוֹ 'you shall meditate on' (Josh. 1.8) and similar
cases. The compression may occur in a word that does not have

ישעיה ושמתי כדכד ופי ספר ירמיה ונלאתי כלכל ולא ופי ספר

דניאל וחכמה כחכמת אלהין ומא ערפת פי הולי אלסבעה כלף

ומא עדאהם מן אלכלף אלקאר מכיר פי אלקראה מא אראד מן

אלאכלאף יקרא וליס לאחד אן ירד עליה

II.S.2.4.

65 דפסיק כל מא חצל בין חרף אלאׄוׄיׄה ובין חרף בֹגֹד כֹפֹת פסיק

לא יכון ללאׄוׄיׄה תאתירא מתל יוסף ייי על עמו כהם עשו כלה

ואמתאל דלך וליס עלי הדה אלכאסרה אסתתנא

II.S.2.5.

דדחיק מעני דדחיק הו אן יכון בין אללחן אלדי פי אל (S20:3v)

כלמה אלדי פיהא חרף אלאׄוׄיׄה ובין חרף בֹגֹד כֹפֹת מלך ואחד

70 ולא יתאנא ולא יטול פי אלנטק בדלך אלמלך פלאגל הדא

אלמלך אלצׁייק כסר שרט אלאׄוׄיׄה כקולך ואעׄידה בֹם והגׄית בוׄ

ואמתאל דלך וקד יכון <אלצׁיק> חאצל פי כלמה ליס פיהא

---

61 ושמתי] וסמתי 62 הולי] האולאי S15:1v 63 אלקראה]

קראתה S15:1v 68 אלדי] אלתי S15:2r 71 אלצׁיק] הדא אלצׁיק

S15:2r 72 ואמתאל דלך] ומא מאתל האולאי S15:2r S29:1r

אלצׁיק S4:1v אלצׁיק] S20

an accent but is a small word, as in מַה־תֹּאמַר נַפְשְׁךָ 'whatever your soul says' (1 Sam. 20.4), זֶה־בְּנִי הַחָי 'This is my son that is alive' (1 Kings 3.23), and other similar cases in which the vowel is pronounced compressed. Surely you see in אֲשֶׁר הוֹרַדְתֵּנוּ בּוֹ 'through which you let us down' (Josh. 2.18), in which the vowel after the accent is pronounced long with exhalation of breath, the same, or approximately the same, as other (long) vowels, the *bet* of בּוֹ does not have *dagesh*. If you examine this closely, you will discern the difference.

II.S.2.6.

ʾAthe me-raḥiq is the opposite of the previous type of case that breaks the rule, because this one (i.e. *ʾathe me-raḥiq*) is on account of what is far and that one (i.e. *di-dhḥiq*) is on account of what is near. This (i.e. *ʾathe me-raḥiq*) arises from the fact that due to the distance of the accent (from the preceding conjunctive accent), one comes upon it (the accent) like a ballista and so the בֹּגֹדֹכֹפֹת letters are pronounced with *dagesh*, as in הוּא יִבְנֶה־בַּיִת לִשְׁמִי 'He will build a house for my name' (2 Sam. 7.13), הֲלַמֵּתִים תַּעֲשֶׂה־פֶּלֶא 'Do you work wonders for the dead?' (Psa. 88.11), סוּרָה שְׁבָה־פֹּה 'Turn aside, sit here' (Ruth 4.1). Also (included in this category) are cases in which there is no (conjunctive) accent, so (such cases must be considered) to have a virtual (conjunctive) accent before them in order to conform to (cases such as) הוּא יִבְנֶה־בַּיִת לִשְׁמִי, as in וְאֵלְכָה אֵלֶיהָ וְאֶדְרְשָׁה־בָּהּ 'that I may go to her and inquire of her' (1 Sam. 28.7), and similar cases.

טעם גיר אנהא תכון כלמה צגירה כקולך מה תאמר נפשך זה

בני החי ומא מאתלהמא ממא יגי <אלנטק> באלמלך אלצّייק

אלי תרי אלי קולך אשר הורדתינו בו למא גא פי <אלמלך> 75

אלדי בעד אלטעם תוסע ב<תנפיס> יגרי מגרי מלך אכר או

קריב מנה לם יגי אלבי מן <בו> דגש ואדא תאמלת וגדת

אלפרק

II.S.2.6.

אֲתָא מרחיק באלעכס מן אלבّאסרה אלמתקדמה לאן הדה למא

בֻעֻד ותיד למא קָרֻב והו אן כמא יבעד אללחן ינצב עליה 80

כאלמנגניק פידגש <חרוף> בֻّגֻّד כֻّפֻّת כֻקֻ הוא יבנה בית הלמתים

תעשה פלא סורה שבה פה ומא לם יכון פיה לחן פהו (S20:4r)

בתקדיר לחן קבלה ליגרי מגרי הוא יבנה בית כקוֹ ואלכה אליה

ואדרשה בה ומא מאתלהא

74 אלנטק] S15:2v אלנטק S20   75 אלמלך] S15:2v + צّיק S20

76 תנפיס] S15:2v תפוס S20   77 בו] S15:2v בי S20   81 חרוף]

S15:2v אלצّייק S20

II.S.2.7.

So far four types of cases that break the rule have been discussed. The fifth type of case that breaks the rule is *mappiq he*. The meaning of the term *mappiq he* is the (consonantal) pronunciation of the *he* and its appearance. It is derived from וְדָתָא נֶפְקַת 'and the decree went forth' (Dan. 2.13), that is נָפְקָה. This is because when the *he* is pronounced at the end of a word, the rule of the אֹוֹיֹה letters is broken, as in מַחֲצִיתָה בַּבֹּקֶר 'half of it in the morning' (Lev. 6.13), הִיא וְכָל־אֲשֶׁר אִתָּהּ בַּבַּיִת 'she and all those who are with her in the house' (Josh. 6.17), וְלַהּ גַּפִּין אַרְבַּע 'and it has four wings' (Dan. 7.6), and similar cases. There are no exceptions to this breaking of the rule at all.

II.S.2.8.

The sixth type of case that breaks the rule is *mappiq vav*. This is because every *vav* at the end of a word is pronounced according to the view of the Palestinians as a *bet rafe*, which breaks the rule of the אֹוֹיֹה, as in חֲצֵרֹתָיו בִּתְהִלָּה '(enter) his courts with praise' (Psa. 100.4), אֵלָיו פִּי־קָרָאתִי 'I cried aloud to him' (Psa. 66.17), and similar cases. There are only two words that are exceptions to this breaking of the rule, namely וְנָטָה עָלֶיהָ קַו־תֹהוּ 'He will stretch the line of confusion over it' (Isa. 34.11), וְקוֹל הָמוֹן שָׁלֵו בָהּ 'The sound of a carefree multitude was with her' (Ezek. 23.42).

II.S.2.9.

The seventh type of case that breaks the rule is *mappiq yod*. This is that whenever *yod* occurs at the end of a word and the next word begins with one of the בֹּגֹדֹכֹפֹּתֹ letters, and *ḥireq* or *ṣere*, I mean a dot or two dots, occur under the letter before the *yod*, then the rule of אֹוֹיֹה is observed, as in לִבְנִי בְנוֹ 'Libni his son' (1 Chron. 6.14), כִּי בְקָקוּם 'for they have stripped them' (Nahum 2.3), שָׂרֵי פְלִשְׁתִּים 'the princes of the Philistines' (1 Sam. 18.30),

II.S.2.7.

85 אלאן קד מצֿא ארבעה כואסר אלכאסרה אלכאמסה מפיק הי

מעני מפיק הי הו כרוג אלהי וטֿהורהא ואשתקאקהא מן דָּתָה

נִפְקַת נפקה והו אן אלהי אדֿא טֿהר פי אכר אלכלמה כסר שרט

אלאֹוֹיֹה כך מחציתה בבקר היא וכל אשר אתה ולה גפין

ארבע ומא מאתל דלך ומא עלי הדה אלכאסרה שי מן

90 אלמסתתנא בתה

II.S.2.8.

אלכאסרה אלסאדסה מפיק ואו ודאך אן כל ואו פי אכר כלמה

יכרג עלי ראי אלשאמיין בבי מרפי יכסר עלי שרט אלאֹוֹיֹה

כקולך חצרותיו בתהלה אליו פי קראתי ואמתאלהמא ואלדֿי

יסתתנא עליה הדה אלכאסרה לפצֿתין פקט המא ונטה עליה קו

95 תהו שלו בה

II.S.2.9.

אלכאסרה אלסאבעה יוד והו אן אן יכון פי אכר כלמה

ואול אלאכר חרף מן חרוף בֹגֹדֹ כֹפֹתֿ ותחת אלחרף אלדֿי קבל

אליוד חרק או צרי אעני נקטה או (S20:4v) נקטתין פֿאן שרט

אלאֹוֹיֹה תֿאבת פיה כך לבְנֵי בנו כִי בקקים שָׂרֵי פֿלשתים

and similar cases. If vowels that are different from the aforementioned occur under the aforementioned letter, the *yod* is strengthened and the rule of אֹוֹיֵה is not observed, as in אוּלַי תַּעֲרוֹצִי 'perhaps you may inspire terror' (Isa. 47.12), יָאְתְרַי בְּנוֹ 'Jeatherai his son' (1 Chron. 6.6), כִּי מִי־גוֹי גָּדוֹל 'for what great nation' (Deut. 4.7), and similar cases. One word is an exception to this breaking of the rule.

II.S.2.10.

The eighth type of case that breaks the rule is the succession of two letters. If two *bets* or *kafs*, but not the remaining letters, I mean בֹּגֹדֹכֹפֹת, succeed one another and under the first of them there is a *shewa*, then the rule of אֹוֹיֵה is broken, as in וַיְהִי בְּבוֹאָהּ 'and when she came' (Josh. 15.18), וַתִּתְפְּשֵׂהוּ בְּבִגְדוֹ 'and she caught him by his garment' (Gen. 39.12), הֲלֹא כְּכַרְכְּמִישׁ 'Is it not like Carchemish?' (Isa. 10.9), and other cases. If a vowel occurs under the first of the two instead of *shewa*, the rule of אֹוֹיֵה is observed, as in וְהוּא אִשָּׁה בִבְתוּלֶיהָ יִקָּח 'And he (shall take) a wife in her virginity' (Lev. 21.13), אֲזַלוּ בִבְהִילוּ לִירוּשְׁלֶם 'They went in haste to the Jews' (Ezra 4.23), and similar cases.

II.S.2.11.

The ninth type of case that breaks the rule is *bet* and *pe*. The statement concerning them is similar to the statement regarding the preceding type of case that breaks the rule, without there being any disagreement. This is that when *bet* is followed by *pe* and *shewa* is below the *bet*, the rule of אֹוֹיֵה is broken, as in וְאִכָּבְדָה בְּפַרְעֹה 'and I will get glory over Pharaoh' (Exod. 14.4), וּדְבָרַי אֲשֶׁר־שַׂמְתִּי בְּפִיךָ 'and my words which I have put in your mouth' (Isa. 59.21), and similar cases. If a vowel occurs instead of *shewa*, then the rule of אֹוֹיֵה is observed, as in אַל־יֵרֶא בִפְלַגּוֹת נַהֲרֵי 'He will not look upon the rivers, the streams' (Job 20.17).

ואמתאל דלך פאן צאר תחת אלחרף אלמדכור סוא אלמלכין 100

אלמדכורין אשתד אליוד ולם יתבת שרט אלאَוَّיֹה כקו אולי

תערוצי יאתרי בנו ומי גוי גדול ואמתאל דלך ויסתתני עלי דלך

בלפצֹה ואחדה

II.S.2.10.

אלכאסרה אלתאמנה חרפין מתראדפין כל בֵֿאֵין או כאפין

תראדפא אלוّاحד בעד אלאכר מן דון בקיה אלחרוף אَעני בֹّّגֹ 105

כֹّّפֹת וכאן תחת אלאول מנהמא שוא כסר שרט אלאَוَّיֹה מתל

ויהי בבואה ותתפשיהו בבגדו והלא ככרכמיש אלי גיר דלך פאן

כאן תחת אלاول מנהמא עוֹّّ אלשוא מלך תבת שרט אלאَוَّיֹה

כקו והוא אשה בבתוליה יקח אזלו בבהילו לירושלם

ואמתאלהמא 110

II.S.2.11.

אלכאסרה אלתאסעה בי ו פי אלכלאם פיהא כאלכלאם פי

אלכאסרה אלתי קבלהא מן גיר כלף והו אן כל בי ובעדה פי

אדא כאן תחת אלבי שוא כסר שרט אלاَوَّיֹה כקו ואכבדה

בפרעה אשר שמתי (S20:5r) בפיך ומא מאתלהמא פאن צאר עוֹّ

אלשוא מלך תבת שרט אלاَوَّיֹה כקו אל ירא בפלגות נהרי 115

II.S.2.12.

Take note that seven cases of *kaf* after וַיְהִי are the subject of disagreement, some pronounce them with *dagesh* and others pronounce them with *rafe,* namely וַיְהִי כִשְׁמֹעַ אֲדֹנָיו 'when his master heard' (Gen. 39.19), וַיְהִי כְשָׁמְעוֹ 'and when he heard' (Gen. 39.15), וַיְהִי כִרְאוֹתוֹ 'and when he saw' (Jud. 11.35), וַיְהִי כִרְאוֹת 'and when (the king) saw' (Esther 5.2), וַיְהִי כְהוֹצִיאָם 'and when they brought (them) out' (Gen. 18.17), וַיְהִי כִמְלֹכוֹ 'when he became king' (1 Kings 15.29), וַיְהִי כַאֲשֶׁר־תַּמּוּ 'and when they perished' (Deut. 2.16).[2] The reader makes a choice: if he wants, he strengthens them (with *dagesh*), and if he wants, he pronounces them with *rafe.*

II.S.2.13.

Take note that the criterion of the (rule of) the אוֹיה letters and the בּגֹדכֹפֹת letters should be based on pronunciation and not on writing. For example in וַיַּרְא בָּלָק 'and Balak saw' (Num. 22.2) the *bet* is pronounced with *dagesh,* because the last letter heard when you read וַיַּרְא is *resh.* An opposite case is וְעָשִׂיתָ בַדֵּי עֲצֵי שִׁטִּים 'and you will make poles of acacia wood' (Exod. 25.23). The last letter heard when you read the word וְעָשִׂיתָ is ʾ*alef* or *he,* and therefore the *bet* of בַדֵּי is pronounced *rafe.* This is the principle throughout the reading of Scripture.

---

[2] The fuller citation וַיְהִי כַאֲשֶׁר־תַּמּוּ as opposed to simply וַיְהִי כַאֲשֶׁר in the text of *Hidāyat al-Qāriʾ* is given in *Kitāb al-Khilaf* (ed. Lipschütz, 1965, 19).

II.S.2.12.

ואעלם אן סבעה כאפאת בעד ויהי הי כלף בעץׄ ידגשהא ובעץׄ

ירפיהא והי כשמוע כשמעו כראותו כראות כהוציאם כמלכו

כאשר אלקאר מכייר אן ‹שא› ישד ואן שא ירפי

II.S.2.13.

ואעלם אן אלמעול פי אלאוֹיֹה ובْגֹד כֹפֿתׄ עלי אללפֿטׄ לא עלי

אלכט מתל וירא בלק גא אלבי מדגוש לאן אכר חרף סמע מנך

פי וירא אלריש ובעכסה ועשית בדי עצי אכר חרף סמע מנך פי

ועשית אמא אלף ואמא הי פלדלך גא אלבי מרפי מן בْדי ועלי

הדה אלסירה תסיר פי אלמקרא כלה

II.S.3.0.

(*TAV*)

Take note that *tav* in three places is strengthened with *dagesh* to a greater degree than (other) cases of *tav* with *dagesh*. These are וַיְשִׂימֶהָ תֵּל־עוֹלָם שְׁמָמָה 'He made it an eternal heap of ruins' (Josh. 8.28), וְאֶת־בָּתָּיו וְגִנְזַכָּיו 'and its houses and its treasuries' (1 Chron. 28.11), וְגֻבְרַיָּא אִלֵּךְ תְּלָתֵהוֹן 'and these three men' (Dan. 3.23). Note that there is disagreement concerning every *tav* in the form בָּתִּים, except in וְאֶת־בָּתָּיו וְגִנְזַכָּיו (1 Chron. 28.11). Whoever wishes to pronounce it with the normal *dagesh* of *tav*, may do so and whoever wishes to pronounce it with the heaviness of the *tav* of וְאֶת־בָּתָּיו וְגִנְזַכָּיו (1 Chron. 28.11), may do so, on condition that this is when there is a conjunctive accent and a disjunctive accent in the word without an intervening letter.

ואעלם אן אלתיו ידגש פי תלתה ומואצֵע זאידא ען סאיר

125 אלתֵוֹאת מדגושה והי וישימיה תל עולם שממה ובֹתֿיו וגנזכיו

וגבריא אלך תלתהון ואעלם אן כל תיו פי לשון מא סוא

ובתיו וגנזכיו הו כלף ומן אראד אן יכרגה בדגש אלתיו אלמעהוד

אכרגה ומן אראד יכרגה <בתקל> (S20:5v) תיו ובתיו אכרגה

בשרט אנה אדא כאן פי אללפטֹה כאדם ולחן וליס בינהמא חרף

II.S.4.0.

SECTION CONCERNING THE VOWELS

II.S.4.1.
What is to be said concerning the vowels is manifest and clear, and not obscure, because it is through them that the purpose of a speaker is understood, and without them speech would be nonsense. A letter can be without a vowel, but a vowel cannot be without a letter.

II.S.4.2.
The total number of vowels is seven: אָ, אַ, אֶ, אֵ, אִ, א and אֹ. From within these seven vowels the letters א, ה, ו, and י are pronounced. From *qameṣ*, *pataḥ* and *segol*[3] *ʾalef* and *he* are pronounced, as in עֲבָדֶיךָ, עֲמֶיךָ and קָשֶׁה. If the *he* (in קָשֶׁה) were elided, the *segol* (by itself) would indicate its existence, just as the *qameṣ* in עֲמְךָ, שְׁמְךָ and עֲבָדֶיךָ indicates the existence of *ʾalef* or *he* in full orthography. Likewise שָׁמַר and זָכַר—the *pataḥ* indicates the existence of *ʾalef*. *Ḥolem*[4] indicates the existence of *vav*, as in זוֹכֵר, שׁוֹמֵר and the like. *Ṣere*[5] and *ḥireq*[6] indicate the existence of *yod*, as in עֵינִי, since the *yod* is frequently written defectively but these two vowels indicate its existence.

---

[3] Literally: the three (points). | [4] Literally: the point above. | [5] Literally: the two points. | [6] Literally: the point below.

II.S.4.0.

פצל[S8:2v] פי אלכלאם פי אלמלוך

II.S.4.1.

אלכלאם פי אלמלוך טֹאהר גֹלי גֹיר כפי לאן בהא יפהם ען אלמתכלם גרצֹה ולולאהא לכאן אלכלאם עבתא [S15:3r] פחרף קד יכון בגיר מלך ומלך לא יכון בגיר חרף

II.S.4.2.

וגמיע אלמלוך סבעה והם אָ אַ אֶ אֵ אִ אֹ אֻ ויכרג מן צֹמן הדה אלסבעה חרוף אלאֿוֿיֿהֿ יכרג ען אלקמץ ואלפתח ואלתלאתה אלף והא והי מתל עבדיך <עמיך> קָשֶׁה לו חדף אלהא לכאן אלגֹ קד דלת עליה כמא דלת אלקמץ פי <עמך ושמך וַעֲבָדֶיךָ פי אלמלא עלי אלף או הא> וכדלך שָׁמַר וְזָכַר קד דלת אלפתחה עלי אלף <ואלנקטה מן פוק תדל עלי ואו מתל זוֹכֵר שׁוֹמֵר> ומא מאתלהמא ואלנקטתין <ואלנקטה מן אספל> תדל עלי יוד מתל <עיני> לאן קד יגֹי אליוד פי כתיר מן אלמואצֹע חסר והדין אל

---

136 עמיך] S17:1v עמך S15 137 עמד...138 הא] S17:1v עִמְּכָהֿ וּשְׁמְכָהֿ ופי אלמלא עלי אלף S15 פי עמךָ ושמךָ ועבדיךָ פי אלמלא עלי אלף S16:4r 139 ואלנקטה...שׁוֹמֵר] S17:1v ואלנקטה מן פוק ואלשָׁרוק תדל עלי ואו מתל זוֹכֵר שׁוֹמֵר יָקם כֶּפֶּר S15 140 ואלנקטה...אספל] S18:7r אלחֵרֶק S15 141 עיני] S17:1v עֵנִי S15

Qibbuṣ[7] and *shureq*[8] indicate the existence of *vav* as in קוּמוּ. So what is pronounced from within the seven vowels are the letters א, ה, ו, and י.

---

[7] Literally: the arrowhead. | [8] Literally: the point in the heart of the *vav*.

(S15:3v) אלמלכין ידלאן עליה >ואלזֶג ואלנקטה פי קלב אלואו
ידלאן עלי אלואו מתל קומו< פצאר אלכארג מן צֶמן אלמלוך
אלסבעה אֹהֹוֹוֹ

---

142 ואלזֶג...143 קומו] S18:7r S15 *omitted*

II.S.5.0.

SECTION CONCERNING THE *SHEWA*

II.S.5.1.

The *shewa* is to be classified into two categories: quiescent and mobile. The distinctive feature of the quiescent *shewa* is that it makes quiescent the letter under which it is present and puts it in the group (of letters) that precedes it, as in יִשְׂרָאֵל 'Israel', יֶחְדְּיָהוּ 'Jehdeiah', זִמְרִי 'Zimri', לְמִשְׁעִי 'for cleansing' (Ezek. 16.4), וּפִסְלִי וְנִסְכִּי 'my graven image and my molten image' (Isa. 48.5). So the letter under which it is present has become quiescent, and has been separated from what follows it and conjoined to what is before it. It is also distinctive of its nature that it divides a word into (units that have) the status of words. This is because every letter at the end of word that is without a vowel and quiescent becomes the stopping point of the word and its place of division, like the *tav* in בְּרֵאשִׁית 'in the beginning' and like the *resh* in אוֹר 'light'. Likewise (a quiescent letter) in the middle (of a word) has the status of a stopping point, as in הַמְצַפְצְפִים 'those who chirp' (Isa. 8.19), תִּרְכַּבְנָה 'they (fpl.) ride', תִּשְׁלַחְנָה 'they (fpl.) send'. Each one of these words has the status of three words on account of the quiescent *shewa*. If it were absent, such a division would not be correct.

II.S.5.2.

The distinctive feature of the mobile (*shewa*) is that when it is under a letter, the letter is not static or at rest, as, for example, the *zayin* in זְכוֹר and the *shin* in שְׁמוֹר, and similar cases. Just as a quiescent letter groups with what comes before it, a mobile letter groups with what is after it, the opposite (of what is the

II.S.5.0.

פצל פי אלכלאם עלי אלשוא

II.S.5.1.

אלשוא ינקסם קסמין סאכן ומתחרך עלאמה אלסאכן אנה יסכן
אלחרף אלדי הוא תחתה ויגעלה פי חזב מא תקדמה נחו יִשְׂרָאֵל
יחדיהו זמרי למשעי ופסלי ונסכי פצאר אלחרף אלדי תחתה
סאכנא ואנפצל ממא בעדה ואנטאף אלי מא קבלה ומן
עלאמתה איצֹא אנה יקסם אלכלמה מתאבה כלם לאן כל חרף
הו פי אכר כלמה אדא ערי מן מלך כאן סאכן לאנה יציר מחט
אלכלמה ומקטעהא נחו אלתאו מן בראשית ונחו אלריש פי אור
וכדלך חכמה פי אלוסט יציר מחט עלי וגֹה המצפצפים תרכבנה
תשלחנה צאר (S15:4r) כל כלמה מן האולאי מתאבה גֹ כלם
לאגֹל אלשוא אלסאכן ולו אנעדם לם תצח אלקסמה

II.S.5.2.

עלאמה אלמתחרך הו אנה אדא כאן תחת חרף לא יסתקר דלך
אלחרף ולא יסכן נחו אלזֹאי מן זכור ואלשין מן שמור
ואמתאלהמא וכמא צאר אלסאכן מתחייז אלי מא קבלה כדא
צאר אלמתחרך מתחייז אלי מא בעדה באלעכס מן אלסאכן

case) with a quiescent letter, as in מַלְכְּכֶם 'your (pl.) king', in which the *lamed* is quiescent with a quiescent *shewa* and groups with the *mem*, whereas the *kaf* is mobile with a mobile *shewa* and groups with the next *kaf*. The same applies to וַיִּשְׁכְּבוּ 'and they lay down', וַיִּקְבְּרוּ 'and they buried', and similar cases.

II.S.5.3.

If there is doubt in some cases as to whether the *shewa* is quiescent or mobile, the endowing of heaviness to the letter before the letter with the *shewa* indicates that it is mobile. This applies to הַמְ at the beginning of words. When *shewa* is under the *mem* and *pataḥ* is under the *he* and it (i.e. the *pataḥ*) is made heavy, then the *shewa* is mobile.

II.S.5.4.

The mobility of the *shewa* can also be ascertained by the number of letters of the word. If there are five letters, then the *shewa* is mobile, as in הַמְקַנֵּא 'are (you) jealous?' (Num. 11.29), הַמְחַכֶּה 'the one who waits' (Dan. 12.12), הַמְשַׂמֵּחַ 'one that cheers' (Jud. 9.13), הַמְדַבֵּר 'the one that speaks' (Gen. 45.12, etc.), and similar cases, except for one word, namely מַדּוּעַ בָּא־הַמְשֻׁגָּע הַזֶּה 'why did this madman come' (2 Kings 9.11). The number of letters is five but the *shewa* is not mobile. The reason for this is that the *he* has not been made heavy. If words consist of more than five letters and *he* and *mem* are at their beginning, the *shewa* in them is sometimes quiescent and sometimes mobile. The rule concerning this is that if the accent is on the fifth letter, or one after this, then the *shewa* is quiescent, such as הַמְדַבְּרִים 'the ones

160 מתל מַלְכְּבֶם אלדי אללמד סאכן באלשוא אלסאכן ואנחאז אלי

אלמים ואלכף תחרך באלשוא אלמתחרך ואנחאז אלי אלכף

אלאכר ונחו וישכבו ויקברו ואמתאל דלך

II.S.5.3.

ואדא אשתכל אלשוא פי בעץ אלמואצֵע הל הוא סאכן או

מתחרך פאלתתקיל פי אלחרף אלדי קבל חרף אלשוא ידל עלי

165 אנה (S15:4v) מתחרך מן דלך <הַמְ> פי אואיל אלכלאם אדא

כאן תחת אלמם שוא ותחת אלהא פתחה והו מתקל פאן

אלשוא מתחרך

II.S.5.4.

יעתבר איצֵא תחריך אלשוא בעדד חרוף אלכלמה אן כאנת

כמסה חרוף פאלשוא מתחרך מתל המקנא המחכה הַמְשַׁמֵּחַ

170 המדבר ונחוהם אלא כלמה ואחדה והי מדוע <בא> המשגע

הזה אלעדד כמסה חרוף ולם יתחרך אלשוא ואלסבב פי דלך אן

אלהא גיר מתקל פאן כאן מן אלכלאם אלתי הי אזיד מן כמסה

חרוף ואלהֹמֹ הא ואלמים פי אולהא פאלשוא פיהא תארה סאכן

ותארה מתחרך פאלשרט פי דלך הוא אן כאן אללחן עלי

175 אלחרף אלכאמס (S9:2r) ומא זאד כאן אלשוא סאכן מתל

---

165 הַמְ] S18:8r S7:6v תַמְ S15   170 בא] S15 omitted

speaking' (Exod. 6.27, etc.), הַמְאָרֲרִים (Num. 5.19) 'those that curse' (Num. 5.22, etc.), הַמְצַפְצְפִים 'those who chirp' (Isa. 8.19), apart from the exceptions (to this rule) הַמְבַקְשִׁים (Exod. 4.19) 'those who seek', הַמְצֹרָעִים 'the lepers' (2 Kings 7.8), and similar cases.

II.S.5.5.

The *shewa* on successive identical letters in the middle of a word can also give rise to uncertainty, when *shewa* is on the first of the two, as to whether this is mobile or quiescent. Consideration should be made as to whether there is heaviness in (the vowel of) the letter before them (i.e. the two successive letters). If this occurs, either through a *gaʿya*, or an accent or the lengthening of a vowel, then the *shewa* is mobile, as in וּבָזְזוּ אֶת־בֹּזְזֵיהֶם 'they will plunder those who plundered them' (Ezek. 39.10), וְשָׁלְלוּ אֶת־שֹׁלְלֵיהֶם 'they will despoil those who despoiled them' (Ezek. 39.10), וּלְלַמְּדָם סֵפֶר 'and to teach them the writing' (Dan. 1.4), and similar cases, except for six cases, in which heaviness occurs (on the vowel of the preceding letter) but the *shewa* is not mobile, namely אָז יִקְרָאֻנְנִי וְלֹא אֶעֱנֶה יְשַׁחֲרֻנְנִי וְלֹא יִמְצָאֻנְנִי 'Then they will call upon me, but I will not answer; they will seek me diligently but will not find me' (Prov. 1.28), בַּצַּר לָהֶם יְשַׁחֲרֻנְנִי 'and in their distress they seek me' (Hos. 5.15), אֲנִי אֹהֲבַי אֵהָב וּמְשַׁחֲרַי יִמְצָאֻנְנִי 'I love those who love me, and those who seek me diligently find me' (Prov. 8.17), . זֹבֵחַ תּוֹדָה יְכַבְּדָנְנִי 'He who brings thanksgiving as his sacrifice honours me' (Psa. 50.23).

המדברים המאררים המצפצפים אלא שואד המבקשים

המצורעים ונחוהמא

II.S.5.5.

וקד ילבס אלשוא פי אלחרפין אלמתראדפין פי וסט אלכלמה

אדא כאן תחת אלאול מנהמא שוא אהו מתחרך אם סאכן

פליעתבר באלתתקיל פי אלחרף אלדי קבלהמא אן כאן 180

<חאצל> או בגעיה או בטעם או אסתיפא מלך פאלשוא

מתחרך מתל ובָזְזוּ אֶת בֹּוזְזֵיהֶם וְשָׁלְלוּ אֶת שֹׁלְלֵיהֶם וּלֲלַמְדָם

סֵפֶּר ואמתאל דלך מא סוי סת מואצֹע פאן אלתתקיל חאצל

ומא תחרך אלשוא והם אז יִקְרָאוּנְנִי וְלֹא אַעֲנֶה יְשַׁחֲרֻנְנִי וְלֹא

ימצאונני בצר להם ישחרונני אני אוהבי אהב ומשחרי (S9:2v) 185

ימצאונני זובח תודה יכבדנני:

II.S.5.6.

Take note that a mobile *shewa* never occurs on a second letter
(of a word) that has a silent (following letter), because it (this
second letter) is mobile due to the mobility of the first letter
with *shewa*. A (*shewa* on) the third letter after (an initial mobile)
shewa may be quiescent or mobile, as in לְיִשְׂרָאֵל 'to Israel', בְּיִרְמְיָהוּ
'against Jeremiah' (Jer. 29.27, etc.), לְיָשְׁבְּקָשָׁה 'to Joshbekashah'
(1 Chron 25.24).

II.S.5.7.

Take note that when a letter has a vowel under it, the letter is
mobile and quiescence occurs in the following (letter), for
example in שָׁמַר and קָבַר quiescence occurs on the *ʾalef* that is
pronounced from within the *qameṣ* and the *pataḥ*.

II.S.5.6.

ואעלם אן אלשוא אלמתחרך לא יקע פי אלחרף אלתאני לה

סכון בתה לאנה יתחרך לאגל חרכת אלואו באלשוא ואלתאלת

ללשוא קד יכון סאכן וקד יכון מתחרך מתל לישראל בירמיה

לישבקשה   190

II.S.5.7.

^(S12:1r) ואעלם אן אלחרף אדא כאן תחתה מלך כאן דלך

אלחרף מתחרך ואלסכון קד יקע פי אלתאני מתל שָׁמַר קָבַר

אלסכון יקע פי אלאלף אלכארג֗ מן אלקאמצה ואלפאתחה:

II.S.6.0.

The (discussion of the) mobile *shewa* should be divided into various subsections.

II.S.6.1. The First Subsection

II.S.6.1.1.
This concerns the influence that it undergoes in connection with the letters א, ה, ח and ע. When these four letters are preceded by a letter that is not one of them and under this letter there is *shewa*, this *shewa* is pronounced as a short (vowel) with the pronunciation of the vowel that is under the four letters, unless it is appropriate for *ga'ya* to be combined with it. If this may appropriately be combined with it, it is pronounced with the pronunciation of the vowel equal (in length), as in וְאִם־יִוָּתֵ֣ר 'and if there remains' (Exod. 29.34), וְאִם־כָּ֫כָה 'and if thus' (Num. 11.15), וְאֶת־מִגְרָשֶׁ֔יהָ 'and its surrounding pasture lands' (1 Chron 6.40, etc.), וְאֶת־בָּנָ֑יו 'and his sons' (Gen. 9.1, etc.). This is a sample of cases with *ʾalef*.

II.S.6.1.2.
He: When *shewa* is before *he*, the *shewa* is pronounced (with the same pronunciation) as the pointing of the *he*, for example in וְהָיָה the *vav* is pronounced with a short *qames* and in וְהָיָ֫ה the *shewa* is pronounced with long *qames* on account of the *ga'ya*.

II.S.6.1.3.
Ḥeth: וְחֵ֥שֶׁב אֲפֻדָּתוֹ 'and the skilfully woven band' (Exod. 28.8, etc.), וְחָלָ֥ה חֶ֖רֶב 'and the sword will rage' (Hos. 11.6), כִּי־רְחוֹקָה־הִ֣יא 'because it is far' (Jdg 18.28).

II.S.6.0.

אלשוא אלמתחרך הו אלמפתן באלפנון

II.S.6.1. אלפן אלאול

II.S.6.1.1.

הו מא יחצל לה מן אלתאתיר פי ארבע חרוף אֹהֹחֹעֹ פאן הדה
אלארבע חרוף אדא כאן קבל אחדהא חרף מן סואהא תחתה
שוא כרג דלך אלשוא בכרוג אלמלך אלדי תחת אלארבעה
חרוף (S12:1v) מכפפא אלא אן כאן יחסן מעה דכול אלגעיה פאן
חסן מעה דכולהא כרג בכרוג אלמלך סוא נחו ואם יותר ואם
ככה ואת מגרשיה ואת בניו הדא נמודג פי אלאלף

II.S.6.1.2.

אלהא אדא כאן אלשוא קבל אלהא כרג אלשוא בנקט אלהא
נחו והיה כרג אלואו בקאמצה כפיפה והיה כרג אלשוא
בקאמצה תקילה לאגל אלגעיה

II.S.6.1.3.

אלחֵית וחשב אפדתו וחלה חרב כי רחוקה היא

II.S.6.1.4.

ʿAyin: בָּרוּךְ יְהוָה לְעוֹלָם 'blessed be the Lord for ever' (Psa. 89.53), יְהִי שְׁמוֹ לְעוֹלָם 'may his name be for ever' (Psa. 72.17), בְּעֵינֵי אֱלֹהִים 'in the eyes of God' (Prov. 3.4), וְאִם רַע בְּעֵינֵיכֶם 'and if it is bad in your eyes' (Josh. 24.15).

II.S.6.1.5.

Now this rule is applied to *shewa* with the four letters when the *shewa* is under a letter that is not one of these four. If it is one of the four letters, the rule does not apply, as in יִמְחֲאוּ־כָף 'let them clap their hands' (Psa. 98.8, etc.), אֱלָהֲהוֹן דִּי 'the God of' (Dan. 3.28, etc.).

II.S.6.1.6.

Take note that when *shewa* occurs under *vav* before a letter of (the verbal prefixes) א, י, נ or ת, it is more suitable (to express) the future than the past. When instead of the *shewa* a vowel appears under the *vav*, it is more suitable (to express) the past than the future tense, as in וָאֶעְדֵּךְ עֶדִי וָאֶתְּנָה 'and I decorated you with ornaments and I gave' (Ezek. 16.11), וָאָקֻם בַּבֹּקֶר 'and I rose in the morning' (1 Kings 3.21). If a *shewa* had occurred in place of these *qameṣ* vowels, the verb would have been future. This is one of the functions of the *shewa*.

II.S.6.2. The Second Subsection

II.S.6.2.1.

When *shewa* comes before *yod*, the *shewa* is always pronounced as *ḥireq*, irrespective as to what pointing the *yod* has, as in כִּי בְיַד־אִשָּׁה 'for into the hand of woman' (Jud. 4.9), בְּיוֹם הִקְרִיב 'on the day he consecrated' (Lev. 7.35), לְיַבָּשָׁה 'into dry land' (Psa. 66.6), לְיוֹרָם 'of Joram' (2 Kings 8.16), and similar cases.

II.S.6.1.4.

אלעין ברוך יוי לעולם יהי שמו לעולם בעיני אלהים ואם רע

בעיניכם

II.S.6.1.5.

אלאן הדא אלשרט לאזם פי אלשוא מע אלארבעה חרוף מתי

כאן אלשוא תחת חרף מן סוי אלארבעה פאנה אן כאן מן

אלארבעה בטל הדא אלשרט נחו ימחאו כף אלההום די   210

II.S.6.1.6.

ואעלם אן אדא גֵֿאת אלשוא תחת ואו קבל (S12:2r) חרף אינת

כאנת באלאסתקבאל אחק מן אלמאצֿי ואדא גֵֿא תחת אלואו

עוֹץֿ אלשוא מלך כאן באלמאצֿי אחק מן אלזמאן אלמסתקבל

נחו ואעדך עדי ואתנה ואקום בבקר ולו גֵֿאת אלשוא מוצֵֿע הדה

אלקואמֵֿץ כאן אלפעל מסתקבל והדה הו מן פואיד אלשוא   215

II.S.6.2. אלפן אלתאני

II.S.6.2.1.

אלשוא אדא כאן קבל יוד כרגֵֿ אלשוא אבדא בנקטה מן אספל

ולא יעתבר בנקט אליוד אישיהו מתל כי ביד אשה ביום הקריב

ליבשה ליורם ונחו דלך

II.S.6.2.2.

Take note that when *shewa* occurs before *yod*, it generally indicates the indefinite, whereas a vowel before it indicates the definite, as in בְּיֹום זִבְחֲכֶם 'on the day of your sacrifice' (Lev. 19.6), (which is) indefinite, and בַּיֹּום הַהוּא כֶּרֶם 'on that day, a vineyard' (Isa. 27.2), (which is) definite, and so forth.

II.S.6.3. The Third Subsection

II.S.6.3.1.

The remainder of the primary letters of Hebrew are seventeen, and to these should be added *yod*, so they come to eighteen. When *shewa* is under one of these eighteen at the beginning of a word, or in the middle of a word, where it has the same status (as one at) the beginning (of a word), the *shewa* is pronounced as a short *pataḥ* when it is not accompanied by a *gaʿya* and as a long *pataḥ* when it is accompanied by a *gaʿya*, as in בְּרָב־עָם 'in a multitude of people' (Prov. 14.28), גְּרֻשֹׁתֵיכֶם 'your evictions' (Ezek. 45.9), דְּרָכָיו 'his ways', וְרֹאשׁ־עֹרֵב 'and the head of Oreb' (Jud. 7.25), זְכֹור־יְהוָה 'remember, oh Lord' (Psa. 132.1), טְמֵאַת הַשֵּׁם 'unclean of name' (Ezek. 22.5), יְראוּ אֶת־יְהוָה 'fear the Lord' (Jos. 24.14), and other cases with these eighteen letters.

II.S.6.3.2.

Take note that these eighteen are (pronounced as if) pointed with *pataḥ*, but it is a feature of this *pataḥ* that it is only pronounced short. There is no way of (representing) its shortness other than by combining it with *shewa*. Since, however, the *shewa* according to their principles does not combine with a vowel under these eighteen letters, they have marked the *shewa* by itself. They could not have written the

II.S.6.2.2.

ואעלם אן אלשוא אדא כאן קבל אליוד פי אכתר אלמואצֿע דלת   220
עלי אלמנכר ואלמלך קבלה ידל עלי אלמיודע מתל ביום זבחכם
מנכר ביום ההוא כרם מיודע ונחו דלך

II.S.6.3. אלפן אלתאלת

II.S.6.3.1.

אלבאקי מן (S12:2v) חרוף אלעבראני אלאצול סבעה̈ עשר ותרד
אליהא אליוד תציר תמאניה̈ עשר אדא כאן אלשוא תחת אחד   225
הדה אלתמאניה עשר פי אול אלכלאם או פי וסט אלכלאם
בחית יגרי מגרי אלאבתדא כרג̇ אלשוא בפאתחה כפיפה אדא
לם יכן מעה געיה ובפאתחה תקילה אדא כאן מעה געיה מתל
ברב עם גרושותיכם דרכיו וראש ערב זכר יוי טֻמאת השם יראו
את יוי אלי גיר דלך מן הדה אלתמאניה עשר חרפא   230

II.S.6.3.2.

ואעלם אן הדא אלתמאניה עשר נקטהא הי אלפאתחה ומן חכם
הדה אלפאתחה̈ אלמדכורה לא ינטק בהא אלא כפיפה ולא וגה
לכפתהא אלא כון אלשוא מעהא ולמא לם יכן אלשוא פי
אצולהם יגתמע מע מלך תחת הדה אלתמאניה עשר חרף געלו
אלשוא פקט (S12:3r) ולם ימכנהם אן יגעלו אלפאתחה וחדהא   235

pataḥ by itself, since it would have been pronounced with its full length. I have discussed this subject at length in *The Guide for the Reader*, where you will find the matter explained clearly.

II.S.6.4. The Fourth Subsection

The *shewa* is never combined with a conjunctive or disjunctive accent on the same letter. This is because an accent cannot combine with a quiescent *shewa* on account of the incongruity (of their functions), since a letter is made mobile by an accent, whereas a quiescent *shewa* makes a letter quiescent, and a letter made quiescent by the *shewa* would have to be made mobile by the accent simultaneously, and this is impossible. Furthermore the mobile *shewa* gives a letter a mobility that has no endurance, like the *bet* in בְּרֵאשִׁית and the *zayin* in זְכוֹר, whereas a letter is given a stable mobility by an accent and it is given many different melodies, as in וַיְמַהֲר֣וּ וַיַּשְׁכִּ֔ימוּ 'and they made haste and went out early' (Josh. 8.14). So the mobility of an accent cannot be combined with the mobility of the *shewa* on account of the speed of the mobility of the *shewa*.

II.S.6.5. The Fifth Subsection

A letter following a mobile *shewa* is always *rafe*, as in בְּבֹאָם 'when they enter' (Exod. 28.43, etc.), בְּכָל־פִּנּוֹת 'in every corner' (cf. 2 Chron. 28.24), כְּכַלּוֹת 'on finishing' (Deut. 31.24, etc.), and similar cases. The reason for this is that the *shewa*, since it wishes to have movement and speed, requires the lightness of the letter after it, because *dagesh* introduces a kind of heaviness in the letter.

לאנהא תגّי מסתופאה וקד אסתקצית אלכלאם פי הדא אלמוצّע

פי הדאיّה אלקאר עלי מא אנת תגّדה הנאך מבינא

II.S.6.4. אלפّן אלראבע

אלשוא לא יגّתמע לא מע לחן ולא מע כאדם פי חרף ואחד

מעّא בתה לאן אלטעם לא יגّתמע מע שוא סאכן מן חית

אלמנאקצّה לאן אלטעם יתחרד בה אלחרף ואלשוא אלסאכן

יסכן אלחרף פכّאן אן יכון אלחרף סאכן באלשוא מתחרד

באלטעם פי חאלّה ואחדה והדא פאסד ולאן אלשוא אלמתחרד

יחרّך אלחרף חרכּה לא תבאת פיהא כאלבא מן בראשית

ואלזאי מן זכّור ואללחן יתחרד בה אלחרף מוצّעה וינגם נגמאת

כתירה מתל וימהרו וישכּימו פלא יגّתמע חרכּה אללחן   (S12:3v)

מע חרכّה אלשוא לסרעה אלשוא פי אלחרכה

II.S.6.5. אלפّן אלכّאמס

אלשוא אלמתחרّך לא יכון אלחרף אלתאני מנה אבדא אלא רפי

מתל בבואם בכל פנות ככּלות ונחו דלך ואלّוגה פי דלך אן

אלשוא למא אראד אלתחרّך ואלסרעה אחתאגّ אלי כפّّה

אלחרף אלדי בעדה לאן אלדגש הו תקל פי אלחרף עלי וגّה

II.S.6.6. The Sixth Subsection

II.S.6.6.1.

A mobile *shewa* does not combine with a vowel on any of the Hebrew letters except the four letters א, ה, ח and ע, for example אֲנִי 'I', הֲלֹא הוּא 'not he?', וַחֲנֵה עַל־הָעִיר 'and encamp against the city' (2 Sam. 12.28), עֲלוּ 'go up!', and similar cases. If one sees this on other letters in some codices, this is because the scribe inteneded thereby to remove uncertainty, for example קֳדָם 'before', קֳדָמֵיהוֹן 'before them', מֶשְׁכוּ אוֹתָהּ 'drag her!' (Ezek. 32.20), וְשֶׁדְדוּ 'and destroy!' (Jer. 49.28). It is not, however, the opinion of all (that this practice is permissible). So you see that everybody combines *shewa* with a vowel under the four letters but only a few combine a vowel with *shewa* under the other eighteen letters, there being no consensus as to whether this (practice) be erroneous or not.

II.S.6.6.2.

Take note that if one wishes to remove a vowel from one of the four letters א, ה, ח or ע, and pronounce the *shewa*, that would be permissible. It is not permissible, however, to mark the vowel by itself, since a vowel by itself would be pronounced with its full length. So, understand this!

II.S.6.6. אלפן אלסאדס

II.S.6.6.1.

אלשוא אלמתחרך לא יגׄתמע מע מלך פי חרף מן חרוף

אלעבראני אלא פי ארבעה חרוף אׄהׄחׄע מתל <אֲנִי הֲלֹא הוא   255

וַחֲנָה עַל הָעִיר עָלוּ ונחו דלך ואן ראי מע סוי האולי אלארבעה

פי בעץׄ אלמצׄאחף פאלגׄרץׄ בה מן כאתבה> לירפע <אלאשכאל

מתל קֳדָם קֳדָמֵיהוֹן מָשְׁכוּ אוֹתָהּ וְשָׁדְדוּ> <וליס הדא ראי

אלכל> (S12:4r) ולדלך תרי אלכל יגׄמעו אלשוא מע אלמלך תחת

אלארבעה חרוף ומא סואהא מן בקיה אלחרוף אלאכל יגׄמע   260

אלמלך מע אלשוא פי אלמגׄלטאת ופי גיר מגׄלט מן אלתמאניׄה

עשׁר לא יגׄמע

II.S.6.6.2.

ואעלם אן לו אראדו אן יחדפו מן אלארבעה חרוף אׄהׄחׄע

אלמלך ויסמע אלשוא לגׄאז דלך ולא יגׄז אן יגׄעלו אלמלך וחדה

מן חית אן אלמלך וחדה יסתופא פאפהמה   265

---

255 אֲנִי...257 כאתבה] S20:8r פני יהוה הלא היא [ ] עליו ונחו דלך ואן
ראי מא סוי האולי אלארבעה פי בעץׄ אלמואצׄע פאלגׄרץׄ בה מן כאתבה
S20:8r | 257 לירפע] ליערף S20:8r | אלאשכאל | 258...וְשָׁדְדוּ] S12
אלאשכאל מתל קדם קדמֵיהון משכו אותה S12   258 וליס...259
אלכל[1] S13:3v ולא הו ראי ללכל S12

II.S.6.7. The Seventh Subsection

When a *shewa* is combined with a vowel under a letter, the vowel is prevented from being given its full length, as in חֳרֵם וּבֵית־עֲנָת 'Ḥorem and Betanath' (Josh. 19.38), גַּם כָּל־חֳלִי 'also every sickness' (Deut. 28.61). Take note that the maintenance of the mobility of the *shewa* is more important than the maintenance of the full length because if they did not need to shorten the vowel and (read it) quickly, they would not have marked *shewa* with it.

II.S.6.8. The Eighth Subsection

Shewa is combined with only three vowels. These are *qameṣ*, *pataḥ* and *segol*. This is because these three may be read with pause and also with speed.

II.S.6.9. The Ninth Subsection

When *shewa* is at the beginning of a word, it is always mobile, as in לְעֶת־יֹום 'at the time of (each) day' (1 Chron. 12.23), דְּבַר־מִי 'the word of whom will stand' (Jer. 44.28), כְּחֹם הַיֹּום 'in the heat of the day' (Gen. 18.1), and similar cases. This is because it is not permissible to begin (a word) with a quiescent letter. You will find the issues concerning this aspect explained in *The Guide for the Reader*. God knows best.

II.S.6.10. The Tenth Subsection

A mobile *shewa* is followed by quiescence in the third letter after it, or one greater (in number than the third), as in, לְיָשָׁבְקָשָׁה 'to Joshbekashah' (1 Chron 25.24), לְיָקְמְעָם 'to Jokmeam' (1 Kings 4.12), and the like, and as in cases in which

II.S.6.7. אלפן אלסאבע

אלשוא אדא אגתמע מע מלך תחת חרף מנע אלמלך מן אן
יסתופי חטה מן אלתקל מתל חרם ובית ענת גם כל חלי ואעלם
אן תבות חרכהֿ אלשוא אולי מן תבות אסתיפא אלמלך לאן
(S12:4v) לו לם יחתאגו אלי כטף אלמלך וסרעתה לם יגעלו מעה 270
אלשוא

II.S.6.8. אלפן אלתאמן

לא יגמע אלשוא אלא מע תלתהֿ מלוד פקט והי אלקאמצה
ואלפאתחה ואלסגלה לאן הדה אלתלתה יצח פיהא אלתוקף
ואלסרעה: 275

II.S.6.9. אלפן אלתאסע

אלשוא אדא כאן פי אול אלכלאם יכון אבדא מתחרך מתל לעת
יום דבר מי יקום <כְּחֹם הַיּום> ונחו דלך לאן לא יצח אלאבתדי
בסאכן ואנת תגד אלכלאם פי הדא אלפן משרוחא פי הדאיהֿ
אלקאר ואללה אעלם 280

II.S.6.10. אלפן אלעאשר

אלשוא אלמתחרך יכון בעדה סכון פי אלחרף אלתאלת ומא

זאד נחו לישבקשה ליקמעם ואמתאלהמא ממא אלסכון פי

---

278 כְּחֹם הַיּום [S13:4v כחום היום S12 בססדך

the quiescence is in the third letter and also in what is beyond the third letter, such as אֱלֹהִים 'God' and בְּרוֹשִׁים 'cypresses'.

II.S.6.11. The Eleventh Subsection

A mobile *shewa* does not come next to a (mobile) *shewa* either at the beginning of a word, or in the middle of it, or at its end. This is because a word is mobile (with a vowel) and what attaches to this mobile component when it begins with (a mobile) *shewa* is of a lesser degree of mobility. A quiescent letter may follow these two. Therefore two mobile (*shewas*) are not combined together, in the way that two quiescent ones can combine.

II.S.6.12. The Twelfth Subsection

Two quiescent *shewas* are not combined except at the end of a word, as in וַיִּשְׁבְּ 'and he captured' (Num. 21.1), וְרָחַצְתְּ | וָסַכְתְּ 'and you will wash and anoint yourself' (Ruth 3.3). Take note that when *shewa* under *shin* and *ṣade* is quiescent and *bet* and *tav* remain after it, they must obligatorily be made quiescent, because they do not have a letter next to them to which they could move towards.

II.S.6.13. The Thirteenth Subsection

It is not possible to have a succession of two adjacent *shewas* the first of which is mobile and the second quiescent. Rather the first must be quiescent and the second mobile. Take note that *shewa* may be construed as a successive sequence (of two) even though only one is written, as in מִזְּעֹק 'from crying' (1 Sam. 7.8), מְזַבְּחִים 'sacrificing', מְחַלְּלִים 'playing the pipe' (1 Kings 1.40, etc.), מִמְּלֹךְ 'from being king' (1 Sam. 8.7, etc.), הַכְּמוֹת 'will it be like?' (2 Sam. 3.33). The reason for this is that the letter is pronounced as two letters. This is the custom of Hebrew,

אלתאלת ומא זאד עלי אלתאלת מתל אלהים ^(S12:5r) ברושים

II.S.6.11. אלפן אלחאדי עשר 285

שוא מתחרך לא יגֿאור שוא לא פי אול אלכלאם ולא פי וסטה

ולא פי אכרה לאן אלכלאם אנמא יכון מתחרך ומא ילחק

באלמתחרך פהו אקל חרכה מן אלמתחרך אדא אבתדי

באלשוא ואלסאכן קד יתבעהמא פלדלך לם יכתרנא מתחרכין

כמא יכתרנא אלסאכנין 290

II.S.6.12. אלפן אלתאני עשר

שואין סאכנין לא יכתרנא אלא פי אכר אלכלמה מתל וישֵב

ורחצֿתֿ וסכתֿ ואעלם אן למא סכן אלשוא אלדי תחת אלשין

ואלצדי ובקי בא ותו לם יכן בד מן תסכינהמא לאן ליס להמא

חרף יגֿאורהמא פיתחרכא אליה 295

II.S.6.13. אלפן אלתאלתֿ עשר

שואין מתראדפין אלאול מתחרך ואלתאני סאכן לא יגֿוז

תראדפהמא אלא אן יכון אלאול סאכן ואלתאני מתחרך ^(S12:5v)

ואעלם אן תם שוא בניתה עלי אלתראדף ואן כאן ליס אלא

ואחד מכתוב נחו מזעק מזבחים מחללים ממלך הכמות ואלסבב 300

פי דלך אן אלחרף יכרגֿ בחרפין פהדה סירה פי אלעבראני והוא

namely that every letter with strengthening, I mean with *dagesh*, in the middle of a word, where it does not have the status of beginning (a word or syllable), under which there is *shewa*, is pronounced as two letters.

II.S.6.14. The Fourteenth Subsection

A *shewa* at the end of a word can only be silent, as in דֶּרֶךְ, מֶלֶךְ, and similar cases.

אן כל חרף משדד אעני מדגוש פי וסט כלמה בחית לא יִגרי

מגרי אבתדי ותחתה שוא יכרג בחרפין

II.S.6.14. אלפן אלראבע עשר

305 אלשוא פי אכר אלכלאם לא ימכן אן יכון אלא סאכן נחו דרך
ומלך ואמתאלההמא

SECTION ON THE NAMES OF THE VOWELS
AND THEIR PLACE OF ARTICULATION

II.S.7.1.

The vowels are seven, namely אֹ, אָ, אַ, אֶ, אֵ, אִ, אֻ.

II.S.7.2.

The first is 'the point above' (i.e. *ḥolem*) because it moves along the surface of the whole mouth. Its name is *ḥolem*. The meaning of this is 'fullness', because it fills the whole mouth. They have derived (the name) from one of the languages that they used.

II.S.7.3.

The second is *qameṣ*, which is derived from וְקָמַץ הַכֹּהֵן 'and the priest will grasp' (Lev. 5.12, etc.), because it grips the mouth.

II.S.7.4.

The third is *pataḥ*, which opens the whole mouth, from פְּתַח־פִּיךָ שְׁפָט־צֶדֶק 'open your mouth, judge righteously' (Prov. 31.9).

II.S.7.5.

The fourth is *segol*, which consists of three dots below, as if they were a bunch of grapes.

II.S.7.6.

The fifth consists of two dots below in a line. Its name is *ṣere*,

II.S.7.0.

פצל פי אסמא אלמלוך ומחלהא

II.S.7.1.

אלמלוך סבעה והי אֹ אַ אָ אֶ אֵ אִ

II.S.7.2.

אלאול אלנקטה מן פוק לאנה יסיר עלי סטח אלפם כלה ואסמה

חלם ומענאה (S12:6r) מלו לאנהא תמלא אלפם כלה ואשתקוה

מן בעץֹ אללגֹאת אלתי מעהם

310

II.S.7.3.

אלתאני קאמצה משתקה מן וקמץ הכהֵן לאנהא תקבץֹ אלפם

II.S.7.4.

ואלתאלת אלפאתחה והי תפתח כל אלפם מן פתח פיך שפט

צדק

II.S.7.5.

ואלראבע סגולה והי אלתלתה נקט מן אספל כאנהא ענקוד

315

II.S.7.6.

ואלכֿאמסה הי נקטתין מן אספל מצטפה אסמוהא צֵירי

---

the meaning of which is 'splitting', because it splits between the teeth. They have derived it from the languages that they used.

II.S.7.7.

The sixth is one dot below. Its name is *ḥireq*, from וַחֲרֹק עָלָיו שִׁנָּיו 'and gnashes his teeth against him' (Psa. 37.12). The meaning of this is that the teeth make a squeaking sound with it.

II.S.7.8.

The seventh consists of three dots (written) obliquely. It may be replaced by one dot in the heart of *vav*. Its name is *shureq*, meaning 'whistling', from לִשְׁמֹעַ שְׁרִקוֹת עֲדָרִים 'to hear the whistlings of the flocks' (Jud. 5.16), because it gathers the lips together.

ומענאהא שאק לאנהא תשק בין אלאסנאן וקד אשתקוהא מן

אללגّאת אלתי מעהם

II.S.7.7.

ואלסאדס הי נקטה ואחדה מן אספל ואסמוהא חרק מן וחרק

עליו שניו ומעני דלך אן תצר בהא אלאסנאן צרא

320

II.S.7.8.

ואלסאבע תלתה נקט מוארבה וקד יכון עוצّהא נקטةֹ ואחדה פי

קלב <אלّואו (S12:6v) אסמוהא שרק> במעני אלצפיר מן

<לשמוע> שריקות עדרים לאנהא תגّמע אלשפתין

---

319 חרק] חֶרֶק S1:8r 321 מוארבה] מורב S6:11r 322 אלّואו...
שרק] אלّואו (+ אסמוהא מפק לאנהא תגّמע אלשפתין ואלתלתה נקט
אלמוארבה (S12) אסמוהא שרק S12 S6:11r 323 לשמוע] S6:11r
אלשמע S3:10v S12

II.S.8.0.

DISCUSSION CONCERNING THEIR PLACE OF ARTICULATION

II.S.8.1.
The place of articulation of *holem* is the root of the tongue and the place of swallowing, and it moves over the surface of the entire mouth.

II.S.8.2.
The place of articulation of *qameṣ* is slightly above the root of the tongue, this being the (first) third of the tongue, and its movement is to above the palate.

II.S.8.3.
The place of articulation of *pataḥ* is the surface of the tongue downwards.

II.S.8.4.
The place of articulation of *segol* is the contraction of the sides of the mouth and its movement is upon the lower surface of the mouth.

II.S.8.5.
The place of articulation of *ṣere* is the teeth, without closure.

II.S.8.6.
The place of articulation of *hireq* is the closure of the teeth with force.

II.S.8.7.
The place of articulation of *shureq* is the lips gathered together (as if for) whistling.

II.S.8.0.

אלכלאם פי מחלהא

II.S.9.0.

SECTION CONCERNING THE *GAʿYA*

The *gaʿya* is an exhalation in speech, which conducts the reading along and carries it forward in a beautiful manner, animating the reader and moving him to read more. One reader omits it in some places whereas another reader sustains it. In sum, it has no principle, because it is not an accent, like a disjunctive accent or a conjunctive accent. It is marked on a slant to the right of the reader, similar to the marking of *ṭifḥa* and *mayela*. It is said that the *gaʿya* has no principle. It is never accompanied by *maqqef*, which is a line that links two words on account of the fact that one word does not have a disjunctive or conjunctive accent. This is because any word that has an accent does not have *maqqef*, unless a *gaʿya* can come before the accent, in which case a word may contain an accent and *maqqef* in some places. There are, however, some places from which *gaʿya* cannot be omitted, such as כִּי לֹא יִשְׁנוּ 'for they do not sleep' (Prov. 4.16), which is from 'sleeping and slumber'. If you were to omit it, it would come to mean 'repeating', as in אַחֲרֵי דְבָרִי לֹא יִשְׁנוּ 'after my word they did not speak' (Job 29.22), and similar cases where the meaning changes on account of it.

II.S.9.0.

פצל פי אלגעיה (S12:27r)

אלגעיה הי תנפס פי אלכלאם ותזף אלקראה ותסוקהא אחסן סיאק ותנשט אלקאר ותחרכה אלי אלתזיד פי אלקראה פקאר יחדפהא מן בעץ̇ אלמואצ̇ע וקאר יתבתהא ובאלג̇מלה לא אצל להא לאנהא ליסת בנגמה (S12:27v) כאלאלחאן ואלכדאם <ונצבהא הו נצב בתמייל> אלי ימין אלקאר שביה בנצב אלטפחה ואלמאילה וקד קיל < אין אָב ללגעיה > והי אבדא יכון מעהא אלמקף והי כטה תוצל בין אלכלמתין אדא כאנת אלכלמה ליס פיהא לחן ולא כאדם לאן כל כלמה פיהא טעם לא יכון פיהא מקף אלא אן תג̇י אלגעיה מן קדאם <אלטעם> פיציר פי אלכלמה טעם ומקף פי בעץ̇ אלמואצ̇ע <גיר אן תם מואצ̇ע לא ימכן חדף אלגעיה מנהא> מתל כי לא ישנו אלדי הו מן אלוסן ואלנום ולו חדפת לצאר מן אלתתניה מתל אחרי דברי לא יִשְׁנו ונחוה ממא יתגיר אלמעני לאג̇להא

340 ונצבהא...בתמייל] S2:17v S19:5v וינצבהא פהו נצב בתמ[ ] S12 341 אין...ללגעיה] S26:1v אֵין אָב לל[ ] S24:1v אֵן אָב ללָגָעְיָה S19:5v אין אב ללגעיה S23:16v אין אבל לגעיה S28:3v אין אין אב ללגעיה S12:27v S2:17v 344 אלטעם] S19:5v אלמארכה S12 345 גיר...346 מנהא] S19:5v תם מוצ̇ע לא ימכן חדף אלגעיה מנה S12

COMMENTARY ON *HIDĀYAT AL-QĀRIʾ*

Long Version

➤ II.L.0.0.

The long version opens with an introduction, which presents various aspects of the background of the ensuing work. ʾAbū al-Faraj Hārūn included such authorial paratexts in his other works. His grammatical work *al-Kitāb al-Kāfī* contains a preface and an introduction (ed. Khan, Gallego and Olszowy-Schlanger 2003, 10-19). The abridgement of *al-Kitāb al-Kāfī* known as *Kitāb al-ʿUqūd fī Taṣārīf al-Lugha al-ʿIbrāniyya* 'The Book of Rules regarding the Grammatical Inflections of the Hebrew Language', which was compiled by an anonymous contemporary of ʾAbū al-Faraj Hārūn, likewise contains an introduction (ed. Vidro 2013a, 22–25). ʾAbū al-Faraj Hārūn's glossary of difficult words, which is referred to as *Tafsīr ʾAlfāẓ al-Miqrā* 'Explanation of the words of Scripture' and several variant titles, contains a postface added at the end of the work, which served the same purpose as a preface and an introduction (Goldstein 2014).

Authorial paratexts, in the form of prefaces, introductions and postfaces, are a characteristic feature of contemporary medieval Arabic literary compositions.[1] The addition of such a paratext, therefore, in the works of ʾAbū al-Faraj Hārūn reflects convergence with the Arabic literary models.

---

[1] See Freimark (1967) and the discussion and references in Goldstein (2014).

  https://doi.org/10.11647/OBP.0194.04

An introductory paratext is found in some earlier works written by Jewish scholars, such as the Masoretic treatise *Seder ha-Simanim* (Allony 1965, ‏טו‎) and some works of Saadya in the tenth century, such as his lexicon *ha-ʾEgron* (ed. Allony 1969a, 148–63) and his Bible commentaries (Stroumsa 2007).

The beginning of the introduction to the long version of *Hidāyat al-Qāriʾ* is missing. If we compare it, however, with the corresponding introduction in the short version, which has been preserved in its entirety, it can be safely assumed that only a short amount of text is missing.

The introduction can be divided into various components, many of which contain standard themes in such authorial paratexts. §II.L.0.1. discusses the reasons why the principles of biblical reading need to be studied. §II.L.0.2.—§II.L.0.6 concern the historical background of the Tiberian reading and its antiquity. §II.L.0.7.—§II.L.0.8. describe the history of the discipline of fixing rules for the correct reading. §II.L.0.9. explains the author's motivation to write the work and summarizes its contents.

ʾAbū al-Faraj states in §II.L.0.9. that the purpose of the work was essentially compilatory, in that it brings together in a comprehensive way specialist works and oral teachings of his predecessors, who remain anonymous. This section contains a 'request to compose' without specifying the name of the requester. This is a standard feature of Arabic introductions of the period and it is often no more than a fictional trope (Freimark 1967, 36–40). As is typical, this 'request to compose' is combined with a modesty trope in which the author acknowledges his own imperfections.

In some cases, we know that medieval Karaite works were commissioned by specific individuals. In the postface to his *Kitāb ʾAlfāẓ al-Miqrā*, ʾAbū al-Faraj indicates the name of the requester, viz. ʾAbū al-Ṭayyib Samuel ibn Manṣūr (Goldstein 2014), who commissioned the work for his children. Another case is the short commentary of ʾAbū al-Faraj Furqān ibn ʾAsad (Yeshuʿa ben Yehuda), in the introduction of which it is indicated that the work was commissioned by the wealthy patron ʾAbū al-Ḥasan Dāʾūd ibn ʿImrān ibn Levi (Khan 1993; Polliack 1997, 47–48). An alternative process is attested in the manuscripts containing the grammatical commentary of the Karaite Yūsuf ibn Nūḥ, known as the *Diqduq*, in which there is a document indicating that the author dedicated the work as a pious foundation to the Karaite community (Khan 2000b, 153–54).

The introduction to *Hidāyat al-Qāriʾ* has a particular focus on the accents rather than the consonants and vowels. This suggests that the main interest of ʾAbū al-Faraj in the work were the accents. Indeed one early source that is apparently referring to *Hidāyat al-Qāriʾ* calls it *Kitāb al-ʾAlḥān* 'The Book of the Accents' (see § II.Int.0.3.). One of the later European recensions of the work, furthermore, had the title *Ṭaʿame ha-Miqra* 'The Accents of the Bible' (see vol. 1, §I.0.13.1.).

It should be noted, however, that the adducing of examples of different positioning of accents as a means of demonstrating the importance of the knowledge of correct reading in §II.L.0.1. has a close counterpart in the introduction by ʾAbū al-Faraj Hārūn to his grammatical work *al-Kitāb al-Kāfī*, which demon-

strates the importance of the knowledge of grammar. A large pro-
portion of the introduction of *al-Kitāb al-Kāfī* (ed. Khan, Gallego
and Olszowy-Schlanger 2003, 12-19) concerns the positioning of
accents and, indeed, several of the examples are the same as
those presented in the introduction to *Hidāyat al-Qāriʾ*. The
shared examples, moreover, are used to demonstrate the same
points. These include the following. The accent position can distinguish between past tense, e.g. הַשָּׁבָה (Ruth 2.6) 'who returned'
and present tense, e.g. וְשָׁבָ֫ה (Lev. 22.13) 'and she returns'. The
position of the accent can distinguish between lexical meaning,
e.g. שָׁ֫בוּ 'they have turned back' (Jer. 11.10) but שָׁבְ֫וּ 'they captured' (Gen. 34.29). Furthermore, the same issues of accent position with overlapping examples also occur in §I.1.1. of *al-Kitāb
al-Kāfī* and in a passage in ʾAbū al-Faraj Hārūn's reworking of Ibn
Nūḥ's commentary on the Pentateuch (Goldstein 2014, 367).

It is likely, therefore, that the use by ʾAbū al-Faraj of the
arguments relating to accent position in his introduction to
Hidāyat al-Qāriʾ was to some extent motivated by the fact that
similar argumentation was already at hand in passages in his
other works. Distinction of meaning arising from accent position
was, moreover, a particularly salient demonstration of how pre-
cise knowledge of the language is important for correct interpretation of Scripture.

➤ II.L.0.1.

לגה אלרגוע ... לגה אלסבי

lexical class of 'returning' ... lexical class of 'capturing'

In the linguistic thought of Karaite grammarians of the tenth and eleventh centuries, inflections and derivative forms of a verb were said to belong to a particular lexical class. This was expressed by the Arabic term *lughah* typically followed by an abstract Arabic verbal noun in genitive annexation, as is the case here (*al-rujūʿ* 'returning', *al-saby* 'capturing'), or by the Hebrew term *lashon* followed by a Hebrew, or occasionally Aramaic, abstract noun in annexation, e.g. לשון ברכה 'lexical class of blessing' (§II.L.3.2.7.), לשון דחילה 'lexical class of fearing' (§II.L.3.1.). A lexical class was a class of attested linguistic forms sharing a common kernel of meaning and common letters. Such a lexical class does not include words that are related in meaning but have no letters in common. The common letters that embrace all words belonging to a lexical class are in most cases equivalent to what we would call the root letters. The medieval Karaite grammarians of the tenth and eleventh centuries, however, did not have a fully developed concept of an abstract triliteral root as the base of derivation in their linguistic theory (Khan 2000b, 78–82; 2013a; 2013b).

The use of the term *lashon* with this sense of lexical class is found in earlier Hebrew Masoretic treatises, e.g. *Diqduqe ha-Ṭeʿamim* (ed. Dotan 1967): לשון ברכה 'lexical class of blessing' (§21), לשן אכילה 'lexical class of eating' (§22), לשון ירידה 'lexical class of descending' (§25). The grammatical use of the term *la-shon* ultimately has its origin in the Rabbinic tradition, where it is used broadly in the sense of linguistic form. Such broader usage is still found in the text of *Hidāyat al-Qāriʾ* in cases such as לשון

בתים 'the form בְּתִים' (§II.L.1.9.2.), לשון יחיד 'singular form'
(§II.L.3.2.1.).

> ## II.L.0.2.

> If one were to say 'What do you say concerning the
> formation of these accents?', the response would be that
> they originated by convention among the people of the
> language, by the help of which they fully expressed their
> purposes, as in the aforementioned examples and others.
> They established them by convention, just as they
> established the vowels by convention, as will be explained.

This reflects a rationalist and anthropocentric view of the origin
of language that ᵓAbū al-Faraj expresses elsewhere in *Hidāyat al-
Qārī* and in his grammatical works. According to this view, language did not develop by revelation from God but rather developed among the primeval speech community of humans by convention in order to fulfil their needs of communication. The primeval speech community is referred to as 'the people of the language' (*ᵓahl al-lugha*). It appears that this was intended to be the
primeval community of Hebrew-speakers. Discussion of the conventional origin of language elsewhere in *Hidāyat al-Qārī* is
found in sections concerning the origin of letters and vowels, e.g.
§II.L.1.1.1. §II.L.1.1.2., §II.L.1.4.1., §II.L.1.8.2., §II.L.2.2.1. In
§II.L.2.2.1. there is a discussion of the role of the language of God
in the development of language by conventional agreement. In
his grammar *al-Kitāb al-Kāfī*, ᵓAbū al-Faraj describes how various
aspects of grammatical structure, such as verbal inflections and

the expression of gender and number, would have arisen by convention within the primeval speech community to fulfil their needs of communication.[2]

The notion of the conventional origin of language was adopted by ʾAbū al-Faraj from the rationalist views of language that were espoused by the Muslim theological movement known as the Muʿtazila. The Muʿtazila, in turn, had received this from the Aristotelian tradition of the conventional origin of meaning of sounds in language (Allen 1948; Kretzmann 1974) through the Arabic translations of Aristotelian texts at the period. Muslim philosophers whose thought was based in the Aristotelian tradition also adopted this concept of the origin of language, e.g. al-Fārābī (d. 950), who wrote a commentary on the Arabic version of Aristotle's *De Interpretatione*, where Aristotle expressed his arguments on this question.[3]

The leading Karaite intellectuals of the period adopted many aspects of Muʿtalizite thought (Wolfson 1979; Sklare 2017). They followed in particular the so-called Bahshamiyya Muʿtazilite school of Baṣra, which was founded by students and followers of ʾAbū Hāshim al-Jubbāʾī. In the second half of the tenth century and the eleventh century, they were influenced especially by the central figures of this school such as ʾAbū ʿAlī ibn Khallād and ʿAbd al-Jabbār al-Hamadhānī. Yūsuf ibn Ibrāhīm ha-Kohen al-Baṣīr, a prominent scholar in the Karaite Jerusalem

---

[2] The various passages in *al-Kitāb al-Kāfī* have been gathered together by Gallego (2003).

[3] See this commentary of al-Fārābī (ed. Beirut 1960, 27, 50–51) and Zimmermann's translation (1982, xli, 12).

school, who was a contemporary of ʾAbū al-Faraj Hārūn, was particularly closely engaged with the Bahshamiyya school led by ʿAbd al-Jabbār and wrote refutations of ʿAbd al-Jabbār's opponents (Sklare 2017, 159, 163).

The rationalist notion of the origin of language through conventional agreement among humans can be traced to ʾAbū Hāshim al-Jubbāʾī (d. 933) of the Baṣran Muʿtalizite school and gained ground among the Muʿtazilites through the works of ʿAbd al-Jabbār (d. 1026) and ʾAbū al-Ḥusayn al-Baṣrī (d. 1044) (Weiss 1974, 35). The Muʿtazalite view of the origin of language by convention was adopted by various Karaite scholars of the Jerusalem school other than ʾAbū al-Faraj Hārūn, such as Yūsuf al-Baṣīr (Vajda 1974, 61–62) and ʾAbū al-Faraj Furqān ibn ʾAsad (also known as Yeshuʿa ben Yehudah) (Zwiep 1997, 149–58).

The key Arabic terms that are used by the Muʿtazilites for convention are ʾiṣṭilāḥ and verbal forms from the root w-ḍ-ʿ, especially muwāḍaʿa and tawāḍuʿ. The latter was the term favoured by ʿAbd al-Jabbār in his discussions of the origin of language (Peters 1976, 304–5). ʾAbū al-Faraj Hārūn uses both of these terms in his references to the conventional origin of language. The terms muwāḍaʿa and tawāḍuʿ appear to be literal translations of the Greek term συνθήκη 'convention' in the Aristotelian corpus, all of which have the basic meaning of 'putting together'.

In the passage in §II.L.0.2. the focus is on the origin of the accents, which are said to have arisen by convention among the 'people of the language', just as they established the vowels by convention, to achieve needs such as the distinctions of meaning described in §II.L.0.1. This would relate to stress position rather than musical cantillation and so would be a feature of natural speech. The passage then goes on to say that the arrangement (*tartīb*) of the accents may have been based on the practice of the Levites. This is most likely referring to the fixing of the sequence of different pitch accents in the musical cantillation. In a discussion of the origin of the vowels in §II.L.2.18., it is stated that 'it is possible that the people of the language formed the shapes of the vowels just has they formed the shapes of the letters. It is also possible that the people of the language used to use them in conversation without their knowing any (written) form for them.' In ʾAbū al-Faraj's discussion of the origin of the accents in §II.L.0.2., it is not clear whether he is referring to both the written accent signs and the oral reading or only to the oral reading.

The view of the origin of the accents and vowels by convention was abandoned by later Karaites, after the dispersal of the Karaite Jerusalem school consequent upon the capture of Jerusalem by the Crusaders in 1099. The Karaite Judah Hadassi, who was active in the middle of the twelfth century in Constantinople, for example, adopted a revelationist view of their origin, and argued that the original tablets that were given to Moses on Mount Sinai must have had the vowels and accents:

> ... for without the five vowels, which are [represented by] the vowel signs, a word could not be articulated nor could it be understood without the pronunciation of the vowels and accents.[4]

---

[4] *Sefer ʾEshkol ha-Kofer* (ed. Eupatoria 1836, 70a): כי בלא חמשת הקולות שהם מלכי הנקוד לא תולד המלה ולא תעמוד בפה ולא יודע מה היא כי אם בנועם נקודים וטעמים. See further Khan (1992, 173).

> ➤ **II.L.0.3.**

This section refers to the devastation of Jerusalem by the Romans, who are referred to figuratively as 'wicked Edom', i.e. Esau, the brother and enemy of Jacob. This was a trope that developed early in Rabbinic tradition (Feldman 1992, 47–48). The term here includes also the Byzantine rulers. The reference to pilgrimage to Tiberias and Gaza is evidently referring to the Byzantine period. Pilgrimage to Gaza, Tiberias and Zoar in the Byzantine period are mentioned also by other medieval Karaites.[5] One such reference is by Sahl ben Maṣliaḥ ha-Kohen in the preface to his *Book of Precepts*:

> After having left that place (i.e. Jerusalem), it remained for over five [hundred] years as rubble and dens of jackals, and the Jews could not enter. The Jews who resided in the East would come to the city of Maʿazyah (i.e. Tiberias) in order to pray, while those who lived in the West would come to the city of Gaza for that purpose. Those who dwelt in the South would go to the city of Zoar. In the days of the little horn (i.e. the Islamic empire; cf. Dan. 7.8), God opened His gates of mercy to His people, and brought them to His holy city.

Another reference to such pilgrimage in the Byzantine period is found in the commentary of Daniel al-Qūmisī (end of the ninth century) on Daniel 11.32:

> Before his arrival (i.e. of the Arabs), they (i.e. the Jews) could not enter Jerusalem and would, therefore, come

---

[5] For the full references see Gil (1996, 165–66).

from the four corners of the earth to Tiberias and to Gaza
in order to catch a glimpse of the Temple.

➤ II.L.0.5.

The argument here is that the opinion of the community as a
whole sanctions the authority of the tradition of the accents. This
is similar to the argument of the Karaite al-Qirqisānī that the
agreement of the majority of the community (*ʾijmāʿ*) on the biblical reading tradition is the crucial basis of its authority (Khan
1990).

➤ II.L.0.7.

Surely you see that Muslims, whether they be two or more,
cannot read with the same degree of coordination as the
Jews read, since each one has his own way (of reading).
One makes long a place that another makes it short. One
reads melodically a place that another reads flat.

The crucial difference between the reading of the Hebrew Bible
and the reading of the Qurʾān is that in the former the contour
and sequence of pitch accents are fixed by tradition whereas in
the latter pitch differences are improvised by individual readers
(Nelson 2001).

➤ II.L.0.9.

הדא אלמכתצר

'this short treatise'

The reference is clearly to the long version of *Hidāyat al-Qāriʾ* and
not to the short version, in connection with which ʾAbū al-Faraj

also uses the verb *ikhtaṣara* 'to shorten' (see the introduction to the short version §II.S.0.1.). The term 'short treatise' in the introduction to the long version can be interpreted as a case of formulaic modesty.

➤ II.L.1.1.

The ideas presented in this section correspond closely to the Muʿtazilite views of language, especially those expressed by ʿAbd al-Jabbār in his various works. ʿAbd al-Jabbār's definitions of speech include 'the arrangement together of two or more letters' (*mā intaẓama min ḥarfayn fa-ṣāʿidan*), 'what consists of the specific arrangement of these intuitively known letters, occurring in two letters or (more) letters' (*mā ḥaṣala fīh niẓām makhṣūṣ min hādhih al-ḥurūf al-maʿqūla, ḥaṣala fī ḥarfayn ʾaw ḥurūf*) and a number of other variant formulations (Peters 1976, 293–94). Likewise ʾAbū al-Faraj states that a communicable utterance must consist of a minimum of two letters. Like ʿAbd al-Jabbār, ʾAbū al-Faraj uses forms of the verb *naẓama* to refer to the arrangement of letters (e.g. §II.L.1.1.4., §II.L.1.1.5, §II.L.1.1.7.). Similar statements are made by the anonymous Karaite grammarian in the work *Kitāb al-ʿUqūd*, viz. 'speech is constituted by articulated sounds arranged in a particular type of arrangement' (*al-kalām huwa al-ḥurūf al-muqaṭṭaʿa al-manẓūma ḍarb min al-niẓām*) (ed. Vidro 2013a, 33), and the works of the Karaite Yūsuf al-Baṣīr, e.g. *al-Kitāb al-Muḥtawī* 'The Comprehensive Book': 'articulated sounds and arranged letters that can by convention convey meaning' (*ʾaṣwāt muqaṭṭaʿa wa-ḥurūf manẓūma yaṣiḥḥ ʾan tufīd bi-l-muwāḍaʿa*) (Vajda 1974, 61).

According to ʿAbd al-Jabbār, sounds are accidents (i.e. properties) and not substances. He uses the term *ʿaraḍ* to refer to this concept of accident (Peters 1976, 299). This corresponds to the term *khāṣṣiyya*, which is used by ʾAbū al-Faraj in *Hidāyat al-Qāriʾ* to denote the property of a letter, i.e. its realization in sound. The term *khāṣṣiyya* is found in some *tajwīd* manuals to refer to the distinctive phonetic realization of letters or categories of letters, e.g. *khāṣṣiyyat al-ḥarf al-rakhw … khāṣṣiyyat al-ḥarf al-shadīd* 'the distinctive property of a "soft" letter … the distinctive property of a "strong" letter' in the commentary on al-Dānī's *Kitāb al-Taysīr* by al-Mālaqī (d. 705/1305), *al-Durr al-Nathīr w-al-ʿAdhb al-Namīr* 'Scattered Pearls and Pure Sweet' (ed. Beirut 2002, 183). Al-Dānī uses the corresponding term *ṣifa* 'attribute' in his works, e.g. *al-Taḥdīd fī al-ʾItqān w-al-Tajwīd* 'The Definition of Precision and Excellent Reading' (ed. Amman 2001, 105).

In *Hidāyat al-Qāriʾ* ʾAbū al-Faraj occasionally uses the Hebrew term טעם (literally: 'taste') in the sense of the quality of a letter. In §II.L.1.3.3. this occurs in its Arabicized form טעאם *ṭaʿām*. The terms are sometimes used together, e.g. טעם אלחרף וכאציתה 'the "taste" of the letter and its property' (§II.L.1.1.2.). The Arabic verb *dh-w-q* 'to taste' is used in connection with the pronunciation of consonants in §II.L.1.3.8.: פאדא דקת אלחרף פי מחלה אנמא דקת מנה כאציתה 'If you taste a letter (by pronouncing it) in its place of articulation, you will taste its property.' This suggests that טעם 'taste' is used by ʾAbū al-Faraj to refer to the perceived quality of the letter, whereas *khāṣṣiyya* is its intrinsic property.

It is stated in §II.L.1.1.1. and §II.L.1.1.2. that 'the conventional agreement was initially on the property of the letter', i.e.

the conventional agreement in the primeval speech community was on sounds of letters rather than the names of letters. As remarked, according to ʿAbd al-Jabbār sounds were accidental properties and so speech must be an accident too. The conventional agreement was, therefore, initially on speech.

> ## II.L.1.1.2.

People differ with regard to the number of the letters that are added to the realization of the letter and its property.

This is referring to the variant forms of the names of the letters that were current during the time of ʾAbū al-Faraj.

> ## II.L.1.1.4.

והם אלמלוך אלדי תסמא אנחא

namely the vowels, which are called vocalization

Two terms are used for vowels. The term 'kings' (*mulūk*) expresses its hierarchical relationship viz-à-viz *shewa*, which is referred to as a 'servant' (*khādim*) in some medieval sources, e.g. the anonymous Masoretic treatise CUL T-S NS 301.84. This would be analogous to the relationship of a conjunctive accent, also referred to in the treatises as a *khādim*, with a following disjunctive accent. The Arabic term *ʾanḥāʾ* is the plural of *naḥw*, the primary meaning of which is the grammatical inflection of a word. In Arabic such inflection is expressed by case vowels and the term has been extended to all vowels.

> ## II.L.1.1.7.

פאדן אלחרף וחדה לא יפאד מנה מעני ועלי הדא אלוגה סמא אלדקדוקיין
אלחרף כאדמא

Now, meaning is not expressed by a letter alone and so the Hebrew grammarians have called a 'letter particle' a 'functional particle'.

The word *ḥarf* is the normal term used for 'grammatical particle' in the standard Arabic grammatical tradition of the period. ʾAbū al-Faraj states here that the Hebrew grammarians use the term *khādim*, which literally means 'serving (particle)', or 'subordinate (particle)', to refer to such grammatical elements. This is the term he himself uses in his grammatical works, e.g. *al-Kitāb al-Kāfī* (ed. Khan, Gallego and Olszowy 2003, §I.27.1). The designation *diqdūqiyyūn* is generally used by ʾAbū al-Faraj to refer to the Karaite grammarians of Hebrew who preceded him. They practiced a discipline that was known as *diqduq* 'attention to fine details, careful investigation (of Hebrew Scripture)'. This was associated with the Masoretic activity that produced the early Masoretic treatises. Such activity is sometimes referred to as *diqduq ha-miqra* 'careful investigation of Hebrew Scripture' in the sources, e.g. Allony (1964). Note also the anonymous Judaeo-Arabic Masoretic treatise that is preserved in the Genizah fragment CUL T-S D1.2, which states that its source is ממא בינוה אלמעלמין אלאולין אלצנאדיד פי דקדוק אלמקרא 'what was explained by the early master teachers of the careful investigation of Hebrew Scripture'.

ʾAbū al-Faraj was sometimes at pains to distinguish his own works from the discipline of *diqduq* (Khan 1997; 2000b, 1–25).

One of the reasons for this appears to be that ʾAbū al-Faraj believed that his grammatical works *al-Kitāb al-Mushtamil* and *al-Kitāb al-Kāfī* had a universalist approach that dealt not only with Hebrew but with general issues realting to human language, whereas the *diqdūqiyyūn* were specifically concerned with the Hebrew language of Scripture.

After completing *al-Kitāb al-Kāfī*, ʾAbū al-Faraj wrote a work entitled *Kitāb al-Madkhal ʾilā ʿIlm al-Diqdūq fī Ṭuruq al-Lugha al-ʿIbrāniyya* 'Book of Introduction into the Discipline of Careful Investigation of the Ways of the Hebrew Language', which he states was intended as a guidebook to the terminology of the *diqdūqiyyūn*. This work is still unpublished.[6] In the work ʾAbū al-Faraj states:

> 'Speech that is used (for communication) consists of three components: noun (*ism*), verb (*fiʿl*) and particle (*ḥarf*, literally: letter), which the people of the discipline of *diqduq* call 'serving particle' (*khādiman*).[7]

The manuscript of our passage in *Hidāyat al-Qāriʾ* has the reading חרפא אלכאדם אלדקדוקיין סמא 'the *diqduq* scholars called a "serving particle" (*khādim*) a "letter" (*ḥarf*).' Given the statement in *Kitāb al-Madkhal* and the following context of the passage in the *Hidāya*, it is clear that this reading is a scribal error for סמא אלדקדוקיין אלחרף כאדמא.

---

[6] See Khan, Gallego and Olszowy-Schlanger (2003, xiii) for a list of the extant manuscripts.

[7] II Firkovitch, Evr.-Arab. I 4601, fol. 112 (an autograph of ʾAbū al-Faraj written in Arabic script): الكلام المستعمل ثلثة اقسام اسم وفعل وحرف يسميه اهل علم الدقدوق خادم.

In the published texts of the early Karaite grammarians no specific technical term is attested for 'grammatical particle' (Khan 2000b, 74; 2000a).

פקד אנכתם פי כל לפטׄה חרף אלף והו מן חרוף אללין

In each of these words a letter ʾ*alef* is hidden, which is one of the soft letters.

This reflects the theory that long vowels were the result of 'soft letters' (*ḥurūf al-līn*), i.e. vowel letters. Such a theory was borrowed from the Arabic grammatical tradition and developed more systematically by the Hebrew grammarian Ḥayyūj, who was active in Spain in the early eleventh century (Basal 2013). Unlike in Arabic, these vowel letters were sometimes elided in the orthography; cf. the discussion in *Hidāyat al-Qāriʾ* in §II.L.1.8.

➤ II.L.1.2.

וינצׄאף אלי אלאצול כמסה חרוף והי אלתי יסמונהא פשוטות והם דְׄמֹנְפְֿץׄ

To the basic letters are added five letters, which are called "straight", namely דְמׄנְפֿץ.

The Hebrew term פָּשׁוּט 'straight' for the long final letters has its origin in Rabbinic literature; cf. Jastrow (1903, 1138).

ינצׄאף אלי אלאצול איצׄא סתה חרוף והי בֹֿגֹֿדֹֿכֹֿפֿתֿ אלטבראניין יזידו עלי הדה אלסתה אחרף חרף ריש ויגעלונהא בֹֿגֹֿדֹֿכֹֿפֿרֿתֿ

To the basic letters are added six letters, namely בגדכפת. The Tiberians add to these six letters the letter *resh*, making it (i.e. the group of non-basic letters) בגדכפרת.

The reference here is to the fricative variants of the בגדכפת consonants and the alveolar trill variant of the *resh* (vol. 1, §I.1.20), all of which were regarded by ʾAbū al-Faraj as secondary variants of the consonants in question. *Sefer Yeṣira* refers to שבע כפולות בגדכפרת 'the seven double letters בגדכפרת' (Hayman 2004, 24). According to Morag (1960), this is referring to the Babylonian pronunciation tradition, in which there was a variation in the realization of *resh* that was different in nature from that of the Tiberian tradition. The fricative variants of the בגדכפת consonants were regarded as secondary also in a Masoretic treatise published by Allony and Yeivin (1985, 97).

זאי מכרוך

For the *zāy makrūkh* see vol. 1, §I.1.7.

> **II.L.1.3.2.**

The Hebrew term בית הבליעה 'place of swallowing' is found in Hebrew Masoretic treatises, e.g. §5 and §6 in Baer and Strack's (1879) corpus. It is attested already in Rabbinic literature (Jastrow 1903, 173).

For the four cases of *dagesh* in *ʾalef* in the standard Tiberian tradition see vol. 1, §I.1.1.

> **II.L.1.3.3.**

For the meanings of the terms טעם and *khāṣṣiyya* see the comments to §II.L.1.1. above.

➢ **II.L.1.3.4.**

טֹהוּר

appearance

Cf. the use of the Arabic term *ẓāhir* 'appearing' to designate *he* with *mappiq* in the Masoretic treatise published by Allony and Yeivin (1985, 97).

➢ **II.L.1.4.1.**

הי עבּארּאת תֹואצֹּע עליהא ארבּאבּהא ליפהמו אגראאצֹּהם לבּעצֹּהם בּעֹץֹ
ויחתאג אן יעלם קבּל הדא אנהם תֹואצֹּעו עלי חרוּף מכצֹוצה פי מחאל
מכתלפה

It [i.e. language] consists of expressions that its original speakers established by convention among themselves to make their intentions understood to one another. It needs to be known that before this they established by convention specific letters in various places of articulation.

The expression *ʾarbābuhā* 'its [i.e. language's] masters' is synonymous with *ʾahl al-lugha* 'the people of the language'.

The establishment by convention of specific letters (*ḥurūf*) is referring to the phonetic realization of the letters in the form of the production of sound, as was discussed in §II.L.1.1.

➢ **II.L.1.4.2.**

פעל פי אלנפס

intransitive verb

This term, which literally means, 'action on oneself', is taken from the early Karaite grammatical tradition; cf. the *Diqduq* of Ibn Nūḥ (Khan 2000b, 108–11). In the standard Baṣran Arabic grammatical tradition an intransitive verb was called *fiʿl ghayr mutaʿaddin*, which was the term used by ʾAbū al-Faraj in his grammar books (Khan, Gallego, and Olszowy-Schlanger 2003, xliii).

> ➢ **II.L.1.4.5.**

ואלקסם אלראבע מא ינבדל מן מחאל מתגאירה והו יעם אלתצחיף
ואלגמטריא לאן אלדאל ואלריש מן מחלין גירין ואלגמטריא אלבא ואלשין
מן מחלין מתגאורין

The fourth category is what interchanges from different places of articulation, which includes scribal error and ciphers, for *dalet* and *resh* (which are sometimes confused by scribal error) are from two different places of articulation and the cipher of letters (consisting of the interchange of) *bet* and *shin* is from two different places of articulation.

Examples of scribal errors resulting in the interchange of *dalet* and *resh* are given in §II.L.1.5.4. They are discussed by ʾAbū al-Faraj in *al-Kitāb al-Kāfī*, in which he states 'It is a type of letter interchange arising from a mistake in writing on account of the similarity of two letters' (ed. Khan, Gallego and Olszowy-Schlanger 2003, §I.28.3.).

The ciphers referred to are in the encryption code known as א״ת ב״ש, whereby a letter is exchanged for its counterpart in the opposite place in the alphabet, e.g. *ʾalef*, the first letter in the alphabet, for *tav*, the last letter, *bet*, the second letter, for *shin*, the penultimate, and so forth (Campanini 2013, 638).

> ➤ **II.L.1.4.7.**

הַשְּׁלִשִׁי֙ לְאַבְשָׁל֔וֹם

'the third is Absalom' (1 Chron. 3.2).

This is cited by ʾAbū al-Faraj as an example of a *lamed* without meaning also in *al-Kitāb al-Kāfī* (ed. Khan, Gallego and Olszowy-Schlanger 2003, §I.25.45.).

> ➤ **II.L.1.4.8.**

יקאל אנה מכתצר יוד פי יד ותקדירה בידי

It is said that a *yod* has been contracted in יָד, and its virtual
form is בְּיָדִי.

ʾAbū al-Faraj uses here the notion of *taqdīr* ('virtual form', 'imagined form'), which he adopted from contemporary Arabic grammatical thought (Levin 1997). This concept is used to explain the existence of various irregularities in grammatical structure. Underlying the actually attested structure of the biblical text, there was a virtual or imagined *(muqaddar)* structure, which existed in the mind of the author. This imagined structure always conformed to grammatical rules and principles. When the imagined structure deviated from the actually attested structure, it was the imagined structure that constituted the basis of interpretation and translation (Khan 2001, 142–44).

> ➤ **II.L.1.5.**

Some cases of letter interchange that are presented in this section are mentioned by ʾAbū al-Faraj in *al-Kitāb al-Kāfī*, e.g. ed. Khan,

Gallego and Olszowy Schlanger (2013, §I.26.28, §I.27.34, §I.28.3).

> ## II.L.1.5.18.

The intention is that חָמִיץ would be in place of חָמוּס 'treated violently (and therefore bloody)'.

> ## II.L.1.5.21.

ואלמכרת יכון שָׁתוֹם

The disjoined form would be שָׁתָם.

ʾAbū al-Faraj uses the Hebrew terms מֻכְרָת 'disjoined' and סָמוּךְ 'conjoined' alongside the corresponding Arabic terms *qaṭʿ* 'disjoined state' (§II.L.1.4.8.) and *muḍāf* 'conjoined'. For סָמוּךְ see §II.L.2.17. These terms are found in Masoretic treatises, e.g. §37 in the corpus of Baer and Strack (1879). In *Hidāyat al-Qāriʾ* the terms are generally used in the sense of 'absolute' and 'construct' forms of a noun respectively. In Karaite grammatical literature the terms are used also to denote pausal and context forms (Khan 2007). The term *qaṭʿ* is used in the sense of pause in *Hidāyat al-Qāriʾ* in §II.L.2.12.14.

ויגב אן יכון אמרה שָׁתוֹם או שְׁתָם

Its imperative would have to be שָׁתוֹם or שְׁתָם.

For the notion of the imperative as the base of morphological derivation see the comments on §II.L.1.10. below.

➢ II.L.1.6.

The letters אויה are intended here to represent long vowels. This reflects the theory that long vowels were the result of 'soft letters' (*ḥurūf al-līn*), i.e. vowel letters; cf. the comments on §II.L.1.1.7. above and the discussion in *Hidāyat al-Qāriʾ* in §II.L.1.8.

Some of the material in this section can be found in other Masoretic treatises, such as §29 in the corpus of Baer and Strack (1879), two of the Judaeo-Arabic treatises published by Allony and Yeivin (1985, 99–101, 112), and various fragments of unpublished texts, e.g. CUL T-S D1.2, Mosseri I, 71.1; Oxford Bod. Heb. d 33, fol. 16.

➢ II.L.1.7.5.

פהו בתקדיר לחן קבלה ליגרי מגרי הֻוא יבנה־בֵּיַת

so (such cases must be considered) to have a virtual (conjunctive) accent before them in order to conform to (cases such as) הֻוא יִבְנֶה־בֵּיַת לִשְׁמֵי.

Here ʾAbū al-Faraj uses the notion of *taqdīr* 'virtual form', 'imagined form' (see the comment on §II.L.1.4.8. above) to explain an apparent irregularity. The idea is that the conjunctive accent existed in the virtual underlying structure, and so this explained the operation of the *ʾathe me-raḥiq*.

➢ II.L.1.7.7.

כל ואו פי אכר כלמה יכרג עלי ראי אלשאמיין בבא מרפי

Every *vav* at the end of a word is pronounced according to the Palestinians as a *bet rafe*.

See vol. 1, §I.1.6. for the pronunciation of the Tiberian *vav*.

> ➢ **II.L.1.7.9.**

For a possible explanation of the phenomenon described in this section, see vol. 1, §I.3.1.10.

> ➢ **II.L.1.7.11.**

For this feature of the reading of Ben Naftali see *Kitāb al-Khilaf* (ed. Lipschütz, 1965, 19).

> ➢ **II.L.1.8.2.**

Yaḥyā ibn Dāʾūd the Maghribī

This is a reference to the Spanish grammarian Yaḥyā ibn Dāʾūd Ḥayyūj (d. c. 1000).

ולא נכליה אלי אן יגו אהל אללגה פנעלם פאידה מא אצטלחו עליה

and we should not abandon it until the people of the language come and we know the function of what they adopted as their convention.

Since the 'people of the language' are the primeval speech community, this would seem to be tantamount to saying that we should never deviate from the customary reading.

> ➢ **II.L.1.9.2.**

For the various degrees of 'heaviness' of *tav* see vol. 1, §I.3.1.11.3.

> ➢ **II.L.1.9.3.**

For the different realizations of *resh*, see vol. 1, §I.1.20.

➢ II.L.1.10.

ואעלם אן אהל אללגה געלו תצאריף אללגה עלי ארבעה אקסאם מן חרף
ואחד אצלי מתל הַכֵּה ונחוה ומן חרפין מתל בְּנֵה ונחוה ומן ג̇ מתל שָׁמֹר
ונחוה ומן ד̇ מתל כרבל ונחוה

Take note that the people of the language made the
conjugations of the language in four categories: from one
root letter, such as הַכֵּה 'hit' and the like, from two letters,
such as בְּנֵה 'build' and the like, from three letters, such as
שָׁמֹר and the like and from four letters, such as כַּרְבֵּל 'wrap',
and the like.

According to the medieval Karaite grammarians, the base of the
process of the derivation of a word was not an abstract root but
rather a concrete structural form consisting of both consonants
and vowels. Such a theory of derivational morphology was
developed in the early Karaite tradition of grammatical thought
in the tenth century, the main extant source for which is the
Diqduq of Ibn Nūḥ. According to Ibn Nūḥ the imperative form is
the derivational base of most verbal forms. The imperative, therefore, was used as the citation form of verbs. This practice of imperative citation forms was continued by ʾAbū al-Faraj in his
grammatical works and *Hidāyat al-Qāriʾ*, in which he uses them
as lemmata to identify and classify verbal conjugations. This was
despite the fact that according to his theory of grammar, adopted
from the mainstream Baṣran school of Arabic grammar, the infinitive was the base of morphological derivation of verbs; cf.
al-Kitāb al-Kāfī (ed. Khan, Gallego, and Olszowy-Schlanger 2003,
§II.16.12-15) and Khan (1997).

Although the Karaite grammarians did not work with a notion of an abstract root that functioned as the source of derivation, they did have a concept of an abstract underlying morphological level, which they referred to as the 'substance' (Arabic *jawhar*) of a word (Khan 2000b, 74–78). Unlike the morphological base, the substance is not an actual linguistic form that can be pronounced. It consists of a series of letters that are regarded as the core of the word. This is what is referred to in this passage in *Hidāyat al-Qārī* as 'root letter' (*ḥarf ʾaṣlī*). Various letters that are present in the morphological base of a word do not belong to the substance and so are not root letters. A final *he* in a verb is not considered to belong to the substance. The substance of imperative bases such as בְּנֵה, therefore, are said to consist of two root letters. A prefix such as the *he* prefix of the *hifꜤil* that does not occur in all inflected forms is not considered to be a root letter. The substance of the verb הַכֵּה 'hit' was considered to consist of only one root letter. For further details see Khan (2013a; 2013b).

ואלחרף איצֿא קד תתקלב פי אללפטֿה ותתגֿאיר מעאניהא

> A letter may also change position in a word with the result
> that its meaning changes.

ʾAbū al-Faraj offers here only one set of examples of such changes of position. In his grammar book *al-Kitāb al-Mushtamil* (see vol. 1, §I.0.13.4), however, he devotes a long section to this question and presents an inventory of sets of lexical forms that share letters in different sequences (Bacher 1895, 247–49). This is known as an anagrammatical lexical arrangement and is attested in other medieval Jewish sources, in particular *Kitāb al-Ḥāwī* 'The

Book of Collection' of Hai Gaon, which is a complete anagrammatical dictionary of Hebrew (Allony 1969b, 1972).

➢ II.L.1.11.

The term 'enhancement' (*tafkhīm*) is used by ʾAbū al-Faraj to refer to the extension of the basic form of a word or affix by the addition of letters without, in principle, bringing about a change in meaning. The list of examples of added letters includes some additions that we would normally interpret as functional affixes, such as directive *he*, e.g. בָּבֶל 'Babylon'—בָּבֶלָה 'to Babylon' (2 Kings 20.17, etc.), or cohortative *he*, e.g. שׁוּב 'return'—שׁוּבָה 'return' (Num. 10.36, etc.). ʾAbū al-Faraj uses the term הא אלתפכים *'he* of enhancement' to refer to cohortative *he* in his grammar book *al-Kitāb al-Kāfī* (ed. Khan, Gallego and Olszowy-Schlanger 2003, §I.27.126), but does not examine there the phenomenon of enhancement systematically. Saadya Gaon, on the other hand, treats the subject extensively in his grammar *Kitāb Faṣīḥ Lughat al-ʿIbrāniyyīn* 'The Book of the Eloquence of the Language of the Hebrews' (Dotan 1997, 142–45). When, however, ʾAbū al-Faraj mentions in *Hidāyat al-Qāriʾ* 'somebody who has discussed enhancement' (§II.L.1.11.5., §II.L.1.12.1.), he does not seem to be referring to Saadya, since the cited examples do not correspond to what is extant in Saadya's work.

➢ II.L.1.11.5.

אלאמר הוֹדֵה הוֹשַׁע

the imperative forms are הוֹדֵה and הוֹשַׁע

The imperative form was regarded by the early Karaite grammarians as the morphological stem on the basis of which verbal inflections were formed. In his grammar *al-Kitāb al-Kāfī*, ʾAbū al-Faraj adopts from the mainstream Baṣran tradition of Arabic grammatical thought the notion that the infinitive was the base of derivation (Khan 1997). This Baṣran Arabic tradition was merged with the early Karaite tradition in the grammatical works of ʾAbū al-Faraj, which sometimes results in apparent inconsistency. He, for example, continued to use the imperative as the citation form of verbs (Khan 2013a). In this passage of *Hidāyat al-Qāriʾ* he appears to be working with the early Karaite notion that the imperative was indeed the stem of derivation.

> ## II.L.1.12.3.

For the term *diqdūqiyyūn* 'diqduq scholars' see the comments above on §II.L.1.1.7.

   The notion of 'auxiliary letter' (*ḥarf mustaʿmal*) is explained by the anonymous Karaite author of *Kitāb al-ʿUqūd* (ed. Vidro 2013a, 51):

> An auxiliary letter is established in the entire conjugation.
> If it is removed, what remains are the letters of the lexical
> class standing without a clear meaning Examples are the
> *lamed* in the lexical class of 'taking', or the *nun* in the
> lexical class of 'going away' and in the lexical class of
> 'approaching', as in נוֹגְעִים, נוֹסְעִים, לוֹקְחִים etc. Here there is
> a clear difference between the removal of the auxiliary *lamed* and that of *ḥet* or *qof*. This holds for each auxiliary

letter. The difference between its removal and the removal
of a root letter is obvious and evident.[8]

I.e. the auxiliary letter is an integral component of the
conjugation but elided in some inflections, as is the case with *nun*
and *lamed* in the cited verbs. This would differ from letters of
enhancement, which are added to the basic letters of a
conjugation, and so are not integral to it.

➢ II.L.1.13.

The 'contraction' (*ʾikhtiṣār*) is the converse of 'expansion', in that
it involves the elision of a letter from the basic form of a word or
affix without changing meaning. The basic form is often referred
to in this section as the 'virtual form' (*taqdīr*), i.e. the expected
regular form (see the comments on §II.L.1.4.8. above). ʾAbū al-
Faraj uses the concept of contraction of letters in *al-Kitāb al-Kāfī*
and, likewise, refers to the uncontracted form as the *taqdīr* of the
word, e.g. ed. Khan, Gallego and Olszowy-Schlanger (2003,
§I.23.7.). This subject is treated systematically by Saadya in his
grammar *Kitāb Faṣīḥ Lughat al-ʿIbrāniyyīn* (Dotan 1997, 140–42).

➢ II.L.2.2.1.

In this passage relating to the origin of vowels, ʾAbū al-Faraj offers a view of the origin of language that differs from the view

---

[8] ואלמסתעמל הו אלד'י יתבת פי אלתצריף כלה ואא זאל בקית חרוף אללגה תّאבתה מן
גיר מעני מסתקר פיהא מתّל אללמאד אלדّי פי לגה אלאכّד ואל[נ]ון פי לגה אלרחיל ולגה
אלדנו בّכّ לוקחים נוסעים נוגעים ואמתّאל דّלך ממא אלפרק בין זّאל אללמאד
אלמסתעמל ובין זّאל אלקוף או אלחית פרקא ואצّחא וכّדّלך כّל חרף מסתעמל אדّא אזّיל
ואזّיל אלחרף אלאצّלי כّאן אלפרק בינהמא בّינא גّליא.

that it has a purely human origin through convention among the primeval speech community known as 'the people of the language' (ʾahl al-lugha), which he presents elsewhere in *Hidāyat al-Qāriʾ* and his grammatical works. In the passage he acknowledges that vowels were an integral part of the original conventional establishment of language ('in the original establishment [of language] by convention they [i.e. the vowels] were indispensable'). He then, however, goes on to associate the origin of language with Adam, according to the biblical account of the origin of language:

וַיָּבֵא אֶל־הָאָדָם לִרְאוֹת מַה־יִּקְרָא־לוֹ וְכֹל אֲשֶׁר יִקְרָא־לוֹ הָאָדָם נֶפֶשׁ חַיָּה הוּא שְׁמוֹ: וַיִּקְרָא הָאָדָם שֵׁמוֹת לְכָל־הַבְּהֵמָה וּלְעוֹף הַשָּׁמַיִם וּלְכֹל חַיַּת הַשָּׂדֶה

'and He (the Lord) brought them (the animals and birds) to the man to see what he would call them; and whatever the man called every living creature, that was its name. The man gave names to all cattle, and to the birds of the air, and to every beast of the field' (Gen. 2.19-20)

ʾAbū al-Faraj suggests various ways of interpreting Adam's activity. He and the angels may have established language by convention. This would, in effect, be extending the notion of the primeval speech community (ʾahl al-lugha) to a community of Adam and the angels rather than original human speakers alone. Another possibility, says ʾAbū al-Faraj, is that the angels taught Adam language. The angels, moreover, would have been taught language by God. The development of language by convention between God and the angels was not possible since such a process requires limbs with which to point to objects and ʾAbū al-Faraj, like his Muʿtazilite contemporaries, rejects anthropomorphisms attributed to God such as human-like limbs.

The teaching of language to Adam by angels, who in turn learnt it from God, is a revelationist view of the origin of language. This was adopted by some Muslim theologians and grammarians of the period (Weiss 1974; Loucel 1963). The process of revelatory teaching of language was known in the Islamic tradition as *tawqīf* 'making known' or *waḥy* 'inspiring' and was based on the Qurʾanic verse: وَعَلَّمَ ءَادَمَ ٱلْأَسْمَآءَ كُلَّهَا 'and He (God) taught Adam all the names (of things)' (2.31).

The fact that ʾAbū al-Faraj presents different versions of the origin of language, conventionalist and revelationist, may have arisen as an attempt to find a synthesis between rationalist Muʿtazilite thought and Jewish biblical tradition.[9] Saadya Gaon, likewise, strove to achieve such a synthesis. Unlike ʾAbū al-Faraj, however, Saadya did not attempt this by offering alternative views, but rather presented a hybrid view. According to Saadya a single primeval human, referred to as 'the establisher of the language' (*wāḍiʿ al-lugha*), fixed arbitrary names for entities and this fixing was subsequently accepted by consensus (*ʾiṣṭilāḥ*)

---

[9] Maimonides followed an Aristotelian view and regarded Adam's act of naming as indicating by itself that languages are conventional, see *Guide of the Perplexed* (transl. Pines 1969, 357). By contrast, Jewish exegetes in medieval Europe adopted a revelationist interpretation. Naḥmanides, at the height of the 'Maimonidean controversy', explicitly rejected Maimonides' notion of convention; cf. Saenz-Badillos (2004, 297).

among people and transmitted to later generations. The 'establisher of the language' that Saadya had in mind was presumably Adam, but he left the name unspecified, possibly to make his theory more universalist and applicable to all human language. According to Saadya, God did not create language but gave Adam the faculty of language (Dotan 1995; 1997, 96–104).

It is also possible that ʾAbū al-Faraj was influenced by some streams of Muslim thought in the eleventh century that attempted a synthesis of the revelationist and conventionalist views (associated with the scholar ʾAbū ʾIsḥāq al-ʾAsfarāʾīnī, d. 1027) or were non-committal and held that neither view could be argued conclusively (associated with the scholar ʾAbū al-Bakr al-Bāqillānī, d. 1013) (Weiss 1974).

> ## II.L.2.3.2.

> ללערב פי לגתהם מן אלאעראב תלתה והי אלרפע והו אלצמה מן פוק
> ואלנצב והו אלפתחה מן פוק ואלכפﬞץ והי אלכסרה מן אספל

> The Arabs have three inflectional vowels in their language. These are 'raising' (*rafʿ*), i.e. the vowel *ḍamma*, which is written above; 'holding level' (*naṣb*), i.e. the *fatḥa* vowel, which is written above; and 'lowering' (*khafḍ*), i.e. the vowel *kasra*, which is written below.

The terms *rafʿ* 'raising', *naṣb* 'holding level' and *khafḍ* 'lowering' derive from a theory of the production of vowels originating in Arabic grammatical thought that involves both the position of buccal organs and the direction of the dynamic flow of air. It was adopted also by Saadya (Dotan 1997, 113–26) and is found in a Hebrew Masoretic treatise published by Baer and Strack (1879, §36), see Eldar (1983) and Posegay (2020). In this section of

Hidāyat al-Qāriʾ ʾAbū al-Faraj is referring to the vowels of Arabic case inflections, which mark syntactic relations. In §II.L.2.4.– §II.L.2.8. he transfers this terminology to categorize Hebrew vowels in morphological patterns. The seven Hebrew vowels are assigned to the three Arabic categories as follows: *rafʿ* (*holem*, *shureq*), *naṣb* (*pataḥ*, *segol*, *qameṣ*), *khafḍ* (*ṣere*, *ḥireq*). A similar practice of applying this three-way classification of vowels to Hebrew morphology is found in the Masoretic treatise §36 of the corpus of Baer and Strack (1879).

> ## II.L.2.4.

ואלנצב ידכל תחתה ‏ِ‏ נגמאת אלפתחה אלכברי והי אָ ואלפתחה אלוסטי
והי אָ ואלפתחה אלצגרי והי אָ

Three vowels correspond to (the Arabic inflectional vowel) 'holding level' (*naṣb*), namely 'big *fatḥa*', i.e. אָ, 'medium *fatḥa*', i.e. אָ, and 'small *fatḥa*', i.e. אָ.

In early Masoretic terminology a basic distinction was made between *pataḥ* (open vowel) and *qameṣ* (vowel with lip-tightening). The vowel *segol* was associated with *pataḥ* and referred to as *pataḥ qaṭan* 'small *pataḥ*'. The vowel *ṣere* was associated with *qameṣ* and referred to as *qameṣ qaṭan* 'small *qameṣ*', see vol. 1, §I.2.1.5. Here in *Hidāyat al-Qāriʾ* a different grouping of the vowels is made based on the perceived proximity of the Hebrew vowels to each of the three Arabic vowels. In the early Masoretic terms *pataḥ qaṭan* and *qameṣ qaṭan*, the attribute 'small' relates to the notion that these vowels were in some way more attenuated and less open than prototypical *pataḥ* and *qameṣ*. This notion can be traced back to Syriac grammatical sources where the Syriac

term *qaṭṭīn* 'narrow' is used to describe the higher front vowels
(Posegay 2020). The terms 'big *fatḥa*', 'medium *fatḥa*' and 'small
fatḥa' seem to relate to varying degrees of lip-spreading. The
vowel *pataḥ* was pronounced with the maximal degree of lip-
spreading and *qameṣ* with the lowest degree, with *segol* exhibiting
an intermediate lip position. The same attributes are used in
§II.L.2.7. and applied to the term *naṣb*, viz. 'big *naṣb*' for *pataḥ*
and 'small *naṣb*' for *qameṣ*.

> ## II.L.2.5.

אלי גיר דלך ממא קד אסתעמל פי אלאמר ואלעבר מתל שׁוֹרֶף שׁוֹרַף
וזנהמא ואסתעמל פי אלאמר מן תצריף כּוֹנֵן נחו סֹב חֹן ואסתעמל פי
אלעבר מן תצריף שירו נחו נוֹדַע נוֹשַׁע

To these should be added forms that are used for the
imperative and the past such as שׁוֹרֶף 'be burnt', שׁוֹרַף 'was
burnt', and other examples of this pattern; those that are
used for the imperative in the conjugaton כּוֹנֵן such as סֹב
'turn', חֹן 'be gracious'; those that are used for the past in
the conjugation שִׁירוֹ, such as נוֹדַע 'be known', נוֹשַׁע 'be
saved'.

The Karaite grammarians regarded the imperative form to be the
morphological base of most verbal forms (see comments on
§II.L.1.10. above). This morphological base enshrined the core
structural features of the inflected forms derived from it.
Although the imperative base is a concrete linguistic form, it is
not necessarily a form that is attested in the corpus of Biblical
Hebrew. The Karaite grammarians held that it is crucial that
there is a close structural relationship between the base and the
inflected form. If there is no attested imperative that is deemed

sufficiently close in structure to the inflected form, a common way of resolving this problem is to propose a hypothetical imperative base.

The imperative base always belongs to the same pattern (*binyan*) as the verbal form derived from it. The notion of pattern (*binyan*) as a unitary abstract category, however, is not found in the morphological theory of the Karaite grammarians. Imperative bases were classified together in groups not on account of sharing of abstract stems but on account of their sharing of actual structural patterns. The imperative form כְּתֹב 'write', for instance, was said to have the same pattern as imperatives such as שְׁמֹר 'guard' and קְצֹר 'harvest'. The imperative שׁוּב 'return' was said to have the same pattern as קוּם 'arise'. The forms כְּתֹב and שׁוּב, however, were not classified together on a more abstract structural level, as became the custom in Hebrew grammar following the teachings of Ḥayyūj.

As remarked, the imperative base had to have a maximally close structural resemblance to the form derived from it. In order to achieve this in some cases the imperative form that is posited as the base of an inflected verb does not actually occur in the language, e.g. נְתֹן for נָתַנּוּ 'we have given' (1 Chron. 29.14), הֲלֹךְ for תְּהֲלֵךְ 'it walks' (Psa. 73.9) and בַּקְשֶׂה for בִּקְשָׂה 'it has sought' (Ecc. 7.28). The motivation for positing an imperative base such as בַּקְשֶׂה is to construe the derivation of the form בִּקְשָׂה, without the *dagesh* in the *qof*, as fully regular and not an anomalous inflection of the imperative base בַּקֵּשׁ, which contains *dagesh*. Such hypothetical imperatives were not used for the writing of creative literature. Indeed, no Karaite author has been found who used these postulated forms in a creative Hebrew text. This reflects the fact that the proposed imperative base of a verb was intended as a purely structural source of derivation. Further evidence for this is that even passive forms expressed by morphological patterns that we now call the *puʿal* and *hufʿal/hofʿal* are regarded by the Karaite grammarians as derived from imperative bases, which cannot be naturally functional in the language, e.g. the past form עֻשֵּׂיתִי 'I was made' (Psa. 139.15) is said to be derived from the imperative form עֲשֵׂה. Here in §II.L.2.5. of *Hidayat al-Qāri⁾* the past form שׂוֹרַף 'was burnt' (inferred from וְהִנֵּה שׂרָף 'and behond it was burnt' Lev. 10.16) is cited alongside the imperative שׂוֹרֵף 'be burnt', which would have been considered to exist hypothetically as its morphological base. Passive imperative bases of *puʿal* and *hufʿal/hofʿal* patterns have *ṣere* in their second syllable by analogy with active *piʿel* and *hifʿil* imperatives. For more details see Khan (2000b, 41–45; 2013a; 2013b).

⁾Abū al-Faraj uses mnemonic symbols to arrange the imperative bases of verbal conjugations into classes. Such a classification is presented systematically in §I.22 of *al-Kitāb al-Kāfī* (ed. Khan, Gallego and Olszowy-Schlanger 2003). These symbols, known in Arabic as *ʿalāma* or *ribāṭ* and in Hebrew as סימן, consisted of bisyllabic Hebrew words in which the first vowel corresponds to the vowel common to all imperatives and the last vowel to the vowel common to all past forms in the class. The vowels in question may be those of the first syllable of the imperative and past forms or those of the last syllable of these forms (Vidro 2013b, 652). The conjugations of the imperatives

הַכֵּה and דַּבֵּר, for example, were assigned to a class designated by the mnemonic symbol גְּנִי, which was based on the first vowel of the imperatives (דַּבֵּר, הַכֵּה) and the past forms (דִּבֶּר, הִכָּה). In a similar way the symbol שִׁירָה included conjugations with imperative bases with the patterns שִׂים and הִכּוֹן, with *ḥireq* in their initial syllable and *qames* in the initial syllable of their past forms, viz. שָׂם and נָכוֹן. The symbol מֵסַב included conjugations in which the imperative had a *ṣere* in the final syllable and the past had a *pataḥ* in the final syllable, e.g. הִמָּלֵט (imperative)—נִמְלַט (past).

This system of classification originated in the early Karaite tradition and was developed by ʾAbū al-Faraj. It was subsequently elaborated still further in some other Karaite works, such as the anonymous treatises *Kitāb al-ʿUqūd* (Vidro 2011; 2013a) and *Meʾor ʿAyin* (Zislin 1990). The classification of verbal conjugations and the systematization of rules for their derivation that are found in these works are likely to have had a pedagogical motivation (Vidro 2011, 165–79).

Just as hypothetical imperative bases were posited for certain past forms, e.g. נְתֹן for נָתַנּוּ 'we have given', so hypothetical past forms were in some cases posited for attested imperative forms. This applies, for example, to the first in the class of conjugations represented by the symbol כּוֹנֵן, which is mentioned in §II.L.2.5. of *Hidāyat al-Qāriʾ*—in the manuscript used in the edition for this passage the original *pataḥ* has been replaced by *segol* due to interference from Arabic phonology on the scribe, viz. כּוֹנֶן (cf. vol. 1, §I.4.3.3.). In conjugations represented by the symbol כּוֹנֵן the first vowel of the imperative is *ḥolem* and the first vowel of the past form is *pataḥ*. The imperatives of the class כּוֹנֵן that are given in §II.L.2.5. are סֹב 'turn' and חֹן 'be gracious'. The attested 3ms past forms of סֹב and חֹן are סָבַב and חָנַן. It is assumed, however, that these imperatives have hypothetical 3ms past forms סַב and חַן, in which the first vowel is *patah*, in conformity with the symbol כּוֹנֵן. This is explicitly stated in *al-Kitāb al-Kāfī* (ed. Khan, Gallego and Olszowy-Schlanger 2003, §I.22.19) and *Kitāb al-ʿUqūd* (ed. Vidro 2013a, 167). The forms סַב and חַן were inferred from attested inflected forms such as סַבֹּ֫תִי 'I have turned' (1 Sam. 22.22), חַנַּ֫נִי 'he has treated me graciously' (Gen. 33.11) and וְחַנֹּתִ֫י 'and I shall be gracious' (Exod. 22.19).

The other symbol mentioned in §II.L.2.5. is שִׁירוֹ, which is exemplified by the past forms נוֹדַע and נוֹשַׁע, with *holem* in their first syllable. The imperative forms of these are הִוָּדַע and הִוָּשַׁע, with *hireq* in their first syllable. Full details and vocalization are given in *al-Kitāb al-Kāfī* (ed. Khan, Gallego and Olszowy-Schlanger 2003, §I.22.25) and *Kitāb al-ʿUqūd* (ed. Vidro 2013a, 193).

פקד צאר הדא אלקסם אלואחד יסתעמל פי אלפאעלין כמא אסתעמלו
אלערב רפע [הם פ]י אלפאעלין ואסתעמלו אלעבראניין פי גיר אלפאעלין
תוסעא כמא אסתעמלו אלערב רפעהם פי ג[יר] אלפאעלין תוסעא מן נחו
אלאבתדא ואלאסתפהאם וגיר דלך

This category (of *rafʿ*) is used for agents, just as the Arabs use *rafʿ* for agents. The Hebrews use it for forms other than those designating agents by extension, just as the Arabs use their *rafʿ* for forms other than those designating agents by extension, such as initial positioning (of nominal subjects), interrogative constructions, and so forth.

In this passage 'Abū al-Faraj identifies a correspondence between the use of the Arabic and Hebrew *rafᶜ* in their marking of agents. In the case of Arabic, the *rafᶜ* vowel *-u* is a case-vowel marking the agent of the clause and so plays a syntactic role. In Hebrew, by contrast, the use of the *rafᶜ* vowel *ḥolem* plays a morphological role as an element in the morphological pattern of Hebrew agents, e.g. הֹרֵג 'slayer'. According to 'Abū al-Faraj the use of *ḥolem* in Hebrew in other morphological patterns is by a process of extension that is analogous to the extension of the *rafᶜ* case-vowel *-u* in Arabic to items that are not agents, including the subject of nominal (i.e. verbless) clauses and interrogative constructions. The latter is most likely referring to nominal clauses with initial interrogative particles such as *hal al-'amīru fī al-bayti?* 'Is the commander in the house?', in which the item with the *-u* case vowel is not the initial item (*mubtada'*).

➢ II.L.2.6.

The symbol שׁוּעָל includes conjugations in which the first vowel of the imperative is *shureq* and the first vowel of the past form is *qameṣ*, e.g. קָם—קוּם, שָׁב—שׁוּב; cf. *al-Kitāb al-Kafī* (ed. Khan, Gallego and Olszowy-Schlanger 2003, §I.22.18) and *Kitāb al-ᶜUqūd* (ed. Vidro 2013a, 161–65).

➢ II.L.2.7.1.

אלמפעול אלמטלק והו אלמצדר נחו שָׁמֹר זָכֹר בָּנֹה עָשֹׂה ואמתאל דלך

It is used in the 'absolute patient', i.e the infinitive, as in שָׁמוֹר 'guarding', זָכוֹר 'remembering', בָּנֹה 'building', עָשֹׂה 'doing', and the like.

The Arabic 'absolute patient' (*mafʿūl muṭlaq*) is a verbal noun in the accusative case in constructions such as *ḍaraba ḍarban* 'he struck a striking', *sāra sayran* 'he journeyed a journey'. This has the role of an 'inner object', i.e. a syntactic object that does not express the role of the undergoer of the action expressed by the verb but rather the action itself. In *al-Kitāb al-Kāfī* (ed. Khan, Gallego, and Olszowy-Schlanger 2003, §I.21.2.) the Arabic *mafʿūl muṭlaq* is equated by ʾAbū al-Faraj with the Hebrew infinitive. He cites examples there of both the infinitive absolute and also the infinitive construct, which he did not distinguish as separate forms as we do today. In this passage in *Hidāyat al-Qāriʾ* the Hebrew examples are infinitive absolutes.

> ## II.L.2.7.2.

The symbol גִּנִּי represents conjugations that have imperatives with *pataḥ* in their first syllable and past forms with *ḥireq* in their first syllable. This clearly applies to the first two examples cited, viz. הִטָּה—הַטֵּה, הִכָּה—הַכֵּה. It does not apply, however, to the other two imperatives that are cited, viz. הַאֲכֵל and הַעֲמֵד, which have *segol* in the first syllable of their past forms, viz. הֶאֱכִיל and הֶעֱמִיד. For this reason the author of *Kitāb al-ʿUqūd* classified the last two verbal conjugations under the symbol מַכֶּה (ed. Vidro 2013a, 199). In *al-Kitāb al-Kāfī* ʾAbū al-Faraj does not have מַכֶּה in his inventory of symbols. In §I.22.10. of *al-Kitāb al-Kāfī* he includes הַרְאֵה (imperative)—הֶרְאָה (past) in the symbol גִּנִּי, but states that the past form 'does not have a *ḥireq* on account of the *resh*.' He does not mention the imperatives הַאֲכֵל and הַעֲמֵד, but presumably he would have included them in גִּנִּי, as here in *Hidāyat al-Qāriʾ*,

in the same way as הָרְאֵה and explain the *segol* as a change conditioned by the initial guttural.

אלמצאדר אלמסתעארה נחו דבֵר קוֵה לשלום

'transposed infinitives', such as דַּבֶּר 'speak', קַוֵּה לְשָׁלוֹם'(we) look for peace' (Jer. 8.15, etc.)

'Transposed infinitives' (*maṣādir mustaʿāra*) are infinitives whose form originally belongs to a different category, in this case that of an imperative, but has been extended to the function of an infinitive. This type of infinitive is discussed in *Kitāb al-ʿUqūd* (ed. Vidro 2011, 303).

> ## II.L.2.8.2.

The inventory that is given here of past forms in the class of conjugations represented by the symbol גַּנִּי (i.e. conjugations with imperatives with *pataḥ* in their first syllable and with past forms with *ḥireq* in their first syllable; cf. the comments on §II.L.2.7.2., §II.L.2.5. above) is longer than the one given by ʾAbū al-Faraj in the section on גַּנִּי in *al-Kitāb al-Kāfī* (ed. Khan, Gallego and Olszowy-Schlanger 2003, §I.22.6.–§I.22.13.). It does, however, correspond closely to the fuller inventory of conjugations of גַּנִּי that is found in *Kitāb al-ʿUqūd* (ed. Vidro 2103, 96-151). Some of these are hypothetical past forms that require comment.

The list here in *Hidāyat al-Qāriʾ* includes the two forms הִשְׁלִיךְ 'he threw' and הִשְׁלֵיךְ 'he threw'. *Kitāb al-ʿUqūd* (ed. Vidro 2013a, 128-130) distinguishes between the two conjugations הַשְׁלֵךְ (imperative)—הִשְׁלֵךְ (past) and הַשְׁלֵיךְ (imperative)—הִשְׁלֵיךְ (past). The first lacks a *yod* in both imperative and past whereas the second has a *yod* in both forms. The purpose of distinguishing the two conjugations was to account for the lack of *yod* in the attested imperative and short imperfect forms such as וַיַּשְׁלֵךְ 'and he cast' (Jud. 9.17) versus the presence of *yod* in other inflections such as הִשְׁלִיךְ (past), מַשְׁלִיךְ (active participle) and הַשְׁלִיךְ (infinitive). In the first conjugation the past form is hypothetical (הִשְׁלֵךְ) whereas in the second conjugation the imperative is hypothetical (הַשְׁלִיךְ with *yod*). Our passage in *Hidāyat al-Qāriʾ* has the two past forms הִשְׁלִיךְ and הִשְׁלֵךְ. It appears that this is a scribal error in the extant manuscripts and this should read הִשְׁלִיךְ and הִשְׁלֵךְ (without *yod*).

The past form הִפְצַר and its imperative form הַפְצַר are inferred from וְאָוֶן וּתְרָפִים הַפְצַר 'stubbornness is iniquity and idolatry' (1 Sam. 15.23); cf. *Kitāb al-ʿUqūd* (ed. Vidro 2013a, 131), Ibn Nūḥ, *Diqduq* (ed. Khan 2000b, 370–71).

The past form בִּקְשָׁה 'he sought' and its imperative form בַּקְשֶׁה are inferred from attested forms such as מְבַקְשֵׁי פָנֶיךָ 'those who seek your face" (Psa. 24.6), which does not have *dagesh* in the *qof*; cf. *Kitāb al-ʿUqūd* (ed. Vidro 2013a, 138-141), Ibn Nūḥ, *Diqduq* (ed. Khan 2000b, 61) and an early anonymous Karaite treatise (ed. Khan 2000a, 106–15).

The past form הִדְרְכָה 'he bent (a bow)' and its imperative הַדְרְכֶה are inferred from the attested form וַיַּדְרְכוּ אֶת־לְשׁוֹנָם קַשְׁתָּם שֶׁקֶר 'and they bent their tongue like their bow in falsehood' (Jer. 9.2); cf. *Kitāb al-ʿUqūd* (ed. Vidro 2013a, 138-139).

Conjugations represented by the symbol שִׁירָה contain a *ḥireq* in the first syllable of their imperative form and a *qameṣ* in the first syllable of their past form (*al-Kitāb al-Kāfī*, ed. Khan,

Gallego and Olszowy-Schlanger 2003, §I.22.20.–§I.22.24.; *Kitāb al-ʿUqūd*, ed. Vidro 2013a, 172-189, *Meʾor ʿAyin* ed. Zislin 1990, 129), viz. שִׂים (imperative)—שָׂם (past), שִׂיח (imperative)—שָׂח (hypothetical past), הָכוֹן (imperative)—נָכוֹן (past), הָמֵק (hypothetical imperative)—נָמַק (past) inferred from וּלְשׁוֹנוֹ תִּמַּק 'and his tongue will rot' (Zech. 14.12) and הִבְאִישׁוּ נָמַקּוּ חַבּוּרֹתָי 'my wounds have grown foul and have festered' (Psa. 38.6), הָבוּךְ (hypothetical imperative)—נָבוּךְ (hypothetical past)—נָבוּךְ (active participle) inferred from נְבֻכִים הֵם בָּאָרֶץ 'they are entangled in the land' (Exod. 14.3). The imperative form הָסוֹעַ, which is given in this section in *Hidāyat al-Qāriʾ* as an imperative of the symbol שִׁירָה, does not appear in the lists of conjugations in the Karaite grammatical texts and it is not clear from what attested forms it could be inferred. The lists offer other imperatives that are close in form, viz. הָסוֹג inferred from נָסֹגוּ אָחוֹר 'they shall be turned back' (Isa. 42.17) and הָנוֹעַ inferred from כַּאֲשֶׁר יִנּוֹעַ בַּכְּבָרָה 'as it is sieved in a sieve' (Amos 9.9) (*Kitāb al-ʿUqūd* ed. Vidro 2013a, 180-183). It is possible that הָסוֹעַ is a scribal conflation of these two forms.

The symbol מֵסַב included conjugations that had *ṣere* in the final syllable of the imperative and *pataḥ* in the final syllable of the past form (*al-Kitāb al-Kāfī*, ed. Khan, Gallego and Olszowy-Schlanger 2003, §I.22.36; *Kitāb al-ʿUqūd*, ed. Vidro 2013a, 220-42; *Meʾor ʿAyin*, ed. Zislin 1990, 135-36). The *pataḥ* in the hypothetical past form הִתְהַלַּךְ would have been inferred from forms such as הִתְהַלַּכְתִּי 'I walked' (Gen. 24.40).

> ## II.L.2.10.2.

פצאר אלחרף אלדי תחתה אלשוא סאכנא לא יתחרך בתה מהמא הוא
תחתה ופצלה ממא בעדה ואצّאפה אלי מא קבלה

Whatever letter it occurs under is not mobile at all and it
(the quiescent *shewa*) cuts it off from what is after it and
conjoins it to what is before it.

For this function of silent *shewa* see vol. 1, §I.2.5.2.

> ## II.L.2.12.

Some of the material in this section on the mobile *shewa* has parallels in earlier Masoretic treatises such as §11-§15 of Baer and
Strack's (1879) corpus, *Diqduqe ha-Ṭeʿmim* (ed. Dotan 1967, §5,
§14) and the *Treatise on the Shewa* (ed. Levy 1936).

> ## II.L.2.12.1.1.

אלאן אן יחסן מעה דכול אלגעיה כרג בכרוג אלמלך סוא נחו ואם כָּכָה
אלשוא תחת אלואו כרג אלואו בחרק מתל מא תחת אלאלף מכפפא למא
לם תכון מעה אלגעיה

Now, if it is appropriate for *gaʿya* to occur on it, it is
pronounced equal to the vowel (following it), for example,
וְאִם־כָּכָה 'and if thus' (Num. 11.15), in which *shewa* is under
vav and the *vav* is pronounced with *ḥireq* like that which is
under the *ʾalef*, but shortened since it it does not have
gaʿya.

The argument here is that a *shewa* with a *gaʿya* behaves like a full
vowel and so would be long in an open syllable.

> ➤ II.L.2.12.2.1.

פשוא אלד חרוף מקצור עלי מא קבלה ושוא אליוד גיר מקצור עלי מא
בעדה

The *shewa* of the four letters is restricted by what is before
it, but the *shewa* of *yod* is not restricted by what is after it.

The intention here seems to be as follows. When a *shewa* is followed by a guttural consonant, its realization is determined by
whether or not it is preceded by a guttural consonant. The realization of *shewa* before *yod*, however, is not affected by the vowel
that follows the *yod*.

> ➤ II.L.2.12.3.3.

אין אב ללגעיה

The *ga'ya* has no principle.

In modern terminology this is tantamount to saying that the *ga'ya*
has no phonological function but is only an optional phonetic
phenomenon. This applies to cases where, according to the discussion in this passage, the reader has a choice as to whether to
pronounce *ga'ya* or not. It would not apply to cases such as יְשָׁנוּ
'they [do not] sleep' (Prov. 4.16)—וַיִּשְׁנוּ 'and they did it a second
time' (1 Kings 18.34), where the *ga'ya* is obligatory.

> ➤ II.L.2.12.5.

פאן תם אלף מסתעאר פאדא קלת שתים שתי צאר אלשוא סאכן

For if there is an added *'alef* and you say [ʔɛʃ'tʰaːjim] and
[ʔɛʃ'tʰeː], the *shewa* becomes quiescent.

In the available manuscripts, the prosthetic *ʾalef* is not written. It is explicitly written in discussions of this topic in some other Masoretic treatises, e.g. *Treatise on the Shewa* and the other sources discussed by Levy (1936, 31–33).

➢ II.L.2.12.6.

Parallels to this section are found in §14 of Baer and Strack's (1879) corpus of Masoretic treatises and in *Kitāb al-Muṣawwitāt* (ed. Allony 1963, 146; 1983, 116).

For the *ḥatef qameṣ* in the closed syllable of מָשְׁכוּ אוֹתָהּ 'drag her!' (Ezek. 32.20) see vol. 1, §I.2.5.1.

➢ II.L.2.12.9.

The point of adducing שָׁמְרָה נַפְשִׁי וְהַצִּילֵנִי 'Guard my life and deliver me' (Psa. 25.20) and מָשְׁכוּ אוֹתָהּ 'draw her down' (Ezek. 32.20) as an objection seems to be that in some manuscripts the short *qameṣ* in words such as שָׁמְרָה and מָשְׁכוּ was represented by *ḥatef qameṣ*, and this could be construed as a mobile *shewa*, which would be followed by quiescence in the following letter. The response is referring to standard Tiberian vocalization, in which the shortness is not represented by using a *ḥatef qameṣ* in a closed syllable, but there is reliance only on the oral tradition.

➢ II.L.2.12.10.

The argument of this subsection complements that of the ninth subsection. The claim is that a mobile *shewa* has to be followed by a vowel and then, on the third letter, a quiescent *shewa* may occur.

➢ II.L.2.13.1.

See vol. 1, §I.2.5.8.1.

➢ II.L.2.13.2.

For an explanation for the reading of the *shewa* as silent in the six words that deviate from this rule, see vol. 1, §I.2.5.7.3.

➢ II.L.2.13.3.

For the distribution of vocalic *shewa* after conjunctive *vav*, see vol. 1, §I.2.5.8.4.

➢ II.L.2.15.

For the theory of vowel production described in this section, see vol. 1, §I.2.1.3.

➢ II.L.2.16.

In the Karaite grammatical works the term *ʿaraḍ* is normally used to designate a noun referring to an abstract quality that is an attribute of an entity, e.g. Ibn Nūḥ, *Diqduq* (ed. Khan 2000b, 238): בֶּכִי 'weeping' (Psa. 30.6), מֶרִי 'rebellion' (Num. 17.25), also *al-Kitāb al-Kāfī* (ed. Khan, Gallego and Olszowy-Schlanger 2003, xliv). Here the concept of *ʿaraḍ* has been extended to include also finite verbs.

➤ II.L.2.17.

This section is an analysis of the differences between vowels within the framework of the theory of the production of vowels that is adopted elsewhere in *Hidāyat al-Qāriʾ*, see comments on §II.L.2.3. above.

➤ II.L.3.2.1.

Cf. §44 in the Masoretic corpus published by Baer and Strack (1879).

➤ II.L.3.2.3.

Cf. §56 in the Masoretic corpus published by Baer and Strack (1879).

ורבאטהא אקלקני אלעבד כשית אלוגע קתלתה

> Their mnemonic combination is 'The slave has vexed me;
> I have feared pain; I have killed him'.

For such mnemonic devices see Vidro (2013b).

➤ II.L.3.2.4.

Cf. §40 and §72 in the Masoretic corpus published by Baer and Strack (1879); *Seder ha-Simanim* (Allony 1965, כז-כח) and *Kitāb al-Muṣawwitāt* (Allony 1963, 148–50; 1983, 106–9). See also vol. 1, §I.2.11.

> ➤ **II.L.3.2.5.**

Cf. *Diqduqe ha-Teʿamim* (ed. Dotan 1967, §7). For the exceptional cases see the discussion in vol. 1, §I.2.3.2., §I.2.11.

> ➤ **II.L.3.2.6.**

Cf. *Diqduqe ha-Teʿamim* (ed. Dotan 1967, §8). For the exceptional cases see the discussion in vol. 1, §I.2.3.2., §I.2.11.

> ➤ **II.L.3.2.7.**

Cf. *Diqduqe ha-Teʿamim* (ed. Dotan 1967, §21). Cf. vol. 1, §I.2.5.7.5.

SHORT VERSION

> ➤ **II.S.0.0.**

The short version begins with an authorial introduction, in which ʾAbū al-Faraj states that he has been requested to compose a short version of the longer work. As remarked in the comments above on the introduction to the long version, such an indication of a 'request to compose' was a standard component of introductions to Arabic works of the period and may have been fictitious, especially when, as is the case here, the requester remains anonymous.

> ➤ **II.S.1.7.**

In this section ʾAbū al-Faraj adds a comment on the phenomenon that he discussed a length in §II.L.1.5. of the long version. He indicates that he now prefers not to refer to the phenomenon as 'interchange' (*tabdīl*), since it is possible that the change of letters in the forms in question expresses semantic modification.

➤ II.S.2.9.

The one exception that breaks this rule is אֲדֹנָי בָּם 'the Lord in them' (Psa. 68.18); cf. long version, §II.L.1.7.8.

➤ II.S.4.2.

For this notion of the vowels being realizations of 'soft' letters א, ה, ו, and י see vol. 1, §I.2.1.8.

➤ II.S.5.6.

> ואעלם אן אלשוא אלמתחרך לא יקע פי אלחרף אלתאני לה סכון בתה
> לאנה יתחרך לאגל חרכת אלאול באלשוא

> Take note that a mobile *shewa* never occurs on a second
> letter (of a word) that has a silent (following letter),
> because it (this second letter) is mobile due to the mobility
> of the first letter with *shewa*.

I.e. if the first letter of a word has *shewa*, which must be mobile, the second letter cannot have a mobile *shewa*. This second letter has a vowel and this is followed by a silent letter, which is either a normal consonant, e.g. לְכַרְמִי, or a 'soft' letter inside a long vowel (see short version §II.S.4.2.), e.g. לְכוּ.

➤ II.S.5.7.

Both the *qameṣ* and the stressed *pataḥ* of the cited words were pronounced long, so, according to the theory of 'soft' letters (cf.

short version §II.S.4.2.), they contained an *ʾalef*, although this does not appear in the orthography.

> ## II.S.6.11.

The argument here seems to be that a mobile *shewa* is dependent on a mobile letter with a vowel, which, therefore, obligatorily follows a mobile *shewa*. A mobile *shewa* cannot be dependent on another mobile *shewa*. A quiescent *shewa* can come after a sequence of mobile *shewa* and a letter with a vowel, but not immediately after the initial mobile *shewa*.

REFERENCES AND ABBREVIATIONS

ABBREVIATIONS

Bod. = Bodleian Library, University of Oxford

CUL = Cambridge University Library

JRL = John Rylands Library, University of Manchester

NLR = National Library of Russia, St. Petersburg

REFERENCES

ʿAbd al-Wāḥid ibn Muḥammad ibn ʾAbī al-Saddād al-Mālaqī. 2002. الدر النثير والعذب النمير. Edited by ʿĀdil ʾAḥmad ʿAbd al-Mawjūd, ʿAlī Muḥammad Muʿawwaḍ and ʾAḥmad ʿĪsā al-Maʿṣarāwī. Beirut: Dār al-Kutub al-ʿIlmiyya.

ʾAbū ʿAmr ʿUthmān ibn Saʿīd al-Dānī. 2001. التحديد فى الاتقان والتجويد. Edited by Ghānim Qaddūrī al-Ḥamad. Amman: Dār ʿAmmār.

Allen, W. Sidney. 1948. 'Ancient Ideas on the Origin and Development of Language'. *Transactions of the Philological Society*, 35–60.

Allony, Nehemiah. 1963. ' ספר הקולות—כתאב אלמצותאת למשה בן אשר'. *Lěšonénu* 29: 9–23, 136–59.

———. 1964. 'רשימת מונחים קראית מהמאה השמינית'. In ספר קורנגרין, edited by Asher Weiser and Ben-Zion Luria, 324–63. Tel-Aviv: Niv.

———. 1965. 'סדר הסימנים'. *Hebrew Union College Annual* 35: 1-40 (Hebrew section).

——. 1969a. *Ha-ʾEgron Kitāb ʾUṣūl al-Shiʿr al-ʿIbrānī by Rav Sĕʿadya Gaʾon*. Critical Edition with Introduction and Commentary. Jerusalem: Academy of the Hebrew Language (in Hebrew).

——. 1969b. ʾהשיטה האנאגרמטית של המילונות העברית בספר יצירה'. *Proceedings of the World Congress of Jewish Studies* 5: 127–29.

——. 1972. ʾהשיטה האנאגרמטית של המילונות העברית בס' יצירה'. *Temirin* 1: 63–99.

——. 1975. 'שתי רשימות ספרים לרושם אחד במאה ה-13'. *Alei Sefer* 1: 35-58.

——. 1983. ' ספר הקולות (כתאב אלמצוותאת) למשה בן אשר (קטע חדש מגניזות קהיר—כי"ב)'. *Lĕšonénu* 47: 85–124.

Allony, Nehemiah, and Israel Yeivin. 1985. ' מספרות הקולות (אלמצוותאת) (ארבעה קטעים מגניזות קהיר—מארבעה חיבורים)'. *Lĕšonénu* 48–49: 85–117.

Bacher, Wilhelm. 1895. 'Le Grammairien Anonyme de Jérusalem'. *Revue des Études Juives* 30: 232–56.

Baer, Seligmann, and Hermann Leberecht Strack. 1879. *Diḳduḳe Ha-Ṭeʿamim*. Leipzig: L. Pernoy.

Basal, Nasir. 1998. ' החלק הראשון של "אלכתאב אלמשתמל" לאבו אלפרג' הרון ותלותו ב"כתאב אלאצול פי אלנחו" לאבן אלסראג''. *Lešonénu* 61: 191–209.

——. 1999. 'The Concept of Ḥāl in the *al-Kitāb al Muštamil* of Abū al-Faraǧ Hārūn in Comparison with Ibn al-Sarrāǧ'. *Israel Oriental Studies* 19: 391–408.

——. 2013. 'Latent Quiescent (Sākin Layyin)'. In *Encyclopedia of Hebrew Language and Linguistics*, edited by Geoffrey Khan,

Shmuel Bolozky, Steven E. Fassberg, Gary A. Rendsburg, Aaron D. Rubin, Ora R. Schwartzwald, and Tamar Zewi, 2:484–90. Leiden-Boston: Brill.

Becker, Dan. 1996. 'A Unique Semantic Classification of the Hebrew Verb Taken by the Qaraite ʾAbū Al-Faraj Hārūn from the Arab Grammarian ʾIbn al-Sarrāj'. *Jerusalem Studies in Arabic and Islam* 20: 237–59.

Campanini, Saverio. 2013. 'Cryptography'. In *Encyclopedia of Hebrew Language and Linguistics*, edited by Geoffrey Khan, Shmuel Bolozky, Steven E. Fassberg, Gary A. Rendsburg, Aaron Rubin, Ora R. Schwartzwald, and Tamar Zewi, 1:636–40. Leiden-Boston: Brill.

Dotan, Aron. 1967. *The Diqduqé Haṭṭĕʿamim of Ahăron Ben Moše Ben Ašér*. Jerusalem: The Academy of the Hebrew Language (in Hebrew).

———. 1995. 'Particularism and Universalism in the Linguistic Theory of Saadia Gaon'. *Sefarad* 51: 61–76.

———. 1997. *Dawn of Hebrew Linguistics: The Book of Elegance of the Language of the Hebrews*. Jerusalem: ha-Iggud ha-ʿOlami le-Madaʿe ha-Yahadut.

Eldar, Ilan. 1980. 'שער בדבר מקומות החיתוך של העיצורים מתוך הדאיה אלקאר הארוֹך'. *Lěšonénu* 45: 233-59.

———. 1983. 'עיון מחודש בשאלת חלוקת התנועות העבריות לדרך רום, מחקרי לשון: מוגשים לזאב בן־חיים בהגיעו In 'דרך מטה ודרך ניצב לשיבה, edited by Moshe Bar-Asher et al., 43–55. Jerusalem: Magnes.

———. 1987a. ‘ מכֿתצר הדאיה אלקאר": חלק הדקדוק יוצא לאור ע״פ
קטעי גניזה בצירוף מבוא ותרגום עברי, חלק ראשׁוֹן: מבוא '. *Lěšonénu*
50: 214–31.

———. 1987b. ‘ מכֿתצר הדאיה אלקאר": חלק הדקדוק יוצא לאור ע״פ
קטעי גניזה בצירוף מבוא ותרגום עברי, חלק שני: הטקסט ותרגומוֹ '.
Lěšonénu 51: 3–41.

———. 1994. *The Study of the Art of Correct Reading as Reflected
in the Medieval Treatise Hidāyat Al-Qāri*. Jerusalem:
Academy of the Hebrew Language (in Hebrew).

———. 2018. *The Masoretic Accentuation of the Hebrew Bible
According to the Medieval Treatise Horayat Haqore*.
Jerusalem: Bialik Institute (in Hebrew).

Fārābī, ʾAbū al-Naṣr al-. 1960. شرح الفارابى لكتاب ارسطوطاليس فى العبارة.
Edited by Wilheim Kutch and Stanley B. Marrow. Beirut:
Catholic Press.

Feldman, Louis H. 1992. ‘Some Observations on Rabbinic
Reaction to Roman Rule in Third Century Palestine’.
Hebrew Union College Annual 63: 39–81.

Freimark, Peter. 1967. ‘Das Vorwort als literarische Form in der
arabischen Literatur’. Ph.D. Thesis, Münster: University of
Münster.

Gallego, María Ángeles. 2003. ‘Orígenes y Evolución del
Lenguaje Según el Gramático y Exegeta Caraíta Abū l-Faraǧ
Hārūn Ibn al-Faraǧ’. *Sefarad* 63: 43–67.

Gil, Moshe. 1996. ‘The Jewish Community’. In *The History of
Jerusalem: The Early Muslim Period (638-1099)*, edited by

Joshua Prawer and Haggai Ben-Shammai, 163–200. Jerusalem—New York: Yad Izhak Ben-Zvi and New York University Press.

Goldstein, Miriam. 2014. 'Arabic Book Culture in the Work of a Jerusalem Karaite: Abū l-Faraj Hārūn and His Glossary of Difficult Biblical Words'. *Zeitschrift der Deutschen Morgenländischen Gesellschaft* 164: 345–73.

Hadassi, Judah ben Elijah ha-Abel. 1836. ספר אשכול הכופר. Eupatoria: Mordechai Tirisken.

Harviainen, Tapani. 1996. 'The Cairo Genizot and Other Sources of the Firkovich Collection in St. Petersburg'. In *Proceedings of the Twelfth International Congress of the International Organization for Masoretic Studies*, edited by E. John Revell, 25–36. Atlanta, GA: Scholars Press.

Hayman, A. Peter. 2004. *Sefer Yeṣira: Edition, Translation and Text-Critical Commentary*. Tübingen: Mohr Siebeck.

Jastrow, Marcus. 1903. *Dictionary of the Targumim, the Talmud Babli and Yerushalmi, and the Midrashic Literature*. London: Luzac.

Khan, Geoffrey. 1990. 'The Opinions of al-Qirqisānī concerning the Text of the Bible and Parallel Muslim Attitudes towards the Text of the Qurʾān'. *Jewish Quarterly Review* 81: 59–73.

———. 1992. 'The Medieval Karaite Transcriptions of Hebrew in Arabic Script'. *Israel Oriental Studies* 12: 157–76.

———. 1993. 'On the Question of Script in Medieval Karaite Manuscripts: New Evidence from the Genizah'. *Bulletin of the John Rylands University Library of Manchester* 75: 133–41.

————. 1997. ''Abū Al-Faraj Hārūn and the Early Karaite Grammatical Tradition'. *Journal of Jewish Studies* 48: 314–34.

————. 2000a. *Early Karaite Grammatical Texts*. Masoretic Studies 9. Atlanta: Society of Biblical Literature.

————. 2000b. *The Early Karaite Tradition of Hebrew Grammatical Thought: Including a Critical Edition, Translation and Analysis of the Diqduq of ʾAbū Yaʿqūb Yūsuf Ibn Nūḥ on the Hagiographa*. Studies in Semitic Languages and Linguistics 32. Leiden: Brill.

————. 2001. 'Biblical Exegesis and Grammatical Theory in the Karaite Tradition'. In *Exegesis and Grammar in Medieval Karaite Texts*, edited by Geoffrey Khan, 127–49. Journal of Semitic Studies Supplement 13. Oxford: Oxford University Press.

————. 2007. 'The Contextual Status of Words in the Early Karaite Tradition of Hebrew Grammar'. In *Sha'arei Lashon. Studies in Hebrew, Aramaic, and Jewish Languages Presented to Moshe Bar-Asher*, edited by Aharon Maman, Steven E. Fassberg, and Yohanan Breuer, *117-*131. Jerusalem: Bialik Institute.

————. 2013a. 'Morphology in the Medieval Karaite Grammatical Tradition'. In *Encyclopedia of Hebrew Language and Linguistics*, edited by Geoffrey Khan, Shmuel Bolozky, Steven E. Fassberg, Gary A. Rendsburg, Aaron D. Rubin, Ora R. Schwartzwald, and Tamar Zewi, 2:707–12. Leiden-Boston: Brill.

————. 2013b. 'Root: Medieval Karaite Notions'. In *Encyclopedia of Hebrew Language and Linguistics*, edited by Geoffrey Khan,

Shmuel Bolozky, Steven E. Fassberg, Gary A. Rendsburg, Aaron D. Rubin, Ora R. Schwartzwald, and Tamar Zewi, 3:420–24. Leiden-Boston: Brill.

Khan, Geoffrey, María Ángeles Gallego, and Judith Olszowy-Schlanger. 2003. *The Karaite Tradition of Hebrew Grammatical Thought in Its Classical Form: A Critical Edition and English Translation of Al-Kitāb Al-Kāfī fī Al-Luġa Al-ʿIbrāniyya by ʾAbū al-Faraj Hārūn Ibn al-Faraj.* Studies in Semitic Languages and Linguistics 37. Leiden: Brill.

Kretzmann, Norman. 1974. 'Aristotle on Spoken Sound Significant by Convention'. In *Ancient Logic and Its Modern Interpretations*, edited by John Corcoran, 3–21. Boston: Reidel.

Levin, Aryeh. 1997. 'The Theory of al-Taqdīr and its Terminology'. *Jerusalem Studies in Arabic and Islam* 21: 142–66.

Levy, Kurt. 1936. *Zur Masoretischen Grammatik.* Bonner Orientalistische Studien 15. Stuttgart: Kohlhammer.

Lipschütz, Lazar. 1965. *Kitāb al-Khilaf: Mishael Ben Uzziel's Treatise on the Differences between Ben Asher and Ben Naphtali.* Publications of the Hebrew University Bible Project 2. Jerusalem: Magnes Press.

Loucel, Henri. 1963. 'L'origine du Langage d'après les Grammairiens Arabes II'. *Arabica* 10: 253–81.

Makkī ibn ʾAbī Ṭālib al-Qaysī. 1996. الرعاية لتجويد القراءة وتحقيق لفظ التلاوة. Edited by Aḥmad Ḥasan Farḥāt. Amman: Dār ʿAmmār.

Morag, Shelomo. 1960. 'שבע כפולות בגדכפר״ת'. In: ספר טור־סיני: מאמרים בחקר התנ״ך מוגש לכבוד הפרופ׳ נ״ה טור־סיני למלאת לו

שבעים שנה, edited by Menahem Haran and Ben-Tsiyon Lurya, 207–43. Jerusalem: Kiryath Sepher.

Nelson, Kristina. 2001. *The Art of Reciting the Qur'an*. American University in Cairo Press.

Peters, Johannes, R. T. M. 1976. *God's Created Speech: A Study in the Speculative Theology of the Muʿtazilî Qâḍî l-Quḍât Abû l-Ḥasan ʿAbd al-Jabbâr bn Aḥmad al-Hamaḏânî*. Leiden: Brill.

Pines, Shlomo. 1969. *The Guide of the Perplexed: Moses Maimonides*. Second American Edition. The University of Chicago Press.

Polliack, Meira. 1997. *The Karaite Tradition of Arabic Bible Translation: A Linguistic and Exegetical Study of Karaite Translations of the Pentateuch from the Tenth and Eleventh Centries C.E.* Études sur le Judaïsme Médiéval 17. Leiden: Brill.

Posegay, Nicholas. 2020 (to appear). 'Connecting the Dots: The Shared Phonological Tradition in Syriac, Arabic, and Hebrew Vocalisation'. In *Studies in Semitic Vocalization and Reading Traditions*, edited by Geoffrey Khan and Aaron Hornkohl. Cambridge Semitic Languages and Cultures. Cambridge: University of Cambridge & Open Book Publishers.

Saenz-Badillos, Angel. 2004. 'The Origin of the Language and Linguistic Pluralism according to Medieval Jewish Exegetes'. In *Verbum et Calamus; Semitic and Related Studies in Honour of the Sixtieth Birthday of Professor Tapani Harviainen*, edited by Hannu Juusola, Juha Laulainen, and Heikki Palva, 293–303. Helsinki: Finnish Oriental Society.

Sklare, David. 2017. 'Muʿtazili Trends in Jewish Theology'. *İslâmî İlimler Dergisi* 12: 145–78.

Stroumsa, Sarah. 2007. 'A Literary Genre as an Historical Document: On Saadia's Introductions to his Bible Commentaries'. In *"A Word Fitly Spoken:" Studies in Qurʾan and Bible Exegesis Presented to Haggai Ben-Shammai*, edited by Meir M. Bar-Asher, Simon Hopkins, Sarah Stroumsa, and Bruno Chiesa, 193–204. Jerusalem: Ben-Zvi Institute and Hebrew University.

Vajda, Georges. 1974. 'La Parole Créée de Dieu d-après le Théologien Karaïte Yūsuf al-Baṣīr'. *Studia Islamica* 39: 59–76.

Vidro, Nadia. 2011. *Verbal Morphology in the Karaite Treatise on Hebrew Grammar: Kitāb al-ʿUqūd fī Taṣārīf al-Luġa al-ʿIbrāniyya*. Études sur le Judaïsme Médiéval 51. Leiden: Brill.

———. 2013a. *A Medieval Karaite Pedagogical Grammar of Hebrew: A Critical Edition and English Translation of Kitāb al-ʿUqūd fī Taṣārīf al-Luġa al-ʿIbrāniyya*. Études sur le Judaïsme Médiéval 62. Leiden: Brill.

———. 2013b. 'Mnemonics'. In *Encyclopedia of Hebrew Language and Linguistics*, edited by Geoffrey Khan, Shmuel Bolozky, Steven E. Fassberg, Gary A. Rendsburg, Aaron D. Rubin, Ora R. Schwartzwald, and Tamar Zewi, 2:650–53. Leiden-Boston: Brill.

Weiss, Bernard G. 1974. 'Medieval Muslim Discussions of the Origin of Language'. *Zeitschrift der Deutschen Morgenländischen Gesellschaft* 124: 33–41.

Wolfson, Harry. 1979. *Repercussions of the Kalam in Jewish Philosophy*. Cambridge, MA: Harvard University Press.

Zimmermann, Fritz W. 1982. *Al-Farabi's Commentary and Short Treatise on Aristotle's De Interpretatione*. Classical and Medieval Logic Texts 3. London: Oxford University Press.

Zislin, Meir N. 1990. *Me'or 'Ayin*. Moscow: Nauka.

Zwiep, Irene E. 1997. *Mother of Reason and Revelation: A Short History of Medieval Jewish Linguistic Thought*. Amsterdam Studies in Jewish Thought 5. Amsterdam: J.C. Gieben.

INDEXES

BIBLICAL VERSES IN HIDĀYAT AL-QĀRIʾ (LONG VERSION)

(Numbers refer to paragraphs)

Genesis

Gen. 18.17: II.L.1.7.11.

Gen. 18.21: II.L.1.7.3.

Gen. 19.20: II.L.1.5.7.

Gen. 20.5: II.L.2.12.6.

Gen. 20.13: II.L.1.4.4.

Gen. 23.10: II.L.2.12.1.4.

Gen. 24.21: II.L.1.9.7.

Gen. 24.32: II.L.1.9.7.

Gen. 25.34: II.L.1.13.

Gen. 26.11: II.L.2.12.3.2.

Gen. 27.19: II.L.3.2.7.

Gen. 27.24: II.L.1.4.8.

Gen. 29.21: II.L.1.13.

Gen. 32.8: II.L.1.12.2.

Gen. 34.29: II.L.0.1.

Gen. 39.12: II.L.1.7.9.

Gen. 39.15: II.L.1.7.11.

Gen. 39.19: II.L.1.7.11.

Gen. 42.10: II.L.1.8.1.

Gen. 43.26: II.L.1.3.2.

Gen. 45.12: II.L.2.13.1.

Gen. 46.3: II.L.1.11.2.

Gen. 46.26: II.L.0.1.; II.L.0.1.

Gen. 46.27: II.L.0.1.; II.L.0.1.

Gen. 49.6: II.L.1.6.

Gen. 49.11: II.L.1.4.7.

Gen. 49.13: II.L.1.5.12.

Gen. 49.26: II.L.3.2.7.

Exodus

Exod. 4.19: II.L.2.13.1.

Exod. 5.1: II.L.1.12.2.

Exod. 6.27: II.L.2.12.8.2.;
II.L.2.13.1.

Exod. 8.20: II.L.1.10.

Exod. 14.4: II.L.1.7.10.

Exod. 14.30: II.L.1.7.2.

Exod. 15.1: II.L.1.7.2.

Exod. 15.4: II.L.3.2.1.

Exod. 15.16: II.L.1.7.2.

Exod. 17.6: II.L.1.5.2.

Exod. 22.4: II.L.1.10.

Exod. 23.31: II.L.1.11.6.

Exod. 28.8: II.L.2.12.1.3.

Exod. 28.43: II.L.2.12.5.

Exod. 32.1: II.L.1.12.2.

Exod. 32.11: II.L.3.2.3.

Exod. 32.20: II.L.1.13.

Leviticus

Lev. 4.23: II.L.2.16.

Lev. 5.5: II.L.1.5.12.

Lev. 6.13: II.L.1.7.6.

Lev. 11.15: II.L.1.10.

Lev. 14.11: II.L.1.4.2.;
II.L.1.4.2.

Lev. 15.25: II.L.3.2.4.

Lev. 19.5: II.L.1.9.7.

Lev. 19.6: II.L.2.12.2.2.

Lev. 20.2: II.L.1.9.7.

Lev. 21.13: II.L.1.7.9.

Lev. 22.13: II.L.0.1.

Judges

Jud. 1.27: II.L.2.12.1.1.

Jud. 3.25: II.L.1.12.2.

Jud. 5.12: II.L.0.1.;
  II.L.2.12.8.2.

Jud. 5.16: II.L.2.14.

Jud. 5.23: II.L.1.12.2.

Jud. 5.28: II.L.3.2.1.

Jud. 7.19: II.L.1.12.3.

Jud. 7.25: II.L.1.10.;
  II.L.2.12.3.1.

Jud. 11.35: II.L.1.7.11.

Jud. 14.17: II.L.1.13.

Jud. 15.5: II.L.1.10.

Jud. 15.10: II.L.3.2.3.

1 Samuel

1 Sam. 1.6: II.L.1.9.6.

1 Sam. 7.8: II.L.2.12.12.

1 Sam. 8.7: II.L.2.12.12.

1 Sam. 14.4: II.L.2.16.;
  II.L.3.2.4.

1 Sam. 17.5: II.L.1.5.19.

1 Sam. 17.15: II.L.1.9.7.

1 Sam. 17.47: II.L.1.11.5.

1 Sam. 18.11: II.L.1.4.9.

1 Sam. 18.30: II.L.1.7.8.

1 Sam. 20.4: II.L.1.7.4.;
  II.L.3.2.2.

1 Sam. 24.19: II.L.2.16.

1 Sam. 26.23: II.L.1.4.8.

1 Sam. 28.7: II.L.1.7.5.

1 Sam. 28.9: II.L.3.2.3.

1 Sam. 28.15: II.L.3.2.3.

2 Samuel

2 Sam. 3.33: II.L.2.12.12.

2 Sam. 7.13: II.L.1.7.5.

2 Sam. 7.29: II.L.3.2.7.

2 Sam. 10.16: II.L.1.4.4.

2 Sam. 12.28: II.L.2.12.6.

2 Sam. 14.31: II.L.3.2.3.

2 Sam. 19.28: II.L.1.5.11.

2 Sam. 19.44: II.L.1.13.

2 Sam. 22.12: II.L.1.5.20.

2 Sam. 24.2: II.L.1.12.2.

1 Kings

1 Kings 1.40: II.L.2.12.12.

1 Kings 3.23: II.L.1.7.4.

1 Kings 4.12: II.L.2.12.9.

1 Kings 6.9: II.L.1.13.

1 Kings 9.15: II.L.2.12.1.1.

1 Kings 10.2: II.L.1.11.2.

1 Kings 15.29: II.L.1.7.11.

1 Kings 17.2: II.L.1.6.

2 Kings

2 Kings 3.20: II.L.1.5.11.

2 Kings 4.13: II.L.3.2.2.

2 Kings 4.40: II.L.1.5.11.

2 Kings 5.11: II.L.1.12.2.

Ezek. 17.9: II.L.1.5.15.;
  II.L.1.9.7.
Ezek. 20.44: II.L.1.11.1.
Ezek. 22.5: II.L.2.12.3.1.
Ezek. 23.40: II.L.2.10.4.;
  II.L.2.12.14.
Ezek. 32.20: II.L.2.12.6.;
  II.L.2.12.9.
Ezek. 35.15: II.L.2.12.3.2.
Ezek. 40.10: II.L.1.9.2.
Ezek. 40.34: II.L.1.4.3.
Ezek. 45.9: II.L.2.12.3.1.
Ezek. 46.14: II.L.1.12.2.

Hosea

Hos. 5.15: II.L.2.13.2.

Amos

Amos 6.3: II.L.2.13.1.

Obadiah

Obd. 1.20: II.L.1.9.7.

Zephaniah

Zeph. 2.14: II.L.1.12.3.
Zeph. 3.8: II.L.0.1.; II.L.1.1.5.

Zechariah

Zech. 11.17: II.L.1.13.
Zech. 13.9: II.L.1.9.7.

Malachi

Mal. 2.13: II.L.2.12.5.

Psalms

Psa. 2.9: II.L.1.12.2.
Psa. 3.3: II.L.1.11.2.
Psa. 8.7: II.L.1.5.21.
Psa. 17.12: II.L.1.9.7.
Psa. 18.11: II.L.1.13.
Psa. 22.3: II.L.2.6.
Psa. 22.15: II.L.3.2.6.
Psa. 25.20: II.L.2.12.9.
Psa. 27.1: II.L.0.1.
Psa. 28.7: II.L.1.11.5.
Psa. 42.10: II.L.3.2.3.
Psa. 43.2: II.L.3.2.3.
Psa. 45.12: II.L.1.13.
Psa. 47.5: II.L.3.2.5.
Psa. 49.6: II.L.3.2.3.
Psa. 50.20: II.L.2.16.
Psa. 59.12: II.L.1.11.6.
Psa. 60.2: II.L.3.2.5.
Psa. 66.6: II.L.2.12.2.2.
Psa. 66.17: II.L.1.7.7.
Psa. 68.31: II.L.1.4.4.
Psa. 68.35: II.L.1.11.1.
Psa. 72.6: II.L.1.9.7.
Psa. 73.9: II.L.1.5.21.
Psa. 74.6: II.L.1.4.9.
Psa. 82.5: II.L.1.12.2.
Psa. 88.11: II.L.1.7.5.

Proverbs

Job

Song of Songs

Cant. 7.3: II.L.1.5.3.

Cant. 7.10: II.L.2.12.1.3.

Cant. 8.14: II.L.2.13.3.

Ruth

Ruth 2.6: II.L.0.1.

Lamentations

Lam. 1.4: II.L.1.9.7.

Lam. 3.23: II.L.2.17.

Ecclesiastes

Ecc. 11.9: II.L.1.4.2.

Esther

Esther 2.1: II.L.1.12.2.

Esther 5.2: II.L.1.7.11.

Esther 9.3: II.L.2.10.3.

Daniel

Dan. 3.2: II.L.1.7.2.

Dan. 3.5: II.L.1.5.9.; II.L.1.7.2.

Dan. 3.13: II.L.1.4.10.

Dan. 4.27: II.L.2.12.6.

Dan. 6.23: II.L.2.12.8.1.;
    II.L.2.13.3.; II.L.2.13.3.

Dan. 7.6: II.L.1.7.6.

Dan. 9.19: II.L.1.11.2.;
    II.L.1.11.2.

Dan. 10.14: II.L.1.5.5.

Dan. 12.13: II.L.1.5.14.

Ezra

Ezra 1.1: II.L.0.3

Ezra 3.7: II.L.2.12.8.1.

Ezra 4.23: II.L.1.7.9.

Ezra 8.18: II.L.1.3.2.

1 Chronicles

1 Chron. 1.6: II.L.1.5.4.

1 Chron. 1.7: II.L.1.5.4.

1 Chron. 6.6: II.L.1.7.8.

1 Chron. 6.14: II.L.1.7.8.

1 Chron. 6.29: II.L.1.3.4.

1 Chron. 8.12: II.L.2.16.

1 Chron. 12.23: II.L.2.12.8.1.

1 Chron. 12.41: II.L.1.4.9.

1 Chron. 17.11: II.L.1.12.2.

1 Chron. 19.16: II.L.1.4.4.

1 Chron. 28.11: II.L.1.9.2.

1 Chron. 28.18: II.L.1.12.2.

2 Chronicles

2 Chron. 1.12: II.L.1.5.14.

Judges

Jud. 4.9: II.S.6.2.1.
Jud. 5.16: II.S.7.8.
Jud. 7.25: II.S.6.3.1.
Jud. 9.13: II.S.5.4.
Jud. 11.35: II.S.2.12.

1 Samuel

1 Sam. 7.8: II.S.6.13.
1 Sam. 8.7: II.S.6.13.
1 Sam. 18.30: II.S.2.9.
1 Sam. 20.4: II.S.2.5.
1 Sam. 28.7: II.S.2.6.

2 Samuel

2 Sam. 7.13: II.S.2.6.
2 Sam. 12.28: II.S.6.6.1.

1 Kings

1 Kings 1.40: II.S.6.13.
1 Kings 3.23: II.S.2.5.
1 Kings 4.12: II.S.6.10.
1 Kings 15.29: II.S.2.12.
1 Kings 17.2: II.S.2.1.

2 Kings

2 Kings 7.8: II.S.5.4.
2 Kings 8.16: II.S.6.2.1.

Isaiah

Isa. 8.19: II.S.5.1.; II.S.5.4.
Isa. 10.9: II.S.2.10.
Isa. 27.2: II.S.6.2.2.
Isa. 34.11: II.S.2.8.
Isa. 47.12: II.S.2.9.
Isa. 59.21: II.S.2.11.
Isa. 60.1: II.S.0.3.

Jeremiah

Jer. 11.10: II.S.0.3.
Jer. 29.27: II.S.5.6.
Jer. 44.28: II.S.6.9.

Ezekiel

Ezek. 16.4: II.S.5.1.
Ezek. 16.11: II.S.6.1.6.
Ezek. 22.5: II.S.6.3.1.
Ezek. 32.20: II.S.6.6.1.
Ezek. 39.10: II.S.5.5. (2x)
Ezek. 45.9: II.S.6.3.1.

Hosea

Hos. 5.15: II.S.5.5.
Hos. 11.6: II.S.6.1.3.

Zephaniah

Zeph. 3.8: II.S.0.3

ורפאה: 533
רפאהא: 503
ואלרפה: 261
רפי: 512, 536, 1218, 1219,
    1222, 1226
אלרפי: 263, 504
ואלרפי: 214, 215, 263, 294,
    296, 297, 559
רפֵי: 1215
רפע: 119, 7, 734, 757
אלרפע: 720, 739, 747, 761,
    763, 766
[אל]רפ[ע]: 764
ואלרפע: 797
ובאלרפע: 762
פאלרפע: 723
ורפעהא: 126
רפעהם: 759
אלשאם: 52
אלשאמיין: 471
שוא: 488, 494, 548, 561, 703,
    851, 858, 877, 888, 892,
    916, 920, 975, 1035, 1037,
    1061, 1061, 1082, 1087,
    1098
אלשוא: 490, 496, 696, 799,
    799, 803, 804, 809, 818,
    844, 851, 853, 857, 859,
    861, 862, 863, 864, 865,
    866, 868, 870, 873, 874,
    880, 880, 890, 892, 896,

903, 907, 912, 912, 913,
919, 922, 923, 930, 945,
948, 949, 950, 951, 952,
960, 961, 963, 963, 973,
977, 980, 981, 987, 989,
994, 996, 997, 1003, 1006,
1007, 1008, 1010, 1011,
1014, 1018, 1020, 1021,
1027, 1029, 1042, 1047,
1047, 1051, 1057, 1069,
1076, 1079, 1084, 1089,
1090, 1092, 1106, 1108,
1111, 1113, 1115, 1119,
1125, 1126, 1257, 1259,
1260
באלשוא: 1064
ושוא: 894
שוא: 291
ואלשוא: 923, 928, 932, 942,
    983, 1097, 1102, 1262,
    1265, 1267, 1268
וללשוא: 745
ללשוא: 1015
פשוא: 893
פאלשוא: 815, 966
אלשוָא: 743, 744
אלשואין: 1100
אלשופר: 29
שין: 1233
אלשין: 12, 165, 392, 626, 656
בשין: 266

TERMS AND WORDS IN HIDĀYAT AL-QĀRI' (SHORT VERSION)

(Numbers refer to lines)

Cambridge Semitic Languages and Cultures

General Editor Geoffrey Khan

About the series

This series is published by Open Book Publishers in collaboration with the Faculty of Asian and Middle Eastern Studies of the University of Cambridge. The aim of the series is to publish in open-access form monographs in the field of Semitic languages and the cultures associated with speakers of Semitic languages. It is hoped that this will help disseminate research in this field to academic researchers around the world and also open up this research to the communities whose languages and cultures the volumes concern. This series includes philological and linguistic studies of Semitic languages and editions of Semitic texts. Titles in the series will cover all periods, traditions and methodological approaches to the field. The editorial board comprises Geoffrey Khan, Aaron Hornkohl, and Esther-Miriam Wagner.

This is the first Open Access book series in the field; it combines the high peer-review and editorial standards with the fair Open Access model offered by OBP. Open Access (that is, making texts free to read and reuse) helps spread research results and other educational materials to everyone everywhere, not just to those who can afford it or have access to well-endowed university libraries.

Copyrights stay where they belong, with the authors. Authors are encouraged to secure funding to offset the publication costs and thereby sustain the publishing model, but if no institutional funding is available, authors are not charged for publication. Any grant secured covers the actual costs of publishing and is not taken as profit. In short: we support publishing that respects the authors and serves the public interest.

Other titles of the series

Studies in Rabbinic Hebrew
Shai Heijmans (ed.)
doi.org/10.11647/OBP.0164

UNIVERSITY OF
CAMBRIDGE
Faculty of Asian and Middle
Eastern Studies

You can find more information about this serie at:
http://www.openbookpublishers.com/section/107/1